A THIRD WAY

In *A Third Way*, Hillary Hoffmann and Monte Mills detail the history, present context, and future of the ongoing legal fight to protect indigenous cultures in the United States. At the federal level, this fight is shaped by the assumptions that led to current federal cultural protection laws, which many tribes and their allies are now reframing to better meet their cultural and sovereign priorities. At the state level, centuries of antipathy toward tribes are beginning to give way to collaborative and cooperative efforts that better reflect indigenous interests. Most critically, tribes themselves are creating laws and legal structures that reflect and invigorate their own cultural values. Taken together, and evidenced by the recent worldwide support for indigenous cultural movements, events of the last decade signal a new era for indigenous cultural protection. This important work should be read by anyone interested in the legal reforms that will guide progress toward that future.

HILLARY HOFFMANN is Professor of Law at Vermont Law School. She has 15 years of experience in the field of federal Indian law, representing tribal clients in private practice, teaching, researching, and writing about tribal cultural preservation. She also serves on the Vermont Commission on Native American Affairs.

MONTE MILLS is Associate Professor and Director of the Margery Hunter Brown Indian Law Clinic at the Alexander Blewett III School of Law at the University of Montana. He has 16 years of experience working for, with, and on behalf of Indian tribes as general and in-house counsel.

A Third Way

DECOLONIZING THE LAWS OF INDIGENOUS CULTURAL PROTECTION

HILLARY HOFFMANN
Vermont Law School

MONTE MILLS
Alexander Blewett III School of Law at the University of Montana

CAMBRIDGE
UNIVERSITY PRESS

University Printing House, Cambridge CB2 8BS, United Kingdom

One Liberty Plaza, 20th Floor, New York, NY 10006, USA

477 Williamstown Road, Port Melbourne, VIC 3207, Australia

314–321, 3rd Floor, Plot 3, Splendor Forum, Jasola District Centre, New Delhi – 110025, India

79 Anson Road, #06–04/06, Singapore 079906

Cambridge University Press is part of the University of Cambridge.

It furthers the University's mission by disseminating knowledge in the pursuit of
education, learning, and research at the highest international levels of excellence.

www.cambridge.org
Information on this title: www.cambridge.org/9781108482776
DOI: 10.1017/9781108697743

First published 2020

A catalogue record for this publication is available from the British Library.

Library of Congress Cataloging-in-Publication Data
NAMES: Hoffmann, Hillary M., 1975– author. | Mills, Monte, 1977- author.
TITLE: A third way : decolonizing the laws of indigenous cultural protection / Hillary Hoffmann,
Vermont Law School ; Monte Mills, University of Montana School of Law.
DESCRIPTION: Cambridge, United Kingdom ; New York, NY, USA :
Cambridge University Press, 2020. | Includes index.
IDENTIFIERS: LCCN 2019049490 (print) | LCCN 2019049491 (ebook) | ISBN 9781108482776 (hardback) |
ISBN 9781108710923 (paperback) | ISBN 9781108697743 (epub)
SUBJECTS: LCSH: Indians of North America–Legal status, laws, etc. | Cultural property–Protection–Law
and legislation–United States.
CLASSIFICATION: LCC KF8205 .H64 2020 (print) | LCC KF8205 (ebook) | DDC 342.7308/72–DC23
LC record available at https://lccn.loc.gov/2019049490
LC ebook record available at https://lccn.loc.gov/2019049491

ISBN 978-1-108-48277-6 Hardback
ISBN 978-1-108-71092-3 Paperback

To Chad, Anna, Nuala, Isabelle, and Jack, with love.
To Ellery, with hope for a better and more just future.
And to a "third way."

Contents

Figures

Preface

The story of indigenous cultures and the law in the United States has been one of theft, loss, and decimation, at least when that story has been created and told by nonindigenous voices. As this book makes clear, we believe the era of those stories has passed and indigenous people will define the future of indigenous cultures and their protection on their own terms. Therefore, we did not write this book in an attempt to establish normative guidelines of indigenous cultural preservation. Instead, we have set out to provide a framework within which tribes – and those interested in the area of indigenous cultural protection – can glean a basic understanding of the various laws that impede that effort as well as those that advance claims to protect indigenous cultures. To frame this discussion in the chapters that follow, we want to begin with a clear description of our purpose and goals.

We are not Native Americans, and particularly in light of the history of appropriation and exploitation of indigenous people and their cultures, we want to be crystal clear that we write as cultural "outsiders," not from within the indigenous cultures this book describes or relates to. It is neither our place nor our intent to claim any such cultural connections or identities. Rather, in writing this book, we have drawn from our experience – experience advocating for indigenous peoples, serving as in-house legal counsel for an Indian tribe, as counsel for individual tribal members in state and federal court, teaching federal Indian law and related subjects to law and graduate students, testifying in Congress about the impact of public lands and energy bills on tribes, giving talks to lawyers about the field of federal Indian law and how it relates to tribal cultural rights, commenting to media on tribal cultural resource threats, and writing numerous articles addressing various aspects of the cultural assaults that indigenous Americans face in the twenty-first century.

During that time, we have encountered knowledge gaps that surprised us, even among audiences and individuals who were highly educated, and especially among fellow communities of outsiders. One of our many goals is to educate those who lack a basic understanding of the cultural threats that tribes face, and the laws that created, or in some way relate to those threats, with the many examples, cases, and stories in the pages that follow. Another goal is to present a comprehensive set of laws and legal arguments that might be useful to tribes and tribal members seeking to defend against cultural appropriation or other types of cultural threats.

The title of this book draws from a passage in a book, *Tonto's Revenge*, written by renowned Osage and Cherokee scholar Rennard Strickland, in which he spoke with a Lummi tribal elder about life during the termination era, immediately after World War II. The elder recalled the day that a Bureau of Indian Affairs (BIA) agent had called the tribe together to inform them that the tribe would be "terminated" by the federal government. The BIA agent told them that it could happen in one of two ways: either the "easy way," with the tribe cooperating, or the "hard way," if the tribe refused, either one of which would lead to termination. At that point, the elder recalled, her husband, a Marine sergeant who had just returned from the war, stood up and said "No, there is a third way and that is with the tribe saying 'NO' and if necessary, going to the congress to stop you" (quoted in Strickland, *Tonto's Revenge*, p. 49). The third way is what the Lummi chose, and they succeeded.

For tribes, bands, nations, or communities of indigenous people and their allies seeking a "third way" to protect their cultures and cultural connections to this continent in the twenty-first century, their path forward might be in Congress, state legislatures, tribal council chambers, the courts, on social media, in the streets, or, most likely, some combination the above.

We wrote this book to support that movement.

Acknowledgments

Although this work was motivated generally by the authors' shared experience of tribal advocacy, the idea for a dedicated manuscript on the topic of indigenous cultural protection was born out of a class that each of the authors have taught at the Alexander Blewett III School of Law at the University of Montana. That class, offered as part of the school's Summer Indian Law Program, focuses on the laws of cultural protection and how Indian tribes and indigenous people can and do utilize those laws to their advantage. The authors appreciate the opportunity to teach in this area and thank the University of Montana for establishing and supporting that course and for continuing to offer such a depth of curricular offerings for students interested in the study of federal Indian Law and tribal advocacy.

Without excellent professors and mentors, it is impossible to learn a subject as complex as federal Indian law. The authors therefore wish to thank Charles Wilkinson, David Getches, Richard Collins, Sarah Krakoff, and Alexander Skibine, who planted the seeds that eventually grew into this book. Without their generosity of spirit and dedication, this field would not be the extensive and inspirational body of law that it is today. The scholars whose work has continually nourished those seedlings as they matured, whose dedication has proven immeasurably inspirational in times when we questioned whether a third way was possible, and whose work appears throughout this manuscript, with reverence and deep gratitude, are Rennard Strickland, Vine Deloria, Walter Echohawk, Joy Harjo, Winona LaDuke, Matthew L. M. Fletcher, and Rebecca Tsosie. Lastly, we appreciate and are grateful for the important legacy of scholarship, teaching, and service that those named in this paragraph and many others, like Margery Hunter Brown, Ray Cross, Kevin Washburn, and Ralph Johnson to name just a few, have built. The power of their example for Indian Country, and the rest of the country, cannot be emphasized enough, and we humbly strive to carry that legacy forward.

While we are fortunate enough to give credit to a few of those folks here, we would also like to acknowledge the many tribal leaders, officials, citizens, and attorneys who are engaged in the daily work of protecting and advancing tribal sovereignty and indigenous cultures and inspire our work, thinking, and writing. Hopefully, this book supports their efforts.

In addition, the authors wish to thank their respective institutions, Vermont Law School and the Alexander Blewett III School of Law at the University of Montana, for their support of this and other scholarly research. Without the institutional support for scholarship, works like this would not be possible.

Finally, we benefited from helpful and insightful commenters like April Youpee-Roll and excellent research support from dedicated students. For the latter, the authors wish to acknowledge and thank their research assistants: Thomas Flynn, Samantha Doyle, Sarah Mooradian, Margaret Kelly, and Hallee Kansman.

Introduction

Bison, the Legacy of Building an Empire, and Hope

The Fort Peck Indian Reservation encompasses just over 2 million acres of rolling grasslands and prairies along the Missouri River in far northeastern Montana. Rising from the banks of the "Mighty Mo'" in the south and nearly reaching the United States–Canada border in the north, the reservation is vast, alive with undulating terrain and near constant wind. At its southern edge, one can stand on the riverbank, gaze out over the prairies, and almost see history unfolding among the waving grasses. At least, one can see the history one knows.

For many Americans, especially those steeped in this nation's long collective obsession with western movies and the associated mythos, the reservation's land-scape almost immediately calls to mind bison herds, John Wayne, cattle drives and trusty sidekicks, and of course, the ever-present scenes involving cowboys and Indians, battling it out for land, glory, and country. At Fort Peck, that imagery is not as distant as it might be on other reservations. The history of this place is closely connected to many of the elements of those movie westerns, with trappers, cowboys, tribes, and grazing bison forming essential features of the storyline. Today, the main thoroughfare through these tribal lands, US Highway 2, known as the "Hi-Line," parallels the iconic route of the Great Northern Railroad, built during the height of the federal government's western settlement push in the 1800s.[1] Still traversed by Amtrak's Empire Builder train service, the modern rail line takes passengers from the upper Midwest to the Pacific on a journey many may still view as their own personal fulfillment of President James Polk's Manifest Destiny.

---

[1] *See* Burlington Northern Railroad v. Fort Peck Tribal Executive Board, 701 F. Supp. 1493, 1496 (D. Mont. 1988), *aff'd in part, dismissed in part sub nom* Burlington Northern Railroad Co. v. Blackfeet Tribe of Blackfeet Indian Reservation, 924 F.2d 899 (9th Cir. 1991) ("The [railroad] right-of-way passed through lands of the 1874 reservation which were eventually included within the boundaries of the Fort Peck Indian Reservation as established by the Act of May 1, 1888").

But for a whistle-stop in the reservation's main hub of Wolf Point, those train passengers, along with many others passing through the reservation, likely do not linger on the more complex and challenging aspects of its history or even stop to consider what it means to be on a reservation. They probably don't go home and research the tribes who have lived there since history began and who still call this reservation home. They might imagine that any indigenous people they see are members of the same tribe and miss the complexity that has arisen and evolved since members of the Assiniboine nation and the Sisseton, Wahpeton, Yanktonais, and Teton Hunkpapa Sioux bands began sharing this reservation in 1871.[2] And they would likely have no way of knowing that, unlike many other Indian tribes, the tribes of the Fort Peck Reservation were not removed to reservations far from their original homelands. But, while the view of the reservation's landscape from the whistle-stop visit evokes classic tales of the American West for the citizen of mainstream America, the reservation's history also reveals the deeper and more nuanced story of how the American legal system long ago expanded the nation's reach into Indian Country.

That story begins with the region's indigenous peoples – the Assiniboine and Sioux tribes – who were first beset by trappers and fur traders traveling along the Missouri and served as real-time witnesses to Lewis and Clark's famed western survey expedition. For them, history grew complicated around the treaty era of the mid-1800s, and that story resonates for many other tribes. The primary motivation behind the mid-century treaties with the Fort Peck tribes was the federal government's dual desire to preserve peace with, yet acquire territory from, the Oceti Sakowin (as the bands of the so-called Great Sioux Nation referred to themselves) in eastern Montana and the Dakotas, so that European American settlers could move through Sioux lands in peace.[3] By treaties signed in 1851, then again in 1868, the United States and various bands of Oceti Sakowin agreed on the terms of passage, settlement, and peace, in what crystallized as a government-to-government relationship.[4] Despite the treaties, this period was fraught with tension, and it was not until after the military conflict at the Battle of Little Bighorn (or Greasy Grass, as many of the plains tribes refer to it) in 1876, the federal government's subsequent taking of the Black Hills from the Sioux, and the forced establishment of other Sioux reservations in the Dakotas, that the Fort Peck Reservation was created in 1886.[5]

Within 25 years, however, the federal government changed the terms of the 1886 agreement, this time by carving up reservation lands and distributing parcels to

[2] *Fort Peck Assiniboine & Sioux Tribal History*, FORT PECK TRIBES, http://www.fortpecktribes .org/tribal_history.html.
[3] Carla F. Fredericks & Jesse D. Heibel, *Standing Rock, the Sioux Treaties, and the Limits of the Supremacy Clause*, 89 U. COLO. L. REV. 477, 501 (2018).
[4] *Id.* at 501–2.
[5] Burlington Northern Railroad, *supra* note 1, at 1496.

individual tribal households.[6] This process, known as allotment, involved offering the individual parcels to tribal members initially, but if none stepped forward to claim the allotments, the statute allowed the government to open up the unclaimed, or "surplus" lands to non-Indian homesteaders.[7] As a result of this law, today's Fort Peck Reservation is mostly owned by non-Indians whose families settled the surplus lands or whose predecessors bought those surplus lands from the federal government.[8] The tribes and some of the estimated 6,000 of their 10,000 members retain less than 1 million surface acres within the reservation's boundaries.[9] On a map, this history leaves the reservation looking like a confusing checkerboard, with tribal, individual Indian, non-Indian, and other lands scattered in different rectangular blocks of color across the entire reservation.

Looking across these lands from the train station, though, one would not see the boundaries, nor could one see or understand the innumerable federal laws, regulations, and court decisions that continue to affect the reservation, its residents, and their daily lives, based largely on who owns which square of the checkerboard. As later chapters discuss, ownership of squares on the checkerboard has come to define the reach of competing sovereigns and that legal framework complicates the rights of indigenous families to raise their children, the rights of tribes to stimulate their economies, and the rights of tribal courts to adjudicate disputes involving tribal members, among other matters.

Beyond the imposition of federal law, those passing through the Fort Peck Reservation also may not recognize the presence of a sovereign government overseeing day-to-day life on the reservation: the government of the Fort Peck Tribes. The tribes first adopted a written constitution in 1927, but their government, culture, and society date back to a period that tribal members call "time immemorial" – or the beginning.[10] Despite centuries of attempts to decimate them, the creation of federal legal authority over their affairs, and the ongoing challenges of governing a reservation owned mostly by non-tribal members, the tribes are engaged in the daily governmental tasks of serving and protecting their communities. Like all governments, some of the challenges facing the tribes are social, including protecting women and children from domestic violence and other crimes; some are environmental, involving development of oil and gas resources nearby, potentially bringing major pipelines; and others involve choices of how to regulate and, sometimes, stimulate the reservation economy.

---

[6] The General Allotment Act period: 1887 to 1934, AMERICAN INDIAN LAW DESKBOOK § 1:12.

[7] *Id.*

[8] COLBY L. BRANCH, INDIAN LANDS – SURFACE ACCESS AND USE, (Rocky Mountain Mineral Law Foundation, Paper No. 7, 2005. n. 201).

[9] *Fort Peck Assiniboine & Sioux Tribal History*, FORT PECK TRIBES, http://www.fortpecktribes .org/tribal_history.html.

[10] *Id.*

Although visitors to the area may not see or feel it, tribal sovereignty courses like the consistent wind through the reservation's hills and waving grasslands. In putting that sovereignty to work for the people of Fort Peck, the tribes have developed all manner of governmental programs. Of those, the effort closest to the heart of the reservation, both geographically and emotionally, might be obvious to those peering out the windows of a passing Empire Builder train. Smack in the center of the reservation's 3,200 square miles, there are 200 freely roaming bison, many of which are genetically pure wild bison relocated from Yellowstone National Park, descend-ants of the wild bison species that once freely roamed the continent's plains. The Turtle Mound Buffalo Ranch is owned and operated by the tribes, who, since reintroducing bison in 1999, have steadfastly worked to expand their numbers and territory across the reservation. As the tribes' Fish and Game Department makes clear to potential hunters who purchase licenses to pursue them, "[t]hese are not penned Buffalo."[11] They are wild animals, roaming the northern plains as their ancestors did for eons before the arrival of the railroad and the mass slaughter that followed.

While these bison are only remnants of the immense historic herds that supported the Sioux and other tribal societies across the Great Plains for centuries, these animals are neither livestock nor simply an effort at economic development for the tribes. Instead, as Robbie Magnan, head of the tribe's Fish and Game Depart-ment remarked when Yellowstone bison first came to the reservation in 2011, the bison represent "the beginning of a whole new chapter for [both] the bison and for [the Tribes]."[12] Reconnecting tribal people to bison "brings us right back to where we were," said Magnan.[13] Like Magnan, another tribal member working to restore bison to different tribes also noted the bison's restorative value: "[r]econnecting with [bison] is a great cultural endeavor [that is] very important for cultural revitalization ... to help heal from atrocities of the past, from genocidal [acts], boarding schools, and the impact of colonization."[14]

Bison restoration efforts like those at Fort Peck are emblematic of tribal efforts to reconnect and revitalize tribal cultures across Indian Country and beyond. Recent decades have seen watershed moments for indigenous Americans in the centuries-long and never-ending battle to preserve their cultural values, identity, and sacred aboriginal lands. Nevertheless, tribes, tribal members, and other indigenous peoples continue to face the long legacy of federal and state laws that conflict with and

---

[11] *Turtle Mound Buffalo Ranch*, FORT PECK TRIBES FISH & GAME DEPARTMENT, http://www .fortpecktribes.org/fgd/buffalo.htm.

[12] Laura Zuckerman, *Montana Tribes Ready for Historic Return of Buffalo*, REUTERS (May 8, 2011, 1:49 PM), https://www.reuters.com/article/us-buffalo-tribes-montana/montana-tribes-ready-for-historic-return-of-buffalo-idUSTRE7471YE20110508.

[13] *Id.*

[14] Angus Thuermer Jr., *In Restoring Buffalo, Tribes Seek to Restore Communities*, NATIONAL PARKS TRAVELER (2012), https://www.nationalparkstraveler.org/2017/09/bison-west-returning-bison-landscape.

frustrate, if not specifically aim to destroy, vital elements of their culture. At Fort Peck, the influence of these destructive laws is seen in the confounding state and federal bureaucracies that classify bison as threats in order to manage and control their interaction with the non-indigenous cattle industry and impede the transfer of wild bison from Yellowstone to the reservation. In fact, each year, hundreds and sometimes thousands of wild bison are legally slaughtered on the edge of Yellowstone in order to maintain a separation between bison and cattle considered so vital to non-tribal ranchers.

Like Fort Peck's bison restoration, over the last generation or so, tribes have developed new tools for enhancing and protecting their cultural values and properties. But, the current legal structure – even laws purporting to protect indigenous cultural identity, cultural resources, and places of cultural significance – remain grounded in broader federal and state interests that severely limit effective consideration of tribal perspectives and values. Indeed, dating to its inception upon the Declaration of Independence, the American government's structure, policies, and legal system have been rooted in the goal of eliminating indigenous peoples and erasing their separate identity. Initially, this goal arose from religious biases and colonial racism. Later, it evolved into the more nuanced – but no less destructive – aim of "assimilation."[15] Targeting indigenous culture has been a particularly effective means of accomplishing these larger goals. In fact, even where Congress has addressed these limitations, the implementation and interpretation of the laws seeking to protect tribal interests often fail to fulfill the purposes that Congress intended for them. And yet, like the bison that once again roam the plains of the Fort Peck Reservation despite their near annihilation a century ago, indigenous cultures are now overcoming the long legacy of those efforts and turning the law to their benefit.

This book aims to empower those who seek to advance tribally driven cultural preservation projects, initiatives, and priorities. Using examples like bison restoration, the battle over sacred sites like those near the Standing Rock Sioux Reservation of North Dakota and the Bears Ears of southeast Utah, and many others, we hope to illustrate the ways in which tribal, state, and federal law can be used to protect and support tribal cultures and cultural objectives. As set out in greater detail in Chapter 4, the central challenge of these efforts is an underlying clash of fundamental values, a challenge reflected in the complex jurisdictional framework applicable to tribal authority (Chapter 2), the seeming inability of federal law to ensure even basic protections for Native American religious practices (Chapter 3), the impotence of federal cultural resource protection laws (Chapter 5), and threats to tribal cultural properties posed by gaps in intellectual property laws (Chapter 8). Beyond highlighting those flaws and disjunctions, however, the book also makes

---

[15] Chad W. Swenson, *South Dakota v. Bourland: Drowning Cheyenne River Sioux Tribal Sovereignty in a Flood of Broken Promises*, 39 S.D. L. REV. 181, 190 (1994).

clear how tribes (Chapter 5) and tribes and states (Chapter 7) are working diligently to reshape historically rigid legal structures in new and innovative ways.

We wrote this book for anyone committed to or interested in developing the next chapters of the ongoing story of indigenous people and their cultures in the United States, especially the tribal leaders, grassroots activists, and lawyers who will lead that effort. Thus far, the story of America's treatment of those who were here first has revealed much about the nation's inability to live up to its founding principles. But, despite immense challenges, the efforts of indigenous populations to protect and revitalize their connections to their homelands, spiritual sites, and places of cultural importance, is a story of survival, hope, and even success. As attorneys and scholars of the law, we believe that the next part of the story will require creative approaches to bend American law and the American legal system further toward tribal interests. While recent events have shown the potential for such reform, the future of this country inevitably will see more tribal voices in the halls and courtrooms of non-Indian-controlled governments across the country. As these voices grow in number and in influence, they will ensure that their cultures, which existed before any of those other governments, will continue to thrive well into a distant and uncertain future.

We hope those voices find power in these pages.

1

Legal History and Foundations

Peoplehood is impossible without cultural independence, which in turn is impossible without a land base.

—Vine Deloria Jr.[1]

The story of indigenous cultures in the United States is almost as old as the land itself. By nonindigenous measures, including the anthropological and archaeological records and Western calendars, they are entering at least their tenth millennium.[2] Despite facing ongoing destructive external forces, particularly over the last 500 years, many of these cultures have witnessed thousands of years of evolution on the North American continent. But viewing these cultures by such scientific standards ignores the depth of their connection to the continent, a depth that is reflected in the oral histories passed down by generations of indigenous people. These histories stretch back to what many indigenous people call "time immemorial," or the beginning of time, and tell of the first moments of the planet's existence, the birth of humankind, and the peopling of the land.[3] These stories are central to many aspects of indigenous culture and spirituality in the same way that sacred texts like the Bible or the Quran are central to Christianity or Islam. Unlike those texts, though, these oral traditions and stories, passed down over centuries, evolve with time and collective experience, and they continue to inform the core cultural beliefs and values of many tribes.

Generalization about indigenous cultures is impossible and irresponsible. Each culture is unique, and generalizations necessarily diminish the unique individual history and evolution of each tribe or indigenous nation. Similarly, it is impossible to generalize about oral cultural histories, as all of them originate and evolve according

[1] VINE DELORIA JR., CUSTER DIED FOR YOUR SINS: AN INDIAN MANIFESTO 180 (1969).
[2] John W. Ragsdale Jr., *Time Immemorial: Aboriginal Rights in the Valles Caldera, the Public Trust, and the Quest for Constitutional Sustainability*, 86 UMKC L. REV. 869, 879 (2018).
[3] *Id.* at 893.

to the specific history and collective experience of each tribe, tribal group, band, clan, or family. Within the 574 indigenous nations – or "Indian tribes" as they are labeled under federal law – recognized by the United States as of 2020 and among other indigenous nations and tribal groups, the range of beliefs, mores, practices, and observances constituting their cultures is nearly infinite. At or near their core, however, many of these cultures are intimately connected with the places from which they originated.[4] Across many indigenous communities, the land, waters, and resources of the continent where the people of those communities have existed forever undergird the foundations of their cultures, beliefs, and spirituality, even when the people have been forcibly removed from those places by the federal government or due to the pressures of nonindigenous encroachment. That inherent connection between people and place is the essence of many indigenous cultures and remains the heart of many tribal efforts to protect and enhance their cultures in modern times.[5]

According to noted Standing Rock Sioux scholar Vine Deloria Jr., "American Indians hold their lands – places – as having the highest possible meaning, and all their statements are made with this reference point in mind."[6] Sioux peoples likely first encountered European Americans when Lewis and Clark's expedition passed through their lands in pursuit of a passage to the Pacific Ocean in 1804.[7] The Oceti Sakowin occupied a massive territory, including most of the Dakotas, parts of eastern Montana, central and southern Minnesota, and northern Iowa, although Sioux hunters ventured hundreds of miles beyond in pursuit of wild game, including bison.[8] To secure safe passage through their territory, European American trappers and explorers had to negotiate with the Oceti Sakowin leaders, a process that was made challenging given that the three main divisions of the nation spoke different languages – Nakota, Dakota, and Lakota.[9] These negotiations were a necessity for the European Americans, though, because the Sioux were so vast in number and so powerful that they, and only they, could potentially secure permanent stability and peaceful passage among the tribes of the Missouri River region, not all of whom were enthusiastic about the growing swell of outsiders venturing in.[10] The Missouri itself was the true heart of the Oceti Sakowin territory, an artery literally coursing through the center of the nation.

---

[4] VINE DELORIA JR., GOD IS RED: A NATIVE VIEW OF RELIGION xvii (2003).

[5] *Id.* at 61.

[6] *Id.*

[7] Carla F. Fredericks & Jesse D. Heibel, Standing Rock, the Sioux Treaties, and the Limits of the Supremacy Clause, 89 Colo. L. Rev. *478, 501* (2018).Teton Sioux Indians, ARIZONA PBS, https://www.pbs.org/lewisandclark/native/tet.html;

[8] *Understanding the Great Sioux Nation*, AKTA LAKOTA MUSEUM & CULTURAL CENTER, http://aktalakota.stjo.org/site/News2?page=newsArticle&id=9017.

[9] *Id.*

[10] Fredericks & Heibel, *supra* note 7, at 502.

The value of this arterial passageway was also obvious to the Europeans and Americans scouting it as a potential passage to the Pacific Ocean, a source of fur-bearing animals to trap and hunt, and later, of water for irrigation and energy projects. In fact, most of the western great rivers were viewed similarly. Because of this great commercial interest in large rivers, the federal government early in its history established a legal right to control them, called the federal "navigation servitude."[11] This power, derived from the Commerce Clause of the US Constitution, allows the federal government not only to regulate activity on rivers but to control access to them, to condemn property rights on their banks, and perhaps the most devastating for Indian Country, to construct dams and authorize the construction of dams by private corporations.[12] It was this power that the federal government used to authorize the construction of the Oahe Dam on the Missouri River, which began in 1948 and concluded in 1959.[13] When it began generating hydroelectric power in 1962, President Kennedy dedicated this great colonial achievement to the American people.

For the people of Standing Rock, and elsewhere in the lands of the Oceti Sakowin, the building of Oahe Dam, and the other dams along the Missouri, had the ironic impact of submerging their lands under their sacred waters. This irony might not have been so difficult for the tribes to navigate, culturally speaking, except for the vast legal power that they lost along the way, which rendered them nearly powerless to make decisions involving their treaty-protected lands and waters. Despite several treaties guaranteeing them rights in the Missouri, for instance, the federal navigation servitude imposed a superseding legal authority. This had various consequences over the years, but perhaps none more visible than when the Texas company Dakota Access proposed a pipeline to transport crude oil from the Bakken region of North Dakota to an oil terminal in Illinois in the early 2000s.[14] From the beginning of the navigational servitude in the early 1820s until the point at which the Standing Rock Sioux Tribe opposed the pipeline's construction in the first decade of the 2000s, the Tribe had lost almost every source of legal authority to regulate or stop it. The pipeline crossed former Oceti Sakowin lands that had been ceded by treaty, stolen, or subordinated to the federal navigational servitude.[15] It crossed waters that were ostensibly protected by treaties but subject to the adjudication of those treaty "interests" by a powerful federal

---

[11] Gibbons v. Ogden, 22 U.S. (9 Wheat.) (1824).

[12] Genevieve Pisarski, *Testing the Limits of the Federal Navigational Servitude*, 2 Ocean & Coastal L.J. 313 (1997).

[13] Brian Gevik, *Building Oahe Dam – 1948–1959*, South Dakota Public Broadcasting (Mar. 4, 2015, 10:16 AM), http://www.sdpb.org/blogs/images-of-the-past/building-oahe-dam-1948-1959.

[14] Maya Fitzpatrick, *He Needs to Listen to Us: Protestors Call on Trump to Respect Native Sovereignty*, National Public Radio (Mar. 10, 2017, 1:36 PM), https://www.npr.org/sections/thetwo-way/2017/03/10/519628736/he-needs-to-listen-to-us-protesters-call-on-trump-to-respect-native-sovereignty.

[15] Fredericks & Heibel, *supra* note 7, at 517.

agency overseeing the nation's large navigable rivers, the Army Corps of Engineers. And so, despite the protests that rang out across the continent and around the world via dedicated YouTube channels, constant media coverage, and social media accounts, the Tribe could not stop completion of the pipeline, although the litigation over Dakota Access' rights to use it remain uncertain as of 2020.[16]

The battle at Standing Rock demonstrates how, over the five centuries since the arrival of Europeans on the North American continent, the expropriation and exploitation of the abundant resources of the "New World" have largely defined the indigenous relationship to place. From Christopher Columbus's journey to find new trade routes to harvest and market spices to the allotment and assimilation policies of the United States in the late 1800s and beyond, non-Indian people have been driven by a profound and urgent need to secure, control, and consume the lands and resources that nurtured indigenous cultures for millennia. To satiate this need, colonizers erected and imposed systems of law, military power, and social oppression to enforce and insulate the acquisition and development of natural resources by non-tribal interests.[17] As a result, the colonizing nations of Europe and their American descendants succeeded in eviscerating many indigenous cultures using the rule of law; removing their children and forcing them to cut their hair, speak English, and worship a Christian God; taking their lands; and burying oil pipelines through the heart of their homelands. And yet, even for the many tribes that were stripped of their lands and identities, and despite the historical weight of the systems built to oppress and destroy them, indigenous peoples and their cultures remain vibrant, resilient, and ever adaptive, well into the twenty-first century.

At an abstract level, it simply seems impossible that, after 500 years of the most intense and concerted efforts on the part of the most powerful nations on earth to destroy them, indigenous peoples and their cultures remain a vital part of the fabric of American society, yet uniquely separated from it. The 574 federally recognized tribes, and even some of those unrecognized by the federal government, are governed by their own political bodies, with sovereign authority recognized by the US Supreme Court, and live under their own laws, with their own justice systems and individual systems of maintaining cultural independence. The story of ongoing indigenous legal and cultural pluralism, which is a true American tale of survival and resilience, is best told by indigenous voices and is not the direct focus of this book. Instead, the chapters that follow aim to explain how, in a legal system committed to the foundational ideals of liberty, equality, and justice, the law has largely promoted, excused, or ignored the destruction of indigenous cultures. By elucidating the history and evolution of these shortcomings, this and the following two chapters provide the foundation for understanding the remaining chapters, which explore how, despite these challenges, tribes, states, and the federal

---

[16] For more on the battle over the Dakota Access Pipeline, *see* Chapter 5.
[17] DELORIA, *supra* note 4, at 63.

government can rely on the law to sustain and perhaps reinvigorate indigenous cultures. Like many of those cultures, this story begins with the land.

The roots of European colonial presence in America are interlaced with tribal relations and the rights of North America's indigenous peoples.[18] Because European colonizers imported their own legal traditions that were subsequently incorporated into American legal doctrine, the foundations of the body of laws that arose out of this relationship, referred to as Federal Indian Law, and the law of protecting indigenous cultures can be traced to the medieval crusades, through papal doctrines, the law of Spanish conquest, and British imperial policies, which British authorities implemented in North America until the Revolutionary War and the founding of the United States of America.[19] Importantly, though the American legal system set its own course in an attempt to find a "new and better rule, better adapted to the actual state of things" in the so-called New World,[20] two fundamental concepts embedded deep within these original legal structures are critical to the modern work of protecting indigenous cultures: (1) the role of treaties and (2) the fallacy of indigenous cultural inferiority.

1.1 TREATIES: SECURING CONNECTIONS TO THE PAST

The European colonial approach to dealing with the tribes of North America often relied upon treaty making, an approach that necessarily "implied recognition of tribes as self-governing peoples."[21] As Professor Robert A. Williams describes it, these colonial era encounters required "adaptation to radically new circumstances," and in many instances, both European colonists and indigenous groups used a collaborative approach – "linking arms together" – to develop and cement new alliances.[22] Though each treaty could vary depending upon the terms negotiated by and between the colonial and tribal representatives, those agreements regularly served to define the geographic, military, and trade boundaries between the two sovereign entities, to the exclusion of other colonial powers.[23] As each colonial government signed more treaties, it theoretically secured alliances that allowed its influence on the continent to grow. The early treaties were negotiated at arms-length, and reflected a mutual level of respect between the signatories, owing to the relative power of the indigenous nations and the relative weakness of the small colonial governments attempting to secure a foothold on the vast North American continent with little support from distant parent countries. These agreements allowed for the

---

[18] *See* David H. Getches, Charles F. Wilkinson, Robert A. Williams Jr., Matthew L. M. Fletcher, & Kristen A. Carpenter, Cases and Materials on Federal Indian Law 47 (West Academic 7th ed. 2017).

[19] *See id.* at 47–71.

[20] Johnson v. M'Intosh, 21 U.S. 543, 591 (1823).

[21] Getches et al., *supra* note 18, at 85.

[22] Robert A. Williams, *Linking Arms Together*, 82 Cal. L. Rev. 981, 984–85 (1994).

[23] *Id.*

purchase and settlement of indigenous lands by European colonists with the consent of the indigenous signatories and also provided the tribes with an opportunity to protect and reserve important rights.[24] Often, these reserved rights included possession of ongoing and permanent homelands and perpetual rights to continue various culturally important activities, such as traveling, hunting, gathering, and fishing, both within those homelands and across broad swaths of historically tribal territories that were ceded away by their indigenous occupants through treaties.[25] Complicating the implementation of the treaty terms was the fact that they were written in a foreign language that many tribal members did not understand, not to mention the fact that they were often concealed or miscommunicated by and between governments.[26] While the colonists viewed indigenous people and lands as available for exploitation,[27] the practice of treaty making began a unique sovereign-to-sovereign relationship that would continue to define the legal basis on which native nations would relate to outside governments for centuries to come. This relationship has protected many enduring powers ever since.

At the time the eastern tribes were making treaties, though, the continent was in the midst of near-constant change, including dramatic nonindigenous immigration and population growth and various wars between European powers, vying for power and land in North America. During the French and Indian and Revolutionary Wars, American colonists fighting against the British relied upon alliances with indigenous people secured through use of treaties, and faced opposition from many who chose to fight alongside France or Great Britain.[28] Either way, the federal government had to secure allegiance from these nations in the postwar years or face its immediate demise. The result was the first of hundreds of treaties by and between a burgeoning independent United States and the original inhabitants of those lands. This form of government-to-government diplomacy marked relations between the European colonists and indigenous peoples during the critical period of constitutional drafting, negotiation, and ratification, and for years beyond.[29]

After the challenges and failures of the Articles of Confederation, America's Founders cemented the preeminent importance of treaties into the Constitution

---

[24] *See* Cohen's Handbook of Federal Indian Law § 1.02, at 12–14 (Nell Jessup Newton ed., 2012).

[25] *Id.*

[26] Kristen A. Carpenter, *Interpretive Sovereignty: A Research Agenda*, 33 Am. Indian L. Rev. 111, 113 (2009).

[27] *See, e.g.*, Williams, *supra* note 22, at 984.

[28] *See, e.g.*, Robert N. Clinton, *There Is No Federal Supremacy Clause for Indian Tribes*, 34 Ariz. St. L.J. 113, 118–19 (2002).

[29] *Id.* at 119–20 ("In short, the general thrust of the nation's first ratified treaty with an Indian tribe appears to contain all of the hallmarks of international diplomacy."); Treaty with the Delawares, Sept. 17, 1778, 7 Stat. 13.

by making clear that the "all Treaties made, or which shall be made, under the Authority of the United States, shall be the supreme Law of the Land," thereafter binding federal officials, federal and state judges, and states to abide by their terms.[30] In doing so, the Constitution insulated the guarantees made to Indian tribes by the United States from interference by potentially recalcitrant states eager to dislodge tribal communities from within their boundaries. As a legal matter, therefore, treaties provided critical protection for the lands possessed and reserved by Indian tribes and thereby ensured ongoing tribal rights to maintain cultural practices across those lands. However, despite their constitutional supremacy and the exclusive federal–tribal relationship they guaranteed, many treaties were nearly immediately violated by non-Indian settlers and state officials looking to acquire indigenous lands. Rather than protect those solemn agreements from denigration, the United States regularly returned to renegotiate their terms, diminish tribal land holdings, and in the case of many tribes of the eastern seaboard, remove them entirely from their aboriginal territories and relocate them far away.[31]

As nonindigenous immigrants, miners, trappers, and settlers followed their "manifest destiny,"[32] and young America expanded westward, the United States remained committed to treaty making as a means to pry additional lands from tribes. Like the practice that had evolved to the east, early western treaties sought to define boundaries in order to ensure peace and clarify respective tribal territories.[33] A series of these treaties made across the Pacific Northwest, then the territory of Washington, relegated numerous tribes to particular areas of their larger traditional territories and resulted in a dramatic reduction of the traditional land base; but, in exchange, the tribal signatories insisted upon, and ultimately secured, their continuing "right of taking fish at all usual and accustomed grounds and stations . . . in common with the citizens of the territory."[34] Like many agreements of the time, the treaty terms sought to secure vast swaths of tribal land and secure peaceful travel and settlement by non-Indian homesteaders, but tribal leaders negotiating those

---

[30] U.S. CONST., Art. VI, Cl. 2.

[31] Carpenter, *supra* note 26, at 121.

[32] Steven Paul Mcsloy, *"Because the Bible Tells Me So": Manifest Destiny and American Indians,* 9 ST. THOMAS L. REV. 37, 40 (1996).

[33] CAROLE E. GOLDBERG, REBECCA TSOSIE, ROBERT N. CLINTON, & ANGELA R. RILEY, AMERICAN INDIAN LAW: NATIVE NATIONS AND THE FEDERAL SYSTEM 8 (2015) (citing Treaty of Fort Sumner with the Navajo Nation (June 1, 1868)).

[34] Washington v. Washington State Commercial Passenger Fishing Vessel Ass'n, 443 U.S. 658, 662, 662, *modified sub nom.* Washington v. United States, 444 U.S. 816 (1979) (citing Treaty of Medicine Creek (10 Stat. 1132), Treaty of Point Elliott (12 Stat. 927), Treaty of Point No Point (12 Stat. 933), Treaty of Neah Bay (12 Stat. 939), Treaty with the Yakamas (12 Stat. 951), and Treaty of Olympia (12 Stat. 971). The parties to the treaties include the Hoh, Lower Elwha Band of Clallam Indians, Lummi, Makah; Muckleshoot, Nisqually, Nooksack, Port Gamble Band of Clallam Indians, Puyallup, Quileute, Quinault, Sauk-Suiattle, Skokomish, Squaxin Island, Stillaguamish, Suquamish, Swinomish, Tulalip, Upper Skagit, and Yakima Nation.).

treaties contemporaneously sought to protect their land and preserve their ways of life – indeed, their cultures – as much as possible. By the time formal treaty-making ended in 1871,[35] many tribes had entered into a series of such agreements, which often resulted in progressively smaller land bases, but nonetheless preserved critical rights to access areas that tribal ancestors had visited since time immemorial to hunt, fish, and gather. Given their treaty-secured status and the constitutionally supreme status of treaties, these terms would prove to be essential tools for protecting ongoing cultural activities, like fishing and the important ceremonies surrounding the taking of fish, among others.

In 1905, the US Supreme Court took up the first of many cases arising out of conflicts over treaty interpretation. These cases required the Court to interpret the language of Indian treaties to determine whether the rights that tribes reserved in those historic documents survived various subsequent political and legal changes and, if so, what current practices those rights protected. The conflict at the heart of the first case, *United States* v. *Winans*,[36] involved the rights of members of the Yakama Tribe "to take fish at all usual and accustomed places, in common with the citizens of the territory," which the tribe had secured in its treaty of 1855.[37] Tribal members saw their rights impeded by the Winans brothers, two non-native fishermen, who constructed a fish wheel near Celilo Falls on the Columbia River, which was one of those usual and accustomed places for the Yakama Tribe. With license from the State of Washington, the Winans brothers fenced off their property, thereby excluding tribal members and preventing them from accessing their traditional fishing grounds, where their ancestors had fished for generations.[38] In the litigation, the Winans argued that their rights of ownership, based on a patent from the state of Washington, gave them legal permission to fence off their property and exclude the tribal members. Moreover, they contended that Washington's rights to enter the union on an equal footing with all other states, acquiring land underneath and along the banks of navigable rivers as a benefit of admission, like other states before it, would be necessarily limited if treaty rights could cloud the title.[39]

The Supreme Court largely rejected those arguments and upheld the treaty right as a continuing right of access and use, notwithstanding Washington's admission into the union or the Winans' claims of ownership.[40] Beginning with an acknowledgment that the tribe and its members had exercised these rights long before Washington existed, and even longer before the Winans brothers arrived, the Court also recognized that those rights "were not much less necessary to the existence of

[35] *See* Act of March 3, 1871 § 1, 16 Stat. 544, 566.
[36] 198 U.S. 371 (1905).
[37] *Id.* at 380–81.
[38] *Id.* at 379.
[39] *Id.* at 379, 382–83.
[40] *Id.* at 381.

the Indians than the atmosphere they breathed."[41] Despite subsequent changes upon the land, its inclusion within Washington's boundaries, and its private ownership, the Court demanded such rights be preserved in order to honor the word of the United States.[42] In the Court's view, "[n]o other conclusion would give effect to the treaty."[43] ✓

The *Winans* opinion would mark the beginning of a long series of Supreme Court decisions wrestling with, but largely upholding, the rights reserved by tribes in treaties entered in the 1800s. In the Northwest, a number of cases following *Winans* defined the scope of the tribal rights to take fish, ultimately resulting in tribes retaining access to half of the region's available salmon harvest,[44] including hatchery-raised fish,[45] largely free from state regulation,[46] and, most recently, prohibiting state actions that interfere with salmon populations.[47] Similar decisions protected tribal rights to hunt and fish in the Great Lakes region,[48] and tribes continue to assert their treaty-reserved rights as protection for their ongoing connection to culturally important lands and natural resources.[49] As recently as the spring of 2019, the Supreme Court upheld tribal treaty rights to hunt secured by one of these treaties.[50] ✓

Thus, despite the evolution of the treaty relationship between tribes and colonizing forces, from linking arms together to the carving away of massive indigenous land holdings, treaties remain a critical connection for many tribes to secure essential cultural properties, values, and activities. The time-honored bonds these treaties represent have survived the centuries since they were made, despite all that has changed since that nineteenth-century ink originally dried. Through judicial recognition and protection, these treaties ensure that present-day tribal members can engage in some of the same culturally vital activities that their ancestors did. Understanding the important role of treaties and the manner in which they have insulated many tribal cultures from the intervening pressures of changing times, populations, and demographics, is therefore central to the continuing protection of indigenous cultures.

---

[41] *Id.*

[42] *Id.*

[43] *Id.*

[44] Washington v. Washington State Commercial Passenger Fishing Vessel, *supra* note 34, at 685.

[45] Michael C. Blumm & Brett M. Swift, *The Indian Treaty Piscary Profit and Habitat Protection in the Pacific Northwest: A Property Rights Approach*, 69 U. Colo. L. Rev. 407, 409 (1998).

[46] *Id.*

[47] Washington v. United States, 138 S. Ct. 1832, 1833 (2018).

[48] United States v. State of Michigan, 653 F.2d 277, 278 (6th Cir. 1981) ("The treaty-guaranteed fishing rights preserved to the Indians in the 1836 Treaty, including the aboriginal rights to engage in gill net fishing, continue to the present day as federally created and federally protected rights.").

[49] Herrera v. Wyoming, 139 S.Ct. 1686, 1691–93 (2019). ●

[50] *Id.*

1.2 THE FALLACY OF INDIGENOUS CULTURAL INFERIORITY

Contrary to their original commitment to link arms on a sovereign-to-sovereign basis with the original inhabitants of the New World, European colonists imported a conflicting norm that also found its way into positive law. Consistent with prior edicts of the pope and aspects of European religious doctrines, the colonizers brought with them the notion of conquest and its accordant "legal" rights, including the idea that a Christian conqueror is entitled to superior rights of title and ownership than those of indigenous occupants.[51] This religious, racist notion underpinned and promoted the conception of Indians as "merciless Indian savages,"[52] or, in the words of George Washington, "Wild Beasts of the Forest," who would "retire" to the wilderness as superior non-Indian civilization advanced and relieved them of their territories.[53] Since well before Washington's time, there was a definite notion on the part of the European colonizers that, eventually, the indigenous peoples of North America would just go away, either legally, literally, or both. However, when they didn't, legal conflicts continually arose based on the sovereign status of tribes (preserved by treaties) and the perceived superior rights of European "conquerors." These conflicts muddied the status of land claims and property rights across the original colonies and, later, the new United States.[54] Similarly, the inconsistency between entering into treaties to guarantee a sovereign-to-sovereign relationship in perpetuity and the idea that Indians, as a savage and inferior people, would ultimately disappear before the advancement of non-Indian settlers also played a significant role in shaping the U.S. Constitution and later, the field of federal Indian law.[55]

Beyond relying on the Eurocentric fallacy of indigenous inferiority to construct an entire legal system that retained the power to make indigenous claims actually inferior, the articulation of indigenous people as different from and inferior to non-Indians had specific consequences for the legal protection of indigenous cultures and cultural resources. In fact, the concept of (white) American exceptionalism motivated federal policies specifically designed to destroy indigenous people and their cultures. In the late 1800s and early 1900s, for example, the United States

[51] *See, e.g.,* Johnson v. M'Intosh. *supra* note 20, at 571–81 (describing the theory and history of European conquest in America).

[52] Adrian Jawort, *The Declaration of Independence – Except for Indian Savages,* INDIAN COUNTRY TODAY (Sept. 23, 2017), https://newsmaven.io/indiancountrytoday/archive/the-declaration-of-independence-except-for-indian-savages-VeebEvQSVoas6vTpg8_5xg.

[53] Letter from George Washington, Commander-in-Chief, to James Duane, Head of the Committee of Indian Aff. of the Continental Congress (Sept. 7, 1783) (reprinted in GETCHES ET AL., *supra* note 18, at 99–100).

[54] Johnson v. M'Intosh, *supra* note 20, at 543, 573.

[55] *See generally,* Chapter 2 (discussion of plenary power), and George Ablavsky, *The Savage Constitution,* 63 DUKE L.J. 999 (2014) (describing the conflicts to constitutional ratification posed by Georgia and other states, which demanded federal assistance to remove tribes from within their boundaries).

outlawed the religious and spiritual practices of many Indian people, forcing much of their most sacred cultural beliefs underground, if they were to survive at all.[56] During this time, the federal government also supported the wholesale invasion of Indian communities by Christian missionaries in an effort to convert their "heathen" inhabitants to the word of God and help them become true American citizens.[57] These decades were perhaps most tragically marked by the wholesale removal of Indian children from their families in order to place them in often far away boarding school institutions that aimed to "kill the Indian in order to save the man."[58] The boarding school era policies specifically sought to eliminate all traces of "Indianness" in the young pupils, forcing them to cut their hair, wear European clothing, speak English, practice Christianity, and ideally, forget their own cultures. These policies, sometimes justified by "Friends of the Indian," paternalistically promoting Indians' "best interests," succeeded in obscuring ongoing cultural connections for many generations of indigenous people and nearly accomplished the wholesale elimination of indigenous cultures.[59] While federal policy over subsequent decades swung away from such directed efforts and, ultimately, resulted in policies that promote tribal self-determination, the ongoing legacy and trauma of these efforts remain omnipresent specters hovering over present-day indigenous cultures.[60]

In addition to those broader historical federal policies, however, the perception of indigenous inferiority also informed the laws and policies that continue to affect the protection of specific lands and items of sacred or cultural concern. The first of these, the Antiquities Act of 1906, came about during the heyday of the assimilation era described earlier.[61] While federal policies of that time sought to destroy tribal cultures in order to allow Indian people to assume the benefits and obligations of American citizenship, the nation's interest was also piqued by the archaeological wonders of the American Southwest. This interest prompted a desire to gain access to and ownership of the products of indigenous labor and worship, in the form of archaeological relics, curios, and even their ancestors' bodies and homes. The display of antiquities at large exhibitions during the 1890s and the discoveries of enormous and complex ruins at Casa Grande, Mesa Verde, and Chaco Canyon heightened the interests of many nonindigenous people in the historical record – and

---

[56] Allison M. Dussias, *Ghost Dance and Holy Ghost: The Echoes of Nineteenth-Century Christianization Policy in Twentieth-Century Native American Free Exercise Cases*, 49 STAN. L. REV. 773, 787 (1997).

[57] *Id.*

[58] Rennard Strickland, *The Genocidal Premise in Native American Law and Policy: Exorcising Aboriginal Ghosts*, 1 J. GENDER RACE & JUST. 325, 326 (1998).

[59] *See id.*

[60] Lori V. Quigley, *Thomas Indian School Social Experiment Resulting in Traumatic Effects*, 14 JUD. NOTICE 48, 62 (2019).

[61] Antiquities Act, 16 U.S.C. § 431 (2012).

riches – that predated European contact.[62] A desire to protect these resources from widespread looting and desecration, so that they could be enjoyed by nonindigenous visitors, motivated the passage of the Antiquities Act, which authorized the president to protect "historic and prehistoric structures, and other objects of historic or scientific interest that are situated upon the lands owned or controlled by the Government of the United States" as national monuments.[63] The Act also authorized the issuance of "permits for the examination of ruins, the excavation of archaeological sites, and the gathering of objects of antiquity upon the lands," administered by the federal government and provided that the "gatherings shall be made for permanent preservation in public museums."[64] Finally, the Act imposed penalties for anyone who excavated or removed such items from federal or Indian lands without authorization.[65]

While perhaps noble in its goals of conservation and protection of the nation's historic and natural heritage, the Antiquities Act created a legal structure permitting the removal, study, and warehousing of the physical cultural legacy of America's indigenous people. Informed by the ongoing misconception that Indian tribes and their people were inferior and would soon be relegated to the pages of history books, the study of their histories and cultures became the province of archaeology and anthropology – disciplines of the social sciences with little, if any, connection to indigenous cultures. That shift, motivated by popular conceptions like the famous vision of the "End of the Trail" exhibited at Chicago's 1893 World's Columbia Exposition[66] or the iconic images of Edward S. Curtis[67] and integrated into law by the Antiquities Act, continues to pose challenges for tribes and tribal members who seek to recover items of cultural patrimony and the remains of their ancestors from museums and private collections. Such efforts went largely without legal support until Congress's enactment of the Native American Graves Protection and Repatriation Act (NAGPRA) in 1990.[68] However, even after NAGPRA was passed, its implementation, interpretation, and ultimate success remain challenging for indigenous people seeking to rely on the law to overcome this history.[69]

The Antiquities Act also largely failed to prevent the private looting and destruction of historic and prehistoric indigenous cultural resources. The vastness of the

---

[62] *See, e.g.,* Linda Ellis, ed., Archaeological Method and Theory: An Encyclopedia 33–35 (2000).

[63] 16 U.S.C. § 431.

[64] *Id.* at § 433.

[65] *Id.* at § 432.

[66] Rennard Strickland, *Indian Law and the Miner's Canary: The Signs of Poison Gas*, 39 Clev. St. L. Rev. 483, 486 (1991).

[67] *See, e.g.,* Timothy Egan, Short Nights of the Shadow Catcher: The Epic Life and Immortal Photographs of Edward Curtis (2012).

[68] Native American Graves Protection and Repatriation Act, 25 U.S.C. §§ 3001, *et seq.*, 104 Stat. 3048; *see* Chapter 5.

[69] *See* Chapter 5.

massive expanses of federal public land, mostly in the American West and particularly in the Southwest, prevented effective monitoring or enforcement of archaeological and cultural theft and vandalism. In addition, the Antiquities Act provided only minimal penalties – up to 90 days imprisonment and a $500 fine – petty offenses even when charged and prosecuted.[70] Given the interest in such resources, the result is that, by some estimates, nearly 90 percent of the archaeologically valuable sites in the Southwest have been vandalized or looted.[71] Indeed, "pot hunting" has been considered a cultural way of life for generations of non-Indians in certain areas of the Southwest.[72]

Finally, the Antiquities Act empowered presidents to set aside and conserve objects and areas of scientific or historic interest as National Monuments.[73] Enacted at the height of the nascent national conservation movement, this authorization responded to the demands of President Teddy Roosevelt, naturalist John Muir, and others to preserve areas of natural wonder and collective import from various forms of development. Those sentiments led to the creation of Yellowstone as the nation's first national park in 1872 and a number of others before the Antiquities Act in 1906.[74] While laudable from a conservation perspective, these efforts largely ignored or disregarded the fact that indigenous cultures lived, worshiped, and relied on these areas for generations. *yes*.

The reservation era that Roosevelt launched provided non-Indians access to these special places for recreational purposes but completely overlooked the needs of indigenous populations who depended upon these places for their cultural survival. The proclamation establishing Devil's Tower National Monument, for instance, focused on nonindigenous values and needs, despite the area's importance to the Lakota Sioux and other nearby tribes, who value Mato Tipila, or the Lodge of the Bear, as a holy site. According to the Lakota, Mato Tipila should be held "in the light of reverence," reflecting its important sacred qualities to the Lakota people.[75] Unlike the nonindigenous visitors who come to the national monument to climb or recreate, the Lakota believe they are human stewards of the rock, with a spiritual, ancient obligation to protect it from disturbance. That duty of protection is accomplished by visiting the lands around the tower and praying or conducting rituals – practices that are necessarily disturbed by the presence of other visitors, especially those climbing on Mato Tipila itself.

---

[70] *See, e.g.*, United States v. Smyer, 596 F.2d 939, 942 (10th Cir. 1979).

[71] Craig Childs, Pillaging the Past, High Country News (Apr. 28, 2008), https://www.hcn.org/issues/369/pillaging-the-past.

[72] *See id.*; Joe Mozingo, A Sting in the Desert, Los Angeles Times (Sept. 21, 2014), http://graphics.latimes.com/utah-sting.

[73] 16 U.S.C. § 431 (2012).

[74] 17 Stat. 32 (Mar. 1, 1872) (establishing Yellowstone as a "public park or pleasuring-ground for the benefit and enjoyment of the people").

[75] In the Light of Reverence: Protecting America's Sacred Lands (Bullfrog Films, 2001).

But instead of honoring and respecting values like those of the Lakota in Mato Tipila, the laws creating the first national parks expressly forbade any trespassing upon those lands and required the president to remove any individuals who lacked federal permission to enter.[76] In fact, in 1896, the Supreme Court recognized that the establishment of Yellowstone National Park removed certain areas from the "hunting districts" referred to in various treaties with local tribes, thereby, in the Court's view, ending any rights of access or to hunt and fish in those areas.[77] Like the development of modern archaeology and anthropology, the growing conservation ethos of the late 1800s and early 1900s separated indigenous people from their historical connections to the land in favor of serving the broader national interests of protecting certain areas of particular natural beauty or value, primarily for nonindigenous populations.[78] Also, as with the eventual enactment of NAGPRA and its mandated repatriation of human remains and associated items removed from archaeological sites, it would take over a century for Indian tribes to utilize the Antiquities Act to revitalize and protect their sacred lands and those attendant cultural connections.[79] Some of those legal victories took place in courtrooms and some in the White House or in Congress, but each marked an important step toward recapturing essential elements of tribal culture for the victors.

1.3 THE PATH FORWARD

The two foundational concepts described in this chapter, the role of treaties and the law's reliance on the fallacy of indigenous cultural inferiority, help elucidate the potential and shortcomings of the legal framework available for protecting indigenous cultures. The Constitution's Supremacy Clause and the legal system's commitment to honor the word of the US government demonstrate the potential of the American legal structure to insulate historic and traditional rights from the drastic changes wrought by subsequent centuries of oppression and external imposition. At the same time, however, deeply rooted misconceptions of colonial superiority and rightful conquest often serve to justify, even if implicitly, the denigration – if not outright destruction – of indigenous cultures. These justifications can take the form of misguided, if seemingly neutral, laws like the Antiquities Act that have long-lasting

---

[76] *See e.g.,* 17 Stat. 32, 33 (Mar. 1, 1872) (prohibiting trespass in Yellowstone); Pub. L. No. 171, 36 Stat. 354 (May 11, 1910) (establishing Glacier National Park and prohibiting and demanding the removal of trespassers from that area).

[77] Ward v. Race Horse, 163 U.S. 504, 510 (1896); repudiated by Herrera v. Wyoming, 139 S.Ct. 1686 (2019).

[78] *See* Sarah Krakoff, *Public Lands, Conservation, and the Possibility of Justice,* 53 HARV. CIV. RIGHTS-CIV. LIB. REV. 213 (2018).

[79] Bethany Sullivan, *Environmental Justice in Indian Country,* ARIZ. ATT'Y 22, 24 (2019); *see also* Chapter 5.

impacts on the integrity and substance of such cultures and more overt protections in other laws, like trademark and copyright laws.

The fight to protect indigenous cultures and cultural practices takes place between these two opposite poles. Where tribes and their advocates can marshal arguments that tie in principles rooted in broader areas of law, such as treaties sounding in international law and recognized by the Supremacy Clause, those principles are more likely to support protection and even invigoration of ancient cultural practices. But, where the available laws and legal principles are based in or allow for indigenous peoples and their cultures to be viewed as objects or inferior cultures or even simply as uniquely beyond the protections available to all other American citizens, the protections available to indigenous cultures are minimal. Much worse, that misconception of the nation's original inhabitants has been relied upon to excuse the outright and intentional destruction of those cultures and their adherents.

Therein lies the fundamental challenge for tribes and others seeking to protect indigenous cultures: the most effective legal and practical strategy often demands calling upon the broader interests of a legal system that, since its inception, denies that those cultures are worthy of protection. Whether in the Supreme Court's early decisions regarding tribal sovereignty and jurisdiction (Chapter 2), the law's treatment of indigenous religion and religious practices (Chapter 3), or even the current state of federal (Chapter 5) and state and local laws (Chapter 7) offering cultural protections, indigenous claims are most often recognized when they align with broader outside interests. But, while such alignment may maximize the chances of securing legal protections, it can also diminish "pride of difference,"[80] obscuring, if not diluting, the distinct and original aspects of those cultures in the eyes of the law. Ultimately, while history demonstrates that the law expects indigenous peoples and cultures to change in order to secure protection, tribes and their allies are now changing those laws and practices to reflect, incorporate, and invigorate indigenous cultures. Even so, it remains important to recognize and understand these laws so that the process of change does not repeat the patterns of legal history in this area.

[80] Frank Pommersheim, Braid of Feathers: American Indian Law and Contemporary Tribal Life 103 (1995).

2

The Jurisdictional Framework of the Second Way
and the Cherokee Diaspora

My brother in law hung out with white people, went to law school with a perfect record, quit.
Says you can keep your laws, your words.

—Joy Harjo, Poet Laureate[1]

Understanding the laws tribes can use to protect their cultures requires a working knowledge of the jurisdictional framework among the nation's three sovereigns: the federal government, state governments, and tribal governments. This chapter provides some of the essential elements of this foundation by tracing the arc of US Supreme Court cases in which the justices filled in the contours of the Constitution's rough outline of the relationship between these three sovereigns. While the Supreme Court's treatment of tribal authority over this period largely reflected the broader federal interests of a particular era, including the elevation and insulation of exclusive federal authority over Indian affairs in the nineteenth century, Supreme Court decisions of more recent vintage have severely restricted tribal authority, even over areas within the boundaries of present-day reservations, during a period in which the federal government otherwise seemed to embrace a policy of supporting tribal self-government.[2] It is therefore not always possible to discuss individual cases or periods of federal Indian policy in general terms. Moreover, the jurisdictional maze that results from this lengthy history often frustrates attempts to seek legal recognition of inherent tribal authority and confuses even well-versed legal practitioners.

The foundations of the modern jurisdictional framework began in the preconstitutional period and in many ways are reflected in the history of the Cherokee Nation. Before the Revolutionary War, the Cherokee occupied parts of what are now western Georgia, western North and South Carolina, and eastern and central

---

[1] Joy Harjo, In Mad Love and War 5 (1990).
[2] Montana v. United States, 450 U.S. 544, 557 (1981).

Tennessee. Their lands were arable and rich in timber and minerals. As early as the 1770s, European American settlers were not content to negotiate with the Cherokee for access rights to these lands and began forcibly encroaching on the tribe's territory. Some tribal members left to avoid the conflict, but some stayed and fought, and as these skirmishes turned into larger armed conflicts, the federal government saw a need to intervene. In an attempt to establish a more peaceful and organized trade relationship with the Cherokee Nation, the United States signed numerous treaties with the Cherokee. The Treaty of Hopewell, signed in 1785, is perhaps the most notable, as it established the basic legal framework that would guide relations between the two nations during the tumultuous period before, during, and after the ratification of the US Constitution. The primary concerns motivating the treating parties were establishing peace, determining respective land rights and corresponding legal boundaries, and protecting the tribe and its lands from encroaching European American settlers.[4] The treaty sketched a rough outline of the general roles of the three sovereigns with an interest in the Cherokee Nation's territory: the federal government, the state of Georgia, and the Cherokee government. It also accomplished the federal government's goal of appeasing the State of Georgia by containing the Cherokee Nation within a smaller territory than the Cherokee had once occupied.

As described in the previous chapter, treaty terms like these were a necessity for the United States because in the years after the Revolutionary War, uncertainty lingered due to wartime allegiances between tribes and European powers like France and Great Britain.[5] The fledgling American federal government, to the extent it existed at that time, was particularly vulnerable and therefore concerned about these military alliances, which if they continued, could overwhelm the newly independent, land-rich, but cash-strapped nation.[6] Thus, the years leading up to the ratification of the US Constitution in 1789 were fraught with tension, lingering resentments between former allies, and uncertainty for indigenous and colonial citizens alike.[7]

The Treaty of Hopewell, which represented the international-style treaty model of this period, also reflected a Cherokee declaration of allegiance to the United States. In Article III of the treaty, the Tribe agreed to place itself "under the protection of the United States of America, and of no other sovereign whatsoever."[8] In Articles IV and V, the treaty separated Cherokee lands from the lands of the state of Georgia and warned that if any settlers crossed the boundary into the

---

[3] David H. Getches, Charles F. Wilkinson, Robert A. Williams Jr., Matthew L. M. Fletcher, & Kristen A. Carpenter, Cases and Materials on Federal Indian Law 91 (7th ed. 2017).

[4] *Id.*

[5] *Id.*

[6] Robert N. Clinton, *The Dormant Indian Commerce Clause*, 27 Conn. L. Rev. 1055, 1098 (1995).

[7] *Id.* at 1125–26.

[8] Treaty of Hopewell, Art. III.

Cherokee Nation, they would "forfeit the protection" of the laws of the United States and submit themselves to the jurisdiction of the Cherokee courts.[9] The only exception to this bright-line jurisdictional boundary was for capital crimes against US citizens occurring inside Cherokee territory, which the treaty reserved exclusively to the federal courts of the United States.[10] Through treaty provisions like these, the parties hoped that "the hatchet [would] be forever buried," as Article XIII somewhat optimistically declared.[11]

Like most treaties of this early period, the Treaty of Hopewell was silent about matters other than criminal jurisdiction, trade, and territorial boundaries. For instance, it did not address the Cherokee Nation's rights to continue their cultural norms and traditions. It did not contain any terms providing legal protection for Cherokee cultural practices, cultural rights, religious practices, traditional education, Cherokee language, or other important traditions. Given that these early treaties were born of necessity, the lack of these provisions may have reflected that there was no need for these protections at that point in history. It may have also reflected an implicit warrant of cultural protections in the political and legal protections guaranteed by the treaty, for as long as tribes respected the treaty terms and boundary lines, their political and cultural autonomy likely would be respected as well.

Yet, cultural pressure was definitely mounting, and it was tied closely to the loss of land and corresponding political and legal power. At the close of the eighteenth century, and in the early years of the nineteenth, indigenous nations like the Cherokee faced exponentially increasing pressure from external settlement efforts and the accompanying demand for natural resources like timber, water, and minerals located on tribal lands. Use and occupation of land in the states, territories, and Indian Country was also haphazard, largely unregulated, and rife with land speculation and fraud, complicating matters even further.[12] In the first Supreme Court opinion attempting to lay rest to some of the chaos, *Johnson v. M'Intosh*, the Court had to determine which of two parties held a superior title to several parcels of land originally within the expansive British charter establishing Virginia.[13] On the one hand, William M'Intosh claimed title by virtue of a patent from the US government, while on the other, several heirs of Thomas Johnson claimed title through direct acquisition from the Piankeshaw tribe.[14] There was no dispute that both parties held

---

[9]   *Id.* at Art. V.

[10] *Id.* at Art. VI. ("If any Indian or Indians, or person residing among them, or who shall take refuge in their nation, shall commit a robbery, or murder, or other capital crime, on any citizen of the United States, or person under their protection," the tribe was required to deliver said person to the United States for prosecution.).

[11] *Id.* at Art. XIII.

[12] Johnson v. M'Intosh, 21 U.S. 543, 573 (1823).

[13] *Id.*

[14] *Id.*

title, but the Supreme Court had to determine which held greater validity under the laws of the United States.

It was straightforward enough to determine that a patent from the federal government was a valid form of title, but there were many questions swirling around the tribally derived title. To resolve these, Chief Justice Marshall borrowed a Spanish colonial doctrine by which European powers had conquered indigenous nations and seized their lands for centuries. This doctrine, the Doctrine of Discovery, posited that a European power gained "ultimate" legal title to indigenous lands within the scope of the foreign sovereign's charter upon arriving in the chartered territory.[15] In M'Intosh's case, that meant that Great Britain had gained title to the lands eventually acquired by Johnson's heirs through the Virginia Charter. Under Marshall's interpretation of the doctrine, a successor to the original discovering nation assumed the same title and could use the doctrine to acquire additional lands, either "by purchase or conquest."[16] Applying this analytical framework to the controversy between these parties resulted in Marshall concluding that the Piankeshaw were divested of freely alienable title to the lands ultimately sold to Johnson through the acquisition of those lands by the United States from Great Britain upon the signing of the Treaty of Paris. Therefore, under Marshall's reasoning, the Piankeshaw had no legal title that could be recognized outside of the Tribe at the time of the conveyance to Johnson, making his title invalid. For those same reasons, Johnson's conveyance to his heirs was also invalid and therefore, the Court concluded that M'Intosh was the rightful owner.

Pursuant to this sweeping doctrine, as Marshall noted, "our whole country been granted by the crown while in the occupation of the Indians."[17] The doctrine thereby created corollary legal rights: "ultimate" title rested with the superior sovereign, but the "right of occupancy," also subsequently referred to as Indian or aboriginal title, was held by the indigenous occupants.[18] The rationales underlying Marshall's adoption of the Doctrine of Discovery into American law were ostensibly cultural necessity and legal practicality.[19] Drawing on contemporaneous and long-standing notions of indigenous cultural inferiority, Marshall determined that, to maintain a civilized society on the vast, wild, and untamed North American continent, Christianity and European societal order must predominate.[20] Marshall ingrained these ideas of indigenous inferiority directly into the foundations of American law, filling paragraphs of his opinion with a description of "the character and habits of the people whose rights have been wrested from them."[21] These

[15] *Id.*
[16] *Id.* at 545.
[17] *Id.* at 579.
[18] *Id.* at 583.
[19] *Id.* at 589.
[20] *Id.*
[21] *Id.* at 589.

people, Marshall wrote, were "fierce savages, whose occupation was war, and whose subsistence was drawn chiefly from the forest. To leave them in possession of their country, was to leave the country a wilderness; to govern them as a distinct people, was impossible, because they were as brave and as high spirited as they were fierce, and were ready to repel by arms every attempt on their independence."[22] Importantly, the Doctrine of Discovery operated only if the discovering nation or power was Christian and the discovered nation was not. It would not support the conquest of France by the United States, or any other Christian power.[23]

Yet, despite the racist and xenophobic reasoning in *Johnson v. M'Intosh*, Marshall's opinion also recognized an indigenous "right of occupancy."[24] This right incorporated the basic rights to use and possess land, but also something more, which derived from the unusual circumstances of tribal nations existing as governmental entities even after colonization. Marshall described this as "[t]he peculiar situation of the Indians," who were "necessarily considered, in some respects, as a dependent, and in some respects as a distinct people, occupying a country claimed by Great Britain, and yet too powerful and brave not to be dreaded as formidable enemies."[25] The rule of *Johnson* sought to accommodate this unique situation by dividing the legal rights to property between the superior title of the United States, derived from European colonial occupation of North America and the Doctrine of Discovery, and the ongoing right of sovereign possession retained by the land's original indigenous inhabitants. So, although indigenous nations may have lost "complete sovereignty" as a result of this decision, they retained a form of limited title in and sovereign powers over their lands.[26]

These sovereign powers were put squarely to the test in the state of Georgia, where the Cherokee Nation had fled during the Revolutionary War to escape invading settlers in the Tribe's aboriginal homeland of the Carolinas region.[27] Yet Georgia provided only a temporary sanctuary. By 1802, the federal government was negotiating removal of the Cherokee with the state of Georgia because the increasing nonindigenous population was hungry for land, mineral wealth, and timber, all of which were plentiful in Cherokee territory.[28] Complicating the situation was the need for the federal government to mollify the southern states, including Georgia, so

---

[22] *Id.* at 590.
[23] *Id.* It would not be possible for Great Britain to mount a flotilla, sail it to Normandy pursuant to a royal charter, and lawfully claim ownership of France pursuant to the Doctrine of Discovery, for example. The doctrine served only to defeat competing claims to indigenous lands by other colonial powers.
[24] *Id.* at 574.
[25] *Id.* at 596–97.
[26] *Id.* at 574.
[27] Robert S. Davis, *State v. George Tassel: States' Rights and the Cherokee Court Cases, 1827–1830*, 12 J.S. LEGAL HIST. 41, 43 (2004).
[28] *Id.* at 42. The Cherokee conflict years were some of the most tenuous for the new United States, with John Quincy Adams commenting that "the Union is in the most imminent danger of dissolution." GETCHES ET AL., *supra* note 3, at 103.

that the already fraying national Union might stay intact.[29] The federal government therefore promised Georgia that it would solve the population and settlement pressures by removing the Cherokee and other tribes.[30]

Frustrated with the lack of progress on this front, the Georgia legislature took matters into its own hands and began passing legislation asserting jurisdiction over, and ultimately, ownership of the Cherokee lands.[31] An 1829 state law even purported to nullify all actions of the Cherokee Nation government within Cherokee Territory.[32] Meanwhile, tensions on the ground erupted into violence as frustrated Georgia residents protested the arrests of white settlers who had been found illegally prospecting for gold on Cherokee land.[33] A federal militia was brought in to maintain order, but the state government continued to encourage non-Cherokee settlers to defy federal authority by claiming and settling on Cherokee lands.[34]

In 1830, the Cherokee government filed a lawsuit in the Supreme Court, invoking the Court's original jurisdiction under Article III of the Constitution, which relates to matters involving a state and a foreign nation.[35] The Tribe's aim was to prevent the state of Georgia from enforcing state laws within the Cherokee Nation, on lands that the federal government had guaranteed exclusively to the Tribe in the Treaty of Hopewell.[36] In their court filings, the Cherokee described themselves as a "nation of Indians, [and] a foreign state, not owing allegiance to the United States, nor to any state of this union, nor to any prince, potentate or state, other than their own."[37] The Tribe's main legal argument was that although the Doctrine of Discovery ostensibly vested the United States with "ultimate" title to their lands, the Treaty of Hopewell guaranteed their sovereignty and independence from external interference and they retained the Court-recognized rights of use and occupancy.[38] To the Cherokee, this sovereignty included the exclusive right to govern themselves and the freedom from the operation of state *or* federal laws in Cherokee territory.[39] Thus, less than a decade after resolving the matter of "Indian title" posed in *Johnson*, the Supreme Court now faced its second case involving indigenous lands and the legal status of indigenous nations that occupied them.[40]

Chief Justice Marshall's final opinion in this case — *Cherokee Nation v. Georgia* — reflected the Court's broader struggle at the time to define the legal status of these

---

[29] Davis, *supra* note 27, at 42.
[30] *Id.*
[31] *Id.* at 43.
[32] *Id.*
[33] *Id.*
[34] *Id.*
[35] GETCHES ET AL., *supra* note 3, at 104.
[36] Cherokee Nation v. Georgia, 30 U.S. 1, 2 (1831).
[37] *Id.* at 3.
[38] *Id.*
[39] *Id.*
[40] *Id.* at 1.

"nation[s] of Indians" within the Constitution's somewhat nebulous and still ill-defined structure.[41] This was complicated by the lack of concrete references to tribes in the Constitution. In the *Cherokee Nation* complaint, the Tribe cobbled together a legal argument based on the three clauses of the Constitution that related, at least implicitly, to Indians or tribes. First, the Tribe argued that the treaties between the Cherokee and the United States were the supreme law of the land under the Supremacy Clause and as such, they nullified any conflicting state laws.[42] Second, under the Contracts Clause, the Cherokee argued that treaties were contracts and that no state law impairing the obligation of these contracts could survive constitutional scrutiny.[43] Finally, they argued that the Constitution's author-ization for Congress to regulate commerce with the Indian Tribes was an exclusive federal power, with which no state could interfere.[44]

Before the justices could address those substantive arguments, though, they had to answer a threshold question that might prevent the Court from hearing the case at all – whether the Court had jurisdiction over the Tribe's claims under Article III of the Constitution, which limits the Court to hearing only controversies between a state and its citizens, a state and a foreign nation, or a state and citizens of a foreign nation.[45] At the time, there was no clear definition of the status of an Indian tribe like the Cherokee Nation under the Constitution, especially under Article III, and only passing reference to Indian tribes and congressional authority in the commerce clause of Article I.

Marshall therefore had to determine whether the Cherokee, and other indigen-ous nations, fit into one of the categories in Article III.[46] He initially observed that, due to the complex history between tribes and the federal government, "the relations of the Indians to the United States is marked by peculiar and cardinal distinctions which exist no where else."[47] Indigenous nations were separate nation-states, yet, as Marshall noted, they existed within the territorial boundaries of the United States and their treaties acknowledged a special relationship of mutual obligation with the United States.[48] In Marshall's view, this obligation was marked by dependence, due to various treaty provisions indicating that tribes were agreeing to submit to the "protection" of the United States. In what came to be considered perhaps the most significant element of the first Cherokee Nation decision, Marshall made the sweeping declaration that all indigenous nations were legally "domestic dependent nations."[49] In this way, just as *Johnson* v. *M'Intosh* imposed a wholesale qualification of the legal status of indigenous title to property, Marshall's declaration that tribal

---

[41] *Id.*
[42] *Id.* at 6–7.
[43] *Id.* at 7.
[44] *Id.*
[45] *Id.* at 15.
[46] *Id.* at 17–18.
[47] *Id.* at 17.
[48] *Id.*
[49] *Id.*

"SUBNATIONAL"

governments were "domestic dependent nations" legally changed the relationship of every indigenous nation within the United States to a subnational political and legal status, even though these indigenous nations remained separate, sovereign entities.[50]

Justice Marshall further expounded on the legal status of tribes in his final opinion of the Marshall Trilogy, *Worcester v. Georgia*, issued in 1832.[51] Samuel Worcester, the appellant in the case, had sought *habeas corpus* relief after he was imprisoned by the state of Georgia for failing to follow laws passed by the Georgia legislature regulating religious missionary activities within the Cherokee Nation.[52] His argument was that the state laws did not apply to his missionary work because the Cherokee Nation was a sovereign nation, not subject to the laws of any state. This sovereign status was protected, Worcester argued, by treaties and the Supreme Court's recent decision in *Cherokee Nation v. Georgia*.[53] The Supreme Court agreed, noting that the Treaty of Hopewell and subsequent treaties between the Cherokee and the United States "remain in full force, and consequently must be so considered as the supreme laws of the land."[54] According to Justice Marshall's confusing opinion in *Worcester*, "these laws throw a shield over the Cherokee Indians," protecting them from the encroachment of state law.[55] In reality, though this shield would prove too weak to protect the Cherokee, who, along with many indigenous peoples of the southeast, were removed to the Indian Territory on the now infamous Trail of Tears within a few short years of these decisions.[56]

Legally speaking, though, the Marshall Trilogy cases established the broad outlines of the jurisdictional framework for the United States, Indian tribes, and the states of the union, delineating the general scope of jurisdictional authority for each governmental entity. A few salient principles emerged from these cases that still resonate today. For one, the federal government had authority over land cessions and intergovernmental negotiations involving tribes. It also possessed "ultimate" title to tribal lands pursuant to the Doctrine of Discovery, but tribes retained the rights of possession and occupancy in their lands. Also, critically, the Marshall Trilogy cases established that tribal land was not the property of states and that states otherwise lacked jurisdiction or regulatory authority over tribes and tribal lands, absent federal (and in some cases, tribal) consent. The Marshall Trilogy established that tribes possess sovereign authority within their territorial boundaries, even if many tribes lacked the sole authority to determine where this territory would be physically located after the era of removal began in earnest in the 1830s.

---

[50] *Id.* These early-nineteenth-century legal labels follow tribes to this day, limiting their legal rights to repatriation of land and other vital political and cultural values.

[51] 31 U.S. 515 (1832).

[52] *Id.* at 537.

[53] *Id.* at 538.

[54] *Id.* at 595.

[55] *Id.*

[56] GETCHES ET AL. *supra* note 3, at 126.

The Marshall Trilogy opinions further clarified that tribal authority was not solely derived from the tribal relationship with the United States in treaties. There was also independent, inherent tribal sovereignty, stemming from the recognition of tribal governmental authority by tribal members. This form of sovereignty is separate from any authority recognized or conferred by the federal government. As described by Marshall, while tribes were both "domestic" and "dependent," they were also "nations" – distinct political communities with their own languages, customs, cultural norms and values, political and judicial systems, and territory.[57] The Supreme Court recognizes the form of sovereignty that derived from these characteristics – inherent sovereignty – to this day.[58]

Finally, the Marshall Trilogy cemented the importance of treaties as the means by which the United States and tribes would conduct their sovereign-to-sovereign relationship. Justice Marshall relied on these treaties to support the wholesale exclusion of state authority from tribal lands and from US interactions with tribes, almost as an independent legal basis for respecting tribal sovereignty. In this way, as discussed in Chapter 1, treaties provided tribes with an additional source of legal authority for protecting their inherent sovereignty within reserved territories and negotiated sovereign rights to extraterritorial.[59] By virtue of these treaty rights, tribes retained some independence from state and federal authority outside of their territorial boundaries, even after the Marshall Trilogy framework was established.

The Marshall Trilogy cases and the tribal rights they recognized under federal law did not protect indigenous populations from the relentless onslaught of population growth and resource acquisition in the eastern states, though, and these decisions were followed by a series of events that left tribal governments and entire tribal nations in tatters. Within five years of the *Worcester v. Georgia* decision, federal troops began forcibly relocating the Cherokee to an area of dedicated federal territory in what is now Oklahoma. Thousands of Cherokee people died in the removal process along what became known as the Trail of Tears. And, although the Cherokee removal is most well known to most Americans from their primary school history classes, similar removal tragedies devastated tribes in various regions, at different times throughout history.[60] Oddly, though, the legal rights established in the Marshall Trilogy cases followed the tribes to their newly established territories in

---

[57] Cherokee Nation, *supra* note 36, at 17.

[58] *See, e.g.*, Michigan v. Bay Mills Indian Community, 572 U.S. 782, 782 (2014).

[59] If a tribe entered into a treaty with the federal government to cede a portion or all of its aboriginal lands and remove to a smaller reservation, a tribe could retain certain usufructuary rights on the ceded lands, and many tribes did reserve these rights, including the rights to hunt, fish, gather, and cross over ceded lands.

[60] GETCHES ET AL., *supra* note 3, at 127 (discussing indigenous removals in the midwest, southwest, and northwest regions of the country).

the Midwest, so they retained sovereign authority over their land base and their people, even as the land base itself sometimes changed dramatically.

Being forced to move away from their homelands often nearly destroyed tribes culturally, economically, and socially, though. And despite retaining sovereign authority over newly established reservation lands, removal complicated the legal landscape as well. The jurisdictional framework Justice Marshall created in the Trilogy cases no longer fit the circumstances on the ground, because for one, not all tribal members relocated pursuant to the removal statutes and orders.[61] Some died, some hid from authorities and stayed in their traditional homelands, and some joined other tribes. In addition, as Cherokee and other tribal territories were broken up by the federal government and new categories of tribally occupied land were being created, jurisdiction became murkier, especially over former tribal lands that remained subject to treaty and other retained rights. A region of what would become Kansas and Oklahoma was designated as the Indian Territory and later, "Indian Country," which was a place to which many "Indian" peoples were removed and relocated.[62] For the Cherokee and other indigenous nations, the removal era created a cultural diaspora, scattering tribal members across multiple states and sometimes, and often permanently, dividing them from one another.[63]

While the Supreme Court issued early opinions that supported tribal sovereignty in some measure, Congress weighed in with legislation like the Removal Acts of the early and mid-nineteenth century, which further reduced tribal land bases.[64] Meanwhile, Congress passed statutes authorizing settlement and development on tribal lands acquired through treaties, beginning with the Preemption Act in 1841, continuing through the passage of the various mid-century homestead acts and railroad land grants, and concluding with the General Mining Law in 1872.[65] These laws incentivized nonindigenous migration and settlement on a scale the United States had not seen, and the losses to tribes – of the land base in particular – were immense.

It was also difficult for tribes to navigate the increasingly complex body of federal law that developed from the evolving relationships between indigenous nations and the federal government in the nineteenth century, as tribes were forced into smaller territories and federal legal authority over them grew. Tribes relied on their treaty rights and depended on the promises contained in those treaties for their cultural and literal survival. One of the rare success stories of this era arose in a famous

---

[61] *Id.* at 128.

[62] *Id.* at 140.

[63] As of 2019, there are three federally recognized Cherokee tribes, two in Oklahoma and one in North Carolina. *Cherokee Ancestry*, US Department of the Interior, https://www.doi.gov/tribes/cherokee.

[64] Marla E. Mansfield, *A Primer of Public Land Law*, 68 Wash. L. Rev. 801, 821 (1993).

[65] *See id.*

1883 Supreme Court case, *Ex parte Kan-gi-shun-ca* ("Crow Dog").[66] Kan-gi-shun-ca, a Brule Sioux citizen, was charged with murdering a former Brule leader, Sin-ta-ge-le-Scka, on Sioux lands.[67] Federal prosecutors charged Kan-gi-shun-ca with murder under a federal criminal statute, and he argued that the resulting conviction should be set aside because the laws of the United States had no force on Sioux lands, which were protected by various treaty agreements.[68] The lower court held in favor of the federal government, but on appeal, the Supreme Court reversed. Noting that a treaty guaranteeing the Sioux certain sovereign rights in their territory had not been expressly abrogated by the federal criminal statute under which Kan-gi-shun-ca was prosecuted, the Court held that it would be fundamentally unjust to impose that federal law on him with no prior warning.[69] Doing so would subject the Sioux to standards of criminal justice developed "not by their peers, nor by the customs of their people, nor the law of their land, but by superiors of a different race, according to the law of a social state of which they have an imperfect conception, and which is opposed to the traditions of their history [and] to the habits of their lives."[70]

The judicial recognition of tribal cultural and legal sovereignty in the Supreme Court's decision in *Ex parte Kan-gi-shun-ca* was not shared by the late-nineteenth-century Congress, however. In a direct response to this decision, Congress passed the Major Crimes Act, which unilaterally imposed federal jurisdiction over serious crimes committed within the sovereign territory of an Indian nation, imposing a uniform, and foreign, standard.[71] In defining the scope of the new law's applicability, Congress declared that it applied to enumerated crimes committed on any lands "within the limits of any Indian reservation," including those "within the boundaries of any state."[72] Later, Congress amended this definition to include any lands constituting "Indian Country," which is now defined to include reservations, dependent Indian communities, such as the Pueblos of New Mexico, and individual trust allotments.[73] As the Supreme Court later recognized in the 1970s, tribes could still prosecute those and lesser crimes, but only if the defendant

---

[66] *Ex parte Kan-gi-shun-ca*, 109 U.S. 556, 571 (1883).

[67] *Id.* at 557.

[68] *Id.* at 562.

[69] *Id.* at 562–63.

[70] *Id.*

[71] 18 U.S.C. § 1153 (2014).

[72] John Hayden Dossett, *Indian Country and the Territory Clause: Washington's Promise at the Framing*, 68 Am. U. L. Rev. 205, 249 (2018).

[73] 18 U.S.C. § 1151. The full definition is: "(a) all land within the limits of any Indian reservation under the jurisdiction of the United States Government, notwithstanding the issuance of any patent, and including rights-of-way running through the reservation, (b) all dependent Indian communities within the borders of the United States whether within the original or subsequently acquired territory thereof, and whether within or without the limits of a state, and (c) all Indian allotments, the Indian titles to which have not been extinguished, including rights-of-way running through the same."

was "Indian."[74] The matter of jurisdiction over crimes committed by non-Indians in Indian Country was left unresolved, however, and went unaddressed by the courts for decades.[75]

Congressional expansion of federal criminal jurisdiction in Indian Country was ostensibly driven by a federal desire to establish a more uniform system for prosecuting serious crimes committed on tribal lands, where the method of prosecution and the nature of the punishment might vary from one tribe to the next. Yet, it had another effect, too, which was to augment the federal government's power in Indian Country, and this had the corresponding effect of diminishing tribal sovereignty. On the heels of the Major Crimes Act, Congress passed the General Allotment Act, which authorized the President, through the Secretary of Interior, to survey all tribal lands and offer unoccupied lands to nontribal members, without tribal consent.[76] As discussed in the previous chapter, the Secretary of Interior initially divided up surveyed tribal lands into homesteads of between 40 and 160 acres, based on his estimate of how many individual homesteads would be necessary for the number of families in the tribe. These were offered first to tribal members, who were encouraged to "homestead" the land. If they could settle for a period of time and "prove up" their homesteads, tribal heads of household could thereby obtain fee title to the land upon maintaining 25 years of exclusive occupancy. As mentioned, the remaining tribal lands, deemed "surplus" by the Secretary of Interior's survey, were opened to nontribal members and land speculators, to descend upon and attempt to privatize under the various land and resource disposal statutes applicable to federal lands at the time.[77] During this era, which inflicted generations of trauma on indigenous peoples, tribes lost 90 million acres of land, or two-thirds of the existing tribal land base.[78]

Tribes challenging the federal government's implementation of this devastating policy did not fare well in the courts, either. The notable Supreme Court case of *Lone Wolf v. Hitchcock* demonstrated the Supreme Court's position at the time, which was to essentially rationalize and justify the Department of Interior's wholesale seizure of most of the existing tribal land base.[79] *Lone Wolf* challenged Congress's ratification of a fraudulently signed treaty agreement with the Kiowa, Comanche, and Apache Nations, in which the tribes allegedly ceded over 2.1

[74] GETCHES ET AL., *supra* note 3, at 486.

[75] Honorable William C. Canby Jr., *Tribal Court, Federal Court, State Court*, Ariz. Att'y, 7-93, at 24, 36.

[76] 25 U.S.C. § 331 (repealed); County of Yakima v. Confederated Tribes & Bands of Yakima Indian Nation, 502 U.S. 251, 254 (1992).

[77] *Id.*

[78] Charlene Koski, *The Legacy of* Solem v. Bartlett: *How Courts Have Used Demographics to Bypass Congress and Erode the Basic Principles of Indian Law*, 84 WASH. L. REV. 723, 730 (2009).

[79] Lone Wolf v. Hitchcock, 187 U.S. 553 (1903).

million acres of land to the federal government.[80] After Congress passed the statute ratifying the treaty, Secretary of Interior Ethan Hitchcock opened the ceded tribal lands to nontribal settlers.[81] The tribes sued, arguing that the statute was invalid because it was based on an invalid treaty, signed by less than the required minimum number of adult male tribal members.[82] In contrast to the reasoning expressed in earlier cases, such as *Ex parte Kan-gi-shun-ca*, the *Lone Wolf* Court sided with the federal government, holding that Congress had authority to pass legislation of this nature, even when it abrogated earlier treaties.[83] For the first time, in this case, the Court stated that Congress's power "over the tribal relations of the Indians" was "plenary," and the Court indicated it would almost entirely defer to Congress's actions.[84]

Over the next century, Congress passed a number of statutes related to Indian Country and "Indian affairs" that went far beyond criminal jurisdiction and land divestiture. In the twentieth century, Congress passed statutes governing tribal recognition, tribal governmental structures, natural resources development, child welfare, and many other topics.[85] Congress also unilaterally imposed US citizenship on tribal members in 1924.[86] Yet, despite what was essentially two centuries of onslaught from colonial and then American governmental entities, including states, aimed at assimilating tribal members into nonindigenous American society, many tribes retained their "separateness," geographically, culturally, and politically.[87] By the early 1930s, in fact, it was apparent that tribes would not voluntarily assimilate and had little interest in shedding their cultural norms, political autonomy, religious beliefs, and languages in favor of joining the apocryphal melting pot of American society. In partial recognition of this fact, Congress passed the Indian Reorganization Act of 1934, otherwise known as the Wheeler-Howard Act or IRA.[88] This statute formally ended the allotment era, authorized federal funding for tribal economic development, and included a mechanism for expanding tribal land bases by authorizing the Secretary of Interior to take land into trust on behalf of tribes, although it conditioned these "benefits" on the adoption of quasi-federal governmental structures.[89] For tribes that chose to adopt governmental organizational documents such as constitutions, implementing a democratic electoral process, the IRA provided a middle ground between absolute assimilation and total exclusion

---

[80] *Id.* at 559.
[81] *Id.* at 560.
[82] *Id.* at 556. Some of the signatures were also fraudulent, having been penned by federal government officials, rather than adult male tribal members.
[83] *Id.* at 564.
[84] *Id.* at 565.
[85] *Id.*
[86] *Id.* at 223.
[87] GETCHES ET AL., *supra* note 3, at 189–90.
[88] 25 U.S.C. § 461, *et seq.*
[89] *Id.*

from a federal system that offered certain benefits, like economic development funds to their citizens.

In the mid-twentieth century, though, Congress engaged in further legislative backsliding, passing statutes that terminated federally recognized tribes, ending the formal government-to-government relationship that the United States and certain denominated tribes had recognized, in some cases, for over a century.[90] The stated purpose of these statutes was to end the "federal supervision" of tribes and "free" them from the federal oversight imposed by statutes like the IRA.[91] Of the statutes passed during this time, arguably none has had lengthier legal consequences for tribal autonomy and jurisdiction than Public Law 280.[92] Passed in 1953, this statute essentially transferred civil and criminal jurisdiction over Indian Country from the federal government to certain identified states, allowing or requiring states to assume this authority without the consent of the tribes subject to it.[93] Until 1968, when Congress finally mandated tribal consent to state jurisdiction under PL 280, states could assume as much civil and criminal authority over indigenous lands as they were capable of exercising.[94] Further complicating matters, some states initially assumed jurisdiction, but later retroceded it, creating a jurisdictional quagmire that tribes, states, and the federal courts have been trying to sort out ever since.[95] For practitioners and tribes located in PL 280 states, tracing the historical contours of the acquisition and possible retrocession of jurisdiction is a necessary first step to determining the viability of claims involving cultural resource protection, especially under tribal or state law.

In addition to the legal mess and economic devastation that termination statutes created, they also had the social effect of reawakening many tribal cultural practices.[96] Tribes resisted termination vehemently, and the federal policies aimed at achieving assimilation and termination seemed to have exactly the opposite of the intended effect – tribes were galvanized around the greater purpose of preserving their political, social, and cultural autonomy and discovered that their "separateness" gave them power.[97] Tribal calls for federal affirmation of tribal sovereignty led to President Nixon's famous message to Congress in 1970, in which he called upon the United States to condemn forced termination, assimilation, and other federal

---

[90] Getches et al., *supra* note 3, at 200–3.

[91] *Id.* at 201.

[92] *Id.*

[93] *Id.* at 489. PL 280 identified some states as "mandatory" states, requiring them to assert jurisdiction in Indian Country. Other identified states, referred to as "non-mandatory" states, were authorized, but not required to assert jurisdiction in Indian Country.

[94] *Id.*

[95] Pub. L. 280 modified the basic structure of criminal jurisdiction from the Major Crimes Act and subsequent Supreme Court opinions, creating a space for states to exercise criminal jurisdiction over non–major crimes in some states. Getches et al., *supra* note 3, at 484.

[96] *Id.* at 216.

[97] *Id.*

policies that undermined indigenous self-determination.[98] In the 1970s and 1980s, Congress responded, passing statutes aimed at revitalizing tribal economies, spurring economic development in Indian Country, and reversing the trend of forcible adoption of tribal children through state foster systems. Congress also passed amendments to major environmental statutes like the Clean Air Act and Clean Water Act, increasing the role of tribal governments in environmental regulation.[99] Under these statutes, tribes were able to voluntarily opt into the role of primary regulators of intra- and extraterritorial sources of pollution, giving them power in some cases to control off-reservation activities impacting tribal lands. Some tribes have used the legal power derived from these statutes to protect sacred cultural waters.[100]

Yet, while Congress moved to promote tribal sovereignty and self-determination in the 1970s and 1980s, the Supreme Court began to cabin it. In 1978, the Supreme Court issued an opinion that imposed implied limitations on tribal criminal jurisdiction, preventing tribes from prosecuting non-Indians who commit crimes in Indian Country.[101] In 1981, the Court heard arguments in *Montana v. United States*, which involved the Crow Tribe's regulation of duck hunting and trout fishing on the Crow Reservation.[102] The challenged regulation prohibited nonmembers from hunting and fishing on all lands and waters within the boundaries of the reservation.[103] Some of this land was fee land owned by nonmembers, which the state of Montana argued that it should have authority to regulate as "state" land. The state also claimed ownership of the bed and banks of the Bighorn River, which the Supreme Court eventually determined were owned by the state despite the language of the Crow Treaty of 1868.[104] Before the court of appeals, the Tribe's jurisdictional arguments resonated, but the Supreme Court reversed, citing two concerns with allowing tribal regulatory authority over nonmembers on fee lands. First, the Court was concerned that allowing tribal regulations to extend to nonmembers' activity on fee lands was "inconsistent" with the Tribe's "diminished" sovereign status, and following a doctrine that it had used in the preceding decades, the Court held that the Crow Tribe had been impliedly divested of the authority to regulate nonmembers on fee lands because that involved a matter that was "external" to the tribe and regulated historically by the state.[105] The state of Montana had maintained "near-exclusive" regulatory authority over fee lands inside the reservation, which the

---

[98]   *Id.* at 219.
[99]   Elizabeth Ann Kronk Warner, *Tribes As Innovative Environmental "Laboratories,"* 86 U. COLO. L. REV. 789, 806 (2015).
[100]   *See, e.g.,* City of Albuquerque v. Browner, 97 F.3d 415, 424 (10th Cir. 1996).
[101]   Oliphant v. Suquamish Indian Tribe, 435 U.S. 191 (1978).
[102]   GETCHES ET AL., *supra* note 3, at 528.
[103]   450 U.S. 544, 547 (1981).
[104]   *Id.*
[105]   *Id.* at 564.

Tribe had traditionally accommodated, a fiction on which the Court relied to deprive the Tribe of its claims to sovereign authority over these lands.[106]

According to the *Montana* Court, there are only two circumstances in which tribal sovereignty can extend to nonmember activity on non–Indian owned fee lands.[107] The first is when the nonmember has consented to tribal jurisdiction, and the second is when the nonmember conduct "threatens or has some effect on the political integrity, the economic security, or the health and welfare of the tribe."[108] The exceptions theoretically guaranteed tribes some measure of protection for their sovereign authority, although, in the years after the *Montana* opinion was issued, the Supreme Court has only once upheld tribal jurisdiction over nonmembers on non-Indian fee land, in a plurality opinion in 1989 case involving tribal zoning, *Brendale v. Confederated Tribes and Bands of the Yakima Nation.*[109] Therefore, the clear boundary markers drawn by Justice Marshall in *Worcester v. Georgia* were changed not only by the Major Crimes Act but also by the process of removal, the allotment of tribal lands, the passage of time, and the more modern subjectivism of the US Supreme Court.[110] For the Crow Tribe, residing on a reservation dotted with fee lands like a checkerboard, the impact of the *Montana* decision was a blow to the tribal government's power within the Tribe's own reservation and served as recognition from the highest legal authority that state regulation could reach into tribal territory via these fee lands. This, in turn, empowered nonmembers, whose on-reservation conduct the Tribe was largely powerless to regulate.

At the same time the Supreme Court was chipping away at tribal sovereignty through opinions like *Oliphant, Montana*, and the later-issued *Nevada* v. *Hicks* (in which the Court adopted the *Montana* framework to limit tribal civil jurisdiction over claims involving state police activities on tribal lands),[111] the Court continued to recognize Congressional power to set the terms of the federal–tribal–state relationship. Despite a shaky constitutional basis, the twenty-first-century Court describes this as a constitutional power.[112] As recently as 2004, in *United States* v. *Lara,* the Court recognized that "the Constitution grants Congress broad general powers to legislate in respect to Indian tribes, powers that [the Court has] consistently described as 'plenary and exclusive.'"[113] The Court currently recognizes the textual

"Define"-subjectivism? wow

---

[106] *Id.* at 566.
[107] *Id.*
[108] *Id.*
[109] 492 U.S. 408 (1989).
[110] David H. Getches, *Conquering the Cultural Frontier: The New Subjectivism of the Supreme Court in Indian Law*, 84 Calif. L. Rev. 1573 (1996).
[111] 533 U.S. 353 (2001).
[112] 541 U.S. 193, 200 (2004).
[113] *Id.* at 204 (citing *e.g.*, Washington v. Confederated Bands and Tribes of Yakima Nation, 439 U.S. 463, 470–71 (1979); Negonsott v. Samuels, 507 U.S. 99, 103 (1993)); *see* Wheeler, 435 U.S., at 323, 98 S.Ct. 1079; *see also* W. Canby, American Indian Law 2 (3rd ed. 1998) ("[T]he

sources of these "broad general powers" as the Indian Commerce Clause and the Treaty Clause.[114] In *Lara*, the Court declared that "The 'central function of the Indian Commerce Clause,' ... 'is to provide Congress with plenary power to legislate in the field of Indian affairs.'"[115] As for the treaty power, the Court explained that although "The treaty power does not literally authorize Congress to act legislatively, for it is an Article II power authorizing the President, not Congress, 'to make Treaties,' ... treaties made pursuant to that power can authorize Congress to deal with 'matters' with which otherwise 'Congress could not deal.'"[116]

The results of Congress's expansive of "broad general powers" to legislate with regard to Indian Country have been mixed, but certainly prolific. Recent examples are statutes aimed at stimulating tribal economic growth, such as the Indian Gaming Regulatory Act,[117] statutes aimed at rectifying disastrous federal policies of earlier eras, such as the Indian Child Welfare Act,[118] and tribally designed and supported laws that protect tribal cultural values, such as the Native American Graves Protection and Repatriation Act,[119] and the environmental amendments of the 1970s and 1980s, authorizing tribal primacy over the regulatory structure of several major areas of environmental regulation.[120]

Tribal governments, tribal members, and academics have viewed the latter examples of congressional plenary power as beneficial to tribal integrity, culture, and even supportive of tribal sovereignty,[121] but the effects of these statutes must, in this context, be divorced from the underlying legal authority supporting them. This is because the underlying premise for *any* modern federal legislation relating to indigenous peoples, their lands, or their cultures is that Congress possesses authority, whether it is properly characterized as constitutional or extraconstitutional, over tribes and other indigenous nations, despite their legal status as sovereign domestic nations.[122] If the Court continues to recognize this power as valid, and broad, Congress can continue to wield a heavy hand in Indian Country.

independence of the tribes is subject to exceptionally great powers of Congress to regulate and modify the status of the tribes").

[114] Lara, 541 U.S. at 200. (*E.g.,* Morton v. Mancari, 417 U.S. 535, 552 (1974); McClanahan v. Arizona Tax Commission, 411 U.S. 164, 172 (1973); *see also* CANBY, *supra* note 113, at 11–12; F. COHEN, HANDBOOK OF FEDERAL INDIAN LAW 209–10 (1982)).

[115] Lara, *supra* note 114 (citing Cotton Petroleum Corp. v. New Mexico, 490 U.S. 163, 192 (1989); *see also, e.g.,* Ramah Navajo School Board, Inc. v. Bureau of Revenue of New Mexico, 458 U.S. 832, 837 (1982) ("broad power" under the Indian Commerce Clause); White Mountain Apache Tribe v. Bracker, 448 U.S. 136, 142 (1980) (same, and citing Wheeler, *supra* note 113, at 322–23)).

[116] Lara, *supra* note 114, at 201 (quoting U.S. CONST., Art. II, § 2, cl. 2; Missouri v. Holland, 252 U.S. 416, 433 (1920)).

[117] 25 U.S.C. §§ 2701–21 (2012).

[118] *Id.* at §§ 1901–3.

[119] *Id.* at §§ 3001–13.

[120] Kronk Warner, *supra* note 99.

[121] *Id.*

[122] Lara, *supra* note 112, at 200.

At the same time, states have a much greater role in Indian Country than ever before, thanks to the jurisdictional muddle wrought by PL 280, the allotment era, and the policies of removal. As Chapter 7 discusses, states played a horrific role in the near annihilation of their indigenous populations, which the Supreme Court has acknowledged.[123] But today, states are starting to attempt reparations. Maine and California have instituted the first state-based truth and reconciliation commissions in the nation in 2016 and 2019, respectively.[124] Maine's effort sent numerous commissioners across the state to interview members of the Wabanaki Confederacy tribes about the impacts of the state's devastating child removal policies.[125] One discovery the commissioners made was that state agencies continue to apply these policies in individual cases involving Maliseet, Penobscot, Passamaquoddy, Abenaki, and Micmac children, despite the state's official rescission and attempted restitution. On the whole, though, tribes around the country have acknowledged the impact that states' efforts have made in opening up relationships that had been historically traumatic for tribes.

Finally, and critically, tribes remain at the forefront of the battle to preserve their sovereignty and its associated legal rights, like jurisdiction and regulatory authority. They feel the impacts of these jurisdictional rules in their day-to-day lives, at a level that is hard for many nonindigenous Americans to comprehend. Tribes like the Cherokee, who once occupied vast areas encompassing parts of several states, on lands they had inhabited for thousands of years, are now fractured, feeling the multigenerational legal and social effects of a cross-country diaspora. The Cherokee Nation was once governed by one government, subject to the jurisdiction of one court system, speaking one language, occupying one land base, and sharing the same customs and day-to-day rhythms of life. Today, the descendants of eighteenth-century Cherokee families live scattered across many states, some in dedicated Cherokee communities, such as the three federally recognized Cherokee tribes, and others in numerous cities and towns throughout the country.

For the Cherokee Nation in Oklahoma, which numbers more than 500,000 according to the tribe's most recent census, and which contains the largest population of Cherokee of the three recognized Cherokee tribes, the results of removal, allotment, and the jurisdictional evolution in the Supreme Court from the Marshall Trilogy to the modern cases like *Lara and Oliphant* created a legal and practical morass. Like other federally recognized tribes, the nation has its own legal system with adjudicatory authority as delineated and limited by the US Supreme Court. It

---

[123] GETCHES ET AL., *supra* note 3, at 615.
[124] Susan Sharon, *Maine, Tribes Seek "Truth and Reconciliation,"* NATIONAL PUBLIC RADIO (Mar. 12, 2013, 4:00 AM), https://www.npr.org/2013/03/12/174080043/maine-tribes-seek-truth-and-reconciliation; Jill Cowan, *"It's Called Genocide": Newsom Apologizes to the State's Native Americans,* NEW YORK TIMES (June 19, 2019), https://www.nytimes.com/2019/06/19/us/newsom-native-american-apology.html.
[125] Sharon, *supra* note 124.

has inherent sovereign authority over the activities of its members within its territory, but it lacks regulatory authority over nonmembers on non-Indian private lands unless the tribe can demonstrate that it satisfies one of the *Montana* exceptions. The results of this jurisdictional quagmire is that tribes largely lack authority over nonmembers, especially if they are not Indian, even within Indian Country. So, while tribes can develop, adopt, and enforce their own cultural preservation laws, their ability to enforce those laws against non-Indians and adjudicate any disputes that arise under those laws (or other laws) is limited. Because of this, tribes like the Cherokee largely depend on the federal government to adopt laws that criminalize or impose civil penalties on non-Indians in Indian Country. For tribes seeking to protect cultural values or rights outside Indian Country, the path is even more difficult, unless there is a treaty right or statutory right allowing the tribe to regulate or punish harmful behavior by non-Indians.

Yet, it is important to note that the path forward is not impossible, even under the existing framework. Tribes retain viable options for seeking greater cultural protections in the twenty-first century and beyond and, perhaps more importantly, are also forging new legal and political opportunities for change. The following chapters detail these options and opportunities.

3

Religious Freedom, the Value of Sacred Places, and the Price of Cultural Ignorance

Tribal religions are actually complexes of attitudes, beliefs, and practices fine-tuned to harmonize with the lands on which the people live.

—Vine Deloria Jr.[1]

Many indigenous nations, tribes, bands, and communities have unique religions, and although it is difficult to generalize across such a large spectrum, there are certain themes that are useful for the purposes of understanding legal claims involving indigenous religions. For instance, many indigenous religions are place based, centering on a principle of stewardship toward a specific place, like a sacred mountain, river, lake, or geological feature.[2] For place-based indigenous religions, essential religious practices may include pilgrimages and prayer, meditation, and other acts designed to engage and fortify spiritual communion with the place. The religious teachings of these faiths may hold that the sacred place played a role in the origin of the tribe and that it continues to be an essential foundation of the tribe's well-being.

For some indigenous peoples, the sacred place may be sentient, providing protection and ensuring the health, safety, and prosperity of the people on a daily basis. Therefore, communing with, praying to, and meditating near or in the sacred place ensures that the place will continue to protect and care for the people. Simultaneously, as place protects people, people must protect place, both to demonstrate their gratitude for the protection they have received and to maintain the spiritual connections that have existed for millennia and ensure their future health and prosperity. Some of the acts of worship reflecting this relationship can and do occur in homes and communal gathering places, distant from the sacred place. As in Christian, Muslim, Jewish, and other nonindigenous religions, though the distant

[1] VINE DELORIA JR., GOD IS RED: A NATIVE VIEW OF RELIGION 69 (2003).
[2] *Id.* at 66.

acts of worship, devotion, and spiritual caretaking are integrally connected to the sacred place. Also, similar to other religions, the purity of the sacred place is vital to the religion. Any harm befalling the sacred place can strike at the very heart of the religion itself, which in turn threatens the cultural integrity of the population as a whole. This is true regardless of whether the devotees travel to the sacred place to worship – as it would be for Muslim adherents who never make the pilgrimage to Mecca, for instance. Through these acts of worship, stewardship, and communion, place-based indigenous religions ensure the continuing health of the place, which is linked directly to the health of the people.

Some indigenous religions do not center on a place, but rather on one or more sacred species, such as bison, whale, or salmon. The dogma of some of these religions holds that the species gave life to the people at the moment of creation, and since time immemorial, the people have relied on the species for their con- tinued vitality, often quite literally.[3] Hunting, harvesting, or fishing is a religious practice for the followers of these religious faiths, and the acts of tracking, hunting, preparing, and consuming the animal, fish, or whale often involve sacred, ancient rituals and ceremonies that last for days or weeks during certain seasons of the year. For these peoples, the social and cultural patterns of their lives are (or traditionally were) connected to the species, including its migration patterns and life cycle. Therefore, ensuring abundance for the people can involve specific acts of prayer and religious rites throughout the entire year, in which tribal members pray to the species to bring them sufficient sustenance for the coming season or year. Like the place-based religions, the acts of pursuing, preparing, and consuming these animals and fish were traditionally accompanied by prayers and religious acts of gratitude, to ensure that the species would continue to bless the people with health and prosper- ity in the future. Further, for some tribes, the species they worship are considered in many senses to be "people" too, and there is no alienation of people from animals, or animals from community.[4]

There are myriad indigenous religions and religious practices that do not fit within these rough categories, yet across all indigenous religions, there is one universal truism. That is the fact that nonindigenous judges, politicians, and land- management officials with legal authority over sacred places or sacred species often struggle to understand the indigenous religions tied directly to them. There may be many reasons for this, but one of them is likely that indigenous religions do not resemble other major religious faiths, in practice or in theory. Indigenous rituals often cannot be seen, requiring solitude and taking place in remote, isolated areas. Indigenous religious dogma is often secret, held by tribal religious leaders and

---

[3] *Id.* at 88.
[4] *Id.*

prohibited from being shared with others, even other tribal members.[5] To the extent it can be revealed, that is often done orally, not in writing, so there is no Bible or other book of religious teachings that a tribe can submit to a federal land management agency or judge to help explain how the religion works. For decades, these audiences in particular have failed to understand indigenous religions, resulting in multitudes of indigenous religious legal claims being discarded or dismissed. Tribes have therefore suffered immeasurable cultural losses at the hands of outside officials with power over their sacred places and practices. Since indigenous peoples first began raising legal claims involving religion, judges in particular have approached them with skepticism, disbelief, or confusion, rendering this type of legal claim one of the most difficult for tribes to use effectively in court.

The United States has a lengthy history of federal suppression of indigenous religions, which reached its zenith in the late nineteenth century but continues to impact tribal religious practices even today.[6] In the days of *Worcester v. Georgia*, the federal government actively encouraged Christian missionaries to bring the gospel to Indian tribes, although there was at the time no official federal policy of Christianizing Indian Country.[7] By the late 1800s, the federal approach had crystallized into a policy that was to bring Christianity to as many tribes as possible, replacing their traditional religious practices with more "civilized" ones and banning the practice of indigenous religions outright.[8] This policy accompanied the large-scale removal and reservation program discussed in Chapter 2; as tribes were removed from their traditional lands and resettled on reservations, they were expected to take up not only Christian agricultural practices and a Christian lifestyle but the Christian religion itself. By the time the General Allotment Act was passed in 1887, "almost every form of Indian religion was banned on the reservations."[9] This even included funeral ceremonies, which were declared illegal.[10] Outlining the federal policies was the task of the Commissioner of Indian Affairs, who oversaw the individual Indian agents residing on each reservation. Each of these agents was, in turn, charged with enforcing the federal religious suppression and conversion policies.[11]

Tribes resisted religious oppression heartily, though. One form of resistance was the modification of religious practices to appear to conform to and coincide with major Christian religious holidays or major federal or state holidays.[12] Tribes would

---

[5]   Sometimes it is secret as a result of historical federal policies aimed at eradicating indigenous religions as well. *See* DELORIA, *supra* note 1, at 271.

[6]   *Id.* at 271.

[7]   DAVID H. GETCHES, CHARLES F. WILKINSON, ROBERT A. WILLIAMS JR., MATTHEW L. M. FLETCHER, & KRISTEN A. CARPENTER, CASES AND MATERIALS ON FEDERAL INDIAN LAW 91 (7th ed. 2017).

[8]   *Id.* at 238.

[9]   *Id.* at 240.

[10]   *Id.*

[11]   GETCHES ET AL., *supra* note 7, at 727.

[12]   DELORIA, *supra* note 1, at 241.

FIGURE 3.1 Arizona Snowbowl Ski Resort, Nuvatukyaovi, Arizona
(Brian Stablyk/Getty Images)

tell the Indian agent assigned to their reservation that they were holding a celebration honoring the Fourth of July, but their songs, dances, and prayers were the traditional ones, honoring their sacred places or blessing the upcoming hunt, adapted slightly based on their new circumstances and the need for secrecy.[13] Adaptations like these preserved indigenous religions, while creating the appearance that tribes were assimilating into mainstream American society. Some tribes were even fortunate enough, either through the size of their reservations or the political power of their governments, to maintain their religious practices largely unchanged during the era of allotment and assimilation. Tribes like the Navajo, the Pueblos of New Mexico, and the Hopi preserved their religions by holding ceremonies in secret, isolated locations, far from the prying eyes of the Indian agents.[14]

To the Hopi and neighboring tribes, a small mountain range in northeastern Arizona is as sacred as Jerusalem is to Christians.[15] The Hopi call these mountains Nuvatukyaovi (Figure 3.1).[16] For thousands of years before European settlers arrived in the region, the Hopi lived in villages east of Nuvatukyaovi, which they have always believed to be the center of the Hopi universe. This is the place where Hopi

---

[13] *Id.*
[14] *Id.*
[15] Navajo Nation v. U.S. Forest Service, 535 F.3d 1058, 1081 (9th Cir. 2008).
[16] *Id.*

people direct all of their prayers and acts of spiritual devotion.[17] Nuvatukyaovi is particularly important to the Hopi religion because it is the seasonal home of the Kachinas, spirits who bring vital "water, snow and life to the Hopi people."[18] According to Hopi tradition, from late summer through midwinter, the Kachina live in Nuvatukyaovi, and for the remainder of the year, they travel down from the mountains and live among the people in their villages.[19]

The Hopi have made pilgrimages from their villages to these mountains since time immemorial. The small carved Kachina figures in Hopi homes serve as tangible reminders of the Kachina in Nuvatukyaovi and are considered spiritual instruments, which the Hopi look to and think about during "their daily songs and prayers."[20] The figures "are more than artfully crafted dolls. To the Hopi they are spiritual icons that call the rains and their ancestors to bring more water, life, and good fortune for all mankind."[21] The Kachina these figures represent are simultaneously the source of, and recipients of, all-important spiritual and tangible acts of Hopi faith.[22] Because the Kachina call Nuvatukyaovi home for part of the year, the Hopi religious dogma, practices, and beliefs all center in or involve Nuvatukyaovi.[23]

As discussed in Chapter 2, the removal period of the nineteenth century resulted in many tribes being physically removed from their places of origin, which often took them away from the places or species that had anchored their religious faith. The General Allotment Act of 1887 further restricted tribal rights to access these sacred places, and other treaties and statutes impacted tribal rights to harvest species that were vital to tribal religions, through privatization to nonindigenous settlers, railroads, and other corporate interests and also through changing federal land designations under various late-1800 federal disposal statutes.[24] Although the Hopi were not removed from their traditional villages, their access to and use of their sacred mountains was greatly impacted by the establishment of Nuvatukyaovi as a

---

[17] *Id.*

[18] *Id.* at 10 99.

[19] Wilson v. Block, 708 F.2d 735, 738 (D.C. Cir. 1983).

[20] Navajo Nation, *supra* note 15, at 1058, 1099.

[21] Katosha Belvin Nakai, *When Kachinas and Coal Collide: Can Cultural Resources Law Rescue the Hopi at Black Mesa?*, 35 ARIZ. ST. L.J. 1283, 1322 (2003).

[22] Brief of Hopi Nation, Navajo Nation, et al. v. U.S. Forest Service et al., 2006 WL 2429669 (9th Cir. 2008).

[23] One critical function of the Kachina is to bring water to the people, which is why Hopi dress as Kachina and perform Kachina dances during arid periods of the year. Nakai, *supra* note 21, at 1285. This connection between Hopi and water is so vital that one scholar estimates that over half of all Hopi names are connected in some way to water. Nakai, *supra* note 21, at 1287.

[24] Some federal statutes, such as the Bald and Golden Eagle Protection Act, contain provisions allowing tribes to obtain permits under a religious exemption, allowing them to take species that are otherwise protected from hunting or harvesting, but for other species, there is no such mechanism. *See* GETCHES ET AL., *supra* note 7, at 754. Navigating this area requires detailed research into the species at the heart of the religious practice and the history of federal or state restrictions on hunting or harvesting it.

national forest reserve in 1908.[25] The act of Congress creating the Coconino National Forest gave the newly created US Forest Service sole management authority over the forest, including the power to authorize logging, mining, recreation, water diversion projects, and other activities. When the Hopi Reservation was created in 1936 out of traditional village lands more than 100 miles from Nuvatukyaovi, it sealed the boundaries of the Tribe's legal rights to an area far from the sacred mountains, preventing the Tribe from having any legal power to control their use by outsiders.

In 1937, the Forest Service approved a permit to construct a ski area on the tallest peak in Nuvatukyaovi.[26] Since then, it has been in continual seasonal use and slowly expanding, somewhat gradually in the earlier years, but more aggressively since the 1970s.[27] In 1977, the owners submitted a proposal to increase the footprint dramatically, including more ski lifts, expanded parking areas, a larger base of operations, and plans to cut large sections of forest to create additional ski trails.[28] Until this point, the Hopi had generally opposed the ski area's presence on the mountain, but they had not raised any legal challenges. The 1977 expansion simply went too far, though. As stewards of the mountains, with a religious duty to protect their purity, the Hopi decided to bring a legal challenge to attempt to stop the expansion and filed suit against the Forest Service after it approved the 1977 expansion plan. The Tribe's primary argument was that the expansion would violate the tribal members' First Amendment rights to freely exercise their religion.[29]

The First Amendment of the US Constitution restricts Congress's ability to make laws prohibiting the "free exercise" of religion.[30] Courts expanded this to a general prohibition on many other types of government actions, including federal permits authorizing certain activities on federal lands. For the courts, this analysis requires answering the question of whether a law or governmental practice or action discriminates against a religious belief, "inhibits the exercise" of an individual's religious beliefs or otherwise "burdens" it.[31] If the individual can show either, the court will analyze whether the governmental entity had a compelling secular purpose and whether it used the least restrictive means of achieving that purpose.[32] Thus, even when a plaintiff can show that a government action has inhibited the free exercise of the individual's religion, the challenge might not succeed in court, depending on the proffered governmental rationale for the harmful action and how the court views and balances the religious exercise against the governmental purpose and

---

[25] 16 U.S.C. § 482n.

[26] Navajo Nation, *supra* note 15, at 1064.

[27] Wilson, *supra* note 19, at 738.

[28] *Id.*

[29] *Id.*

[30] U.S. Const., Amend. I.

[31] Michael W. McConnell, *The Origins and Historical Understanding of Free Exercise of Religion*, 103 Harv. L. Rev. 1409, 1417 (1990).

[32] *Id.*

rationale.[33] Critically, the analysis that accompanies this legal test depends on how the attorneys explain and present the religious practices and beliefs to the court and how well the reviewing judge understands them.

In the case of the Hopi and the Forest Service approval of the ski area and expansion the Tribe faced devastating threats to its religion from the proposal, which included road construction, parking lot grading and paving, forest clearing, cutting additional ski trails, and also the installation of new ski lifts, expansion of buildings at the base of the ski area. Beyond the initial construction, there were inevitable impacts from the multitudes of additional recreational users attracted by these new amenities. These were acts of desecration that the Hopi were legally powerless to stop on their own; the tribe had no governmental authority or other legal right to participate in the governance decisions involving and affecting Nuvatukyaovi, aside from the rights shared by the general public. The First Amendment offered one of the only potentially viable claims for the Tribe, but the tribe's burden in court was high – it had to explain the Hopi religion in a manner that judges hearing the case would understand, identify the restrictions on religious practice that would flow from the Forest Service's decision to allow the expansion, and then hope that the judges would decide that any governmental interest in approving the ski area expansion was not compelling enough to infringe the tribal member's Free Exercise rights.[34]

The case against the Forest Service began where most Free Exercise claims start – with the task of explaining the Hopi religion in enough detail that the judge might understand how the religious faith is "exercised." This is a critical task because the severity of the impact of the governmental action depends largely on how the religious interest is explained. The task is complicated by the fact that even the Supreme Court has struggled to define what it means to "exercise" one's religion. In recent years, the Court has held that the "exercise of religion" can involve "not only belief and profession but the performance of (or abstention from) physical acts: assembling with others for a worship service, participating in sacramental use of bread and wine, proselytizing, abstaining from certain foods or certain modes of transportation."[35] The Court has therefore held that it would be unlawful for the government "to ban such acts or abstentions only when they are engaged in for religious reasons, or only because of the religious belief that they display," noting by way of example that "[i]t would doubtless be unconstitutional ... to ban the casting of statues that are to be used for worship purposes, or to prohibit bowing down before a golden calf."[36] However, when the religious acts violate a "general law, not aimed at the ... restriction of religious beliefs," the practitioner is not exempted from the

---

[33] *Id.*
[34] Wilson, *supra* note 19, at 735, 740–41.
[35] Employment Division, Department of Human Resources of Oregon v. Smith, 494 U.S. 872, 877–78 (1990).
[36] *Id.*

general law by virtue of the religious Free Exercise claim.[37] In one of the most famous cases to reach the high court involving indigenous religious claims, the Court held that members of the Native American Church, who practiced a religious ritual involving peyote ingestion, were not exempted from a general Oregon statute criminalizing the use of peyote, and the First Amendment also did not protect them from any other consequences of violating that law, which was generally applicable to the entire population of the state.[38] That decision basically obliterated the protections offered by the First Amendment to indigenous religious practitioners, which spurred Congress to restore a similar test and protection for religious exercise through the Religious Freedom Restoration Act (RFRA).[39] The Court has also held that a federal requirement for an indigenous child to obtain a Social Security number prior to receiving public assistance benefits did not violate the parent's Free Exercise rights, even though the parent asserted that assigning his child a unique identifying number would rob her of her essential spirit.[40]

The Hopi case against the Forest Service seemed more concrete, though, in at least in some respects. In their pleadings, the Hopi explained that Nuvatukyaovi was the spiritual center of their religion.[41] They explained the Kachina and their connection to Nuvatukyaovi and to the Hopi people. They also explained that one role of the Kachina is to create the rain and snow that fall on Nuvatukyaovi and funnel down to the Hopi villages, sustaining the people and literally giving them life. They explained that disturbing the mountain by cutting trees, grading roads, paving parking lots, and constructing ski trails would disturb the Kachina and the mountain, and therefore interfere with the delicate religious balance between mountain, Kachina, and people. It might literally stop the rain from coming or the snow from falling. They also explained their religious duty of stewardship toward Nuvatukyaovi, which requires them to protect the mountains from acts of desecration, to keep the time-honored symbiotic relationship intact, and thereby ensure the continuing prosperity of the Hopi people.

The court was not persuaded, though. In the first challenge, which did not resolve until 1983, the court held that while the Hopi petitioners' beliefs were "religious" and "sincerely held," the Forest Service's act of approving the ski area expansion did not directly or indirectly burden them.[42] Specifically, the court noted that "[m]any government actions may offend religious believers, and may cast doubt upon the veracity of religious beliefs, but unless such actions penalize faith, they do not burden religion."[43] In short, the act of the Forest Service

---

[37] *Id.*
[38] *Id.* at 890.
[39] Pub. L. 103-141, 107 Stat. 1488 (Nov. 16, 1993).
[40] *Bowen v. Roy*, 476 U.S. 693, 703 (1986).
[41] *Navajo Nation, supra* note 15, at 1063.
[42] *Wilson, supra* note 19, at 741.
[43] *Id.*

(approving the ski area expansion) did not burden the Tribe's "freedom to believe" in their religion, even if it caused the Hopi petitioners to experience what the court described as "spiritual disquiet."[44]

There were other general pitfalls the Hopi sought to avoid, too. One is that an individual bringing a Free Exercise challenge must show that the infringed activity is religious, as opposed to secular, and that the individual's religious belief is "sincere."[45] The latter is not a particularly onerous legal hurdle, but does require a sufficient showing that the religious exercise in question is part of a sincerely held religious belief, which may require expert testimony from a religious leader or a witness who is intimately familiar with the tenets of the religion.[46] In addition, tension can arise when the government acts to protect the religious practice of one individual or group in a way that acts as a governmental endorsement of that religion, due to the First Amendment's corollary clause prohibiting the establishment of an official state religion.[47] The Supreme Court has struggled to reconcile the tension between the Establishment Clause and the Free Exercise Clause, noting the difficulty of plotting "a neutral course between the two Religion Clauses, both of which are cast in absolute terms, and either of which, if expanded to a logical extreme, would tend to clash with the other."[48]

In 1988, the Supreme Court heard arguments in *Lyng v. Northwest Indian Cemetery Protective Association*, involving claims of the Yurok, Karok, and Tolowa tribes that a proposed logging road passing through a sacred prayer location in what is now the Six Rivers National Forest in northwestern California would violate their Free Exercise rights.[49] The Yurok, Karok, and Tolowa have occupied the area in and around the Six Rivers National Forest since time immemorial.[50] Many members of these tribes, including those who brought the lawsuit against the Forest Service, reside on the Hoopa Valley Indian Reservation, which borders the National Forest to the southwest.[51] Within the Six Rivers National Forest, there is a remote area known as the "high country," which the Yurok, Karok, and Tolowa consider sacred.[52] This area is the holiest place in their religion.[53] According to tribal historians, a specific area within the high country was established by the Creator as the sacred source of religious powers and is the only location in which to engage

---

[44] *Id.*

[45] McConnell, *supra* note 31, at 1417.

[46] Alabama & Coushatta Tribes of Texas v. Trustees of Big Sandy Independent School District, 817 F. Supp. 1319, 1329 (E.D. Tex. 1993) (considering testimony of an anthropologist familiar with Cree religion to determine if requiring a student to cut his hair infringed upon a sincerely held religious belief).

[47] Locke v. Davey, 540 U.S. 712, 718 (2004).

[48] Walz v. Tax Commission, 397 U.S. 664, 668–69 (1970).

[49] Lyng v. Northwest Indian Cemetery Protective Association, 485 U.S. 439, 459 (1988).

[50] *Id.*

[51] Brief for the Indian Respondents, *Lyng*, 1987 WL 880352, at *4 (filed Oct. 22, 1987).

[52] *Id.*

[53] *Id.* at 5.

in direct communion with the Creator.[54] Tribal members and tribal religious leaders use this area for rituals and ceremonies central to their religious belief system.[55] Practitioners use "prayer seats" located on focal sites within the area, as part of these rituals.[56] Under the tenets of their religion, these locales form a geographic hierarchy of power, which correlates with the progress of an individual practitioner's quest for spiritual power through the high country.[57] In a sequenced manner, practitioners can deepen their faith by completing these rituals, under the guidance of a spiritual leader.

If tribal members believe that the Creator has "called them," they make pilgrimages to the high country for prayer, divine guidance, and in quest of personal "power" for individual achievements and concerns.[58] They know when they have been called and what they need to do in response because they were trained as young people in the basic religious beliefs system of the tribe - training that took place in the sacred area within the high country.[59] The high country is thus integral to tribal members' practice of their religion but also to its perpetuation, because it is there that spiritual leaders train young people in the traditional religious beliefs and ceremonies, ensuring that the religion will continue.[60]

Similar to what happened to the Hopi sacred mountains, the Forest Service in 1982 approved a permit to upgrade a section of logging road through the Six Rivers National Forest, connecting the two logging towns of Gasquet and Orleans, located just outside the forest boundaries. These towns serve as gateways to the logging companies with rights to harvest timber in the forest.[61] The Gasquet–Orleans, or G–O, road expansion would pass through the heart of the high country, destroying the seclusion, silence, and tranquility of the area and making it impossible for the Tribes to conduct their ceremonies, and acts of communion and prayer.[62] Making matters worse for the Tribes, at around the same time it approved the permit for the new G–O road, the Forest Service adopted a new management plan for the area that contemplated a significant increase in timber harvesting.[63] Foreseeing the damage to the high country that would flow from these decisions, the tribes sued Secretary of Agriculture Richard Lyng and the Forest Service, claiming that the agency's decision to approve the road construction violated their First Amendment Free Exercise rights.[64] The case ultimately wound its way to the Supreme Court.

---

[54] *Id.*
[55] *Id.*
[56] *Id.* at 6.
[57] *Id.*
[58] *Id.*
[59] *Id.*
[60] *Id.*
[61] Lyng, *supra* note 49, at 442.
[62] *Id.*
[63] *Id.* at 443.
[64] *Id.*

Before the Supreme Court, the Tribes did not fare as well as they had before the more understanding courts below. In an opinion authored by Justice Sandra Day O'Connor, a majority of justices agreed that the permit approving the upgrades to the G–O road did not violate the Free Exercise rights of the tribal members.[65] Despite finding that the impact of constructing and paving the road would be "severe" and even "devastating" to the Tribes' religious practices, Justice O'Connor concluded that the "Constitution simply does not provide a principle that could justify upholding" the Tribes' religious claims.[66] Moreover, Justice O'Connor appeared troubled by the vast amount of forest land the tribal members used for their religious practices and perhaps even cynical about the their motives when she wrote "[n]o disrespect for these practices is implied when one notes that such beliefs could easily require *de facto* beneficial ownership of some rather spacious tracts of public property."[67] Finally, citing the number and complexity of potentially conflicting religious beliefs that might be impacted by a variety of different governmental actions on federal lands throughout the country, Justice O'Connor emphasized that "[t]he Constitution does not, and courts cannot, offer to reconcile the various competing demands on government, many of them rooted in sincere religious belief, that inevitably arise in so diverse a society as ours. That task, to the extent that it is feasible, is for the legislatures and other institutions."[68]

The effect of the *Lyng* decision on tribal religions was devastating and vast.[69] It made tribal religious freedom claims involving federal lands incredibly challenging, if not virtually impossible to assert, and seemingly created a new test only for tribal Free Exercise claims.[70] While traditional religious adherents were able to somewhat easily prevail on Free Exercise claims involving governmental policies infringing a right not to work on the Sabbath, for example, tribes could not, even when the complained of governmental policy threatened to destroy their equivalent of Jerusalem or Mecca.[71]

After *Lyng*, lower courts used the ruling as a basis to deny numerous tribal religious freedom challenges involving federal agency actions on federal land,[72] dismissing tribal religious claims. This included a second Hopi challenge to another Forest Service decision approving expanded ski area operations on Nuvatukyaovi in 2002.[73] Due to decreasing annual snowfall, the operators of the Snowbowl Ski

---

[65] *Id.* The Court also dismissed the tribes' claims under the much-cited American Indian Religious Freedom Act because there was no "judicially enforceable" right in that statute for the Court to apply.

[66] *Id.* at 447, 452.

[67] *Id.* at 453.

[68] *Id.* at 452.

[69] GETCHES ET AL., *supra* note 7, at 737.

[70] *Id.*

[71] Sherbert v. Verner, 374 U.S. 398, 404 (1963); Lyng, *supra* note 49, at 452.

[72] GETCHES ET AL., *supra* note 7, at 737.

[73] Navajo Nation, *supra* note 15, at 1058, 1071.

Resort proposed to increase their snowmaking operations, which required an additional Forest Service permit. In an effort to reduce cost, the Snowbowl operators proposed to use reclaimed wastewater for the snowmaking operations.[74] A pipeline conveying the reclaimed wastewater to the ski resort also would contain various fire hydrants, allowing residents and municipal entities along its path to access water for fire suppression efforts during the summer months.[75] A reservoir containing reclaimed wastewater was proposed for the base of the ski area, to support fire suppression efforts at the ski area.[76]

When the Forest Service issued its decision approving the ski resort's snowmaking and fire suppression plans, the Hopi and several other tribes with religious claims to the same mountains filed suit against the agency in federal court.[77] They alleged that the use of reclaimed wastewater, which contained a small but measurable percentage of human waste, on and near these mountains would desecrate them. This desecration would infringe on the plaintiff tribes' religious duty to protect the mountains from pollution and acts of desecration.

In an attempt to avoid the challenges of adverse precedent like *Lyng* and *Smith*, the tribes relied on RFRA,[78] which ostensibly provided a streamlined pathway to judicial review for "Americans of all faiths."[79] RFRA prohibits the government from imposing a substantial burden on "a person's exercise of religion even if the burden results from a rule of general applicability," unless the government can show that the burden is "in furtherance of a compelling governmental interest" and is the "least restrictive means of furthering that compelling interest."[80] An initial challenge to RFRA's applicability to state government actions was successful, rendering RFRA inapplicable to any claim against state agencies and officials, but it posed an intriguing new option for tribes that had been frustrated in their attempts to bring religious freedom claims.[81]

In the Hopi case against the Forest Service, the Tribe argued that the use of reclaimed wastewater, containing measureable amounts of human waste, on and near Nuvatukyaovi, would impose a substantial burden on the exercise of religion under RFRA.[82] Taking each part of the RFRA test in turn, the Court first noted that it was undisputed that the Hopi exercise of religion was inextricably tied to the area around the Snowbowl Ski Area. Thus, the Tribe had satisfied the first part of the test. In the court's analysis of the second part, though, problems arose when the judges explored

---

[74] *Id.* at 1065.

[75] *Id.*

[76] *Id.*

[77] *Id.*

[78] 42 U.S.C. § 2000bb–2000bb-4.

[79] GETCHES ET AL., *supra* note 7, at 752; *Religious Freedom Restoration Act Signing Ceremony*, FEDERAL NEWS SERVICE (Nov. 16, 1993).

[80] 42 U.S.C. § 2000bb(1)(a) & (b).

[81] City of Boerne v. Flores, 521 U.S. 507 (1997).

[82] Navajo Nation, *supra* note 15, at 1067.

whether the governmental action imposed a "substantial burden" on the tribal exercise of religion.[83] Hewing strictly to the language of two prior Supreme Court cases on which the RFRA test was based, the court established first that "[u]nder RFRA, a 'substantial burden' is imposed only when individuals are forced to choose between following the tenets of their religion and receiving a governmental benefit or coerced to act contrary to their religious beliefs by the threat of civil or criminal sanctions."[84] Applying this more nuanced and detailed standard to the case of the Hopi religious practices, the Ninth Circuit Court of Appeals found that "[t]he presence of recycled wastewater on the [sacred] Peaks does not coerce the Plaintiffs to act contrary to their religious beliefs under the threat of sanctions, nor does it condition a governmental benefit upon conduct that would violate their religious beliefs, as required to establish a 'substantial burden' on religious exercise under RFRA."[85]

By adhering so closely to the Supreme Court's holdings in the earlier cases of *Sherbert v. Verner* and *Wisconsin v. Yoder*, the Ninth Circuit adopted a test for RFRA claims that would be virtually impossible for any indigenous religious adherent to meet.[86] For the Hopi, it was clear that the Forest Service's approval of the reclaimed wastewater snowmaking and fire suppression project would, in fact, coerce the plaintiffs into acting contrary to their religious beliefs. They would be forced to make pilgrimages to Nuvatukyaovi and perform ceremonial acts surrounded by the remnants of human waste and human desecration. Such acts of desecration certainly controvert the Hopi religion, and by failing to stop these acts, the Hopi had violated a central tenet of their religion, which was to protect Nuvatukyaovi.

In addition, although the Hopi would not have to choose between receiving a governmental benefit and practicing their religion, they were faced with the arguably much worse situation of not being able to practice their religion in its original form at all, or potentially modify their religious practices to accommodate the desecration of their sacred mountains, which might have the effect of violating fundamental tenets of their religious faith. As dumping reclaimed wastewater on the Wailing Wall or pumping sewage into the Vatican would potentially destroy the value of those sacred places for Judaism and Catholicism, the use of reclaimed wastewater on Nuvatukyaovi destroyed the spiritual value of this place for the Hopi.

Yet, despite rulings like these, tribes continued to use RFRA as a basis for challenging federal actions impacting their religious places and practices. RFRA was one of the many legal tools used by the Standing Rock Sioux Tribe in the mid-2000s to challenge the construction of the Dakota Access Pipeline.[87] As discussed in

---

[83] 42 U.S.C. § 2000bb(1)(a) & (b).

[84] Navajo Nation, *supra* note 15, at 1069–70.

[85] *Id.* at 1067.

[86] *But see* Burwell v. Hobby Lobby Stores, Inc., 573 U.S. 682 (2014) (relying on RFRA to protect the religious beliefs and esercise of a privately held corporation).

[87] Standing Rock Sioux Tribe v. U.S. Army Corps of Engineers, 239 F. Supp. 3d 77, 88 (D.D.C., Mar. 7, 2017).

Chapter 1, the Tribe was powerless to stop most of the pipeline construction because it was routed almost entirely across private land. Thus much of the construction was allowed to proceed without tribal, federal, or state permitting.[88] The one place where Dakota Access needed to secure federal approval before completing the final section of the pipeline, though, was located half a mile from the Standing Rock Sioux Reservation border, at the edge of Lake Oahe.[89]

Lake Oahe and the waters of the Missouri River more generally are an integral part of various Lakota religious practices.[90] The Lakota originally sought to protect their rights in the waters of Lake Oahe through several environmental and historic preservation statutes, including many discussed in Chapter 4. It seemed that some of these might succeed, and near the end of 2016, the Army Corps of Engineers – the agency with primary permitting authority over the Lake Oahe crossing – paused its approval process to determine the nature of the Tribe's cultural interests and treaty rights in the lake before making any final decision on Dakota Access's application.[91] However, the Army Corps made this announcement after the November 2016 presidential election, in the waning months of the Obama administration. When President Trump took office in January 2017, he sent a presidential memorandum to the Secretary of the Army, directing the agency to expedite all approvals for the pipeline.[92] Shortly thereafter, the Army Corps issued a decision granting the easement for the completion of the pipeline under Lake Oahe.[93]

The Standing Rock Sioux Tribe and the Cheyenne River Sioux Tribe challenged the Army Corps' final approval of the pipeline easement under RFRA.[94] According to the Tribes' court filings, "the mere existence of a crude oil pipeline under the waters of Lake Oahe will desecrate those waters and render them unsuitable for use in … religious sacraments."[95] Further, the Tribes believed "that the pipeline correlate[d] with a terrible Black Snake prophesied to come into the Lakota homeland and cause destruction" and that "the very existence of the Black Snake under their sacred waters in Lake Oahe [would] unbalance and desecrate the water and render it impossible for the Lakota to use that water in their Inipi ceremony."[96] The procedural mechanism that the tribes used to introduce the religious claims was a motion for a preliminary injunction, which could stop construction temporarily while the district court considered the merits of the case. Part of the court's analysis under the rule allowing preliminary

---

88 *Id.*
89 *Id.*
90 *Id.* at 82.
91 *Id.*
92 *Id.*
93 *Id.*
94 *Id.*
95 *Id.*
96 *Id.*

injunctions is an assessment of the likelihood of success on the merits of the plaintiff's claim, so the court analyzed the RFRA argument in some detail, even though it was still only a preliminary stage of the case.[97]

Using a new three-part framing of the RFRA test adopted by the Supreme Court in a 2015 case under a related statute, the Religious Land Use and Institutionalized Persons Act, the *Standing Rock* court analyzed whether the government's policy or action implicated the Tribes' religious exercise, whether the relevant religious exercise was grounded in a sincerely held religious belief, and the degree to which the policy or action substantially burdened that exercise.[98] The tribes presented their religion to the court, to frame the legal arguments, and explained how it involved performing various water-based ceremonies. According to Lakota belief, water is sacred and "clean, pure water is an essential part of the Lakota way of life."[99] Water plays a central role in several Lakota ceremonies, including in the Hanbleceya (vision quest), Wiwanyan Wacipi (birth and renewal ceremony), Isnati Awiciliwanpi (coming-of-age ceremony for young women), Wiping of the Tears (conclusion of mourning), and Inipi (prayer and purification) ceremonies.[100] According to the Cheyenne River tribal historic preservation officer, who submitted testimony supporting the RFRA claims, these ceremonies are essential aspects of the Lakota religion and Lakota adherents "cannot practice [their] religion without [their] ceremonies."[101]

The court seemed to accept that the Tribes' religious beliefs were sincerely held, but did not directly address whether the Army Corps' actions implicated the Tribes' religious beliefs because it determined that the tribes failed on the substantial burden element of the analysis.[102] Following the D.C. Circuit's interpretation of the substantial burden test in RFRA, the *Standing Rock* court noted that "[a] substantial burden exists when government action puts 'substantial pressure on an adherent to modify his behavior and to violate his beliefs.'"[103] Applying this standard to the Dakota Access pipeline easement approval, the court concluded that the Army Corps' decision did not "impose a sanction on the Tribe's members for exercising their religious beliefs," nor did it "pressure them to choose between religious exercise and the receipt of government benefits."[104]

The court therefore denied the motion for a preliminary injunction because the Tribes could not show a likelihood of success on the merits of the RFRA claim. The national focus on the pipeline protest waned as the legal battles continually failed,

[97] *Id.*
[98] *Id.* at 88.
[99] *Id.*
[100] *Id.*
[101] *Id.*
[102] *Id.* at 91.
[103] *Id.*
[104] *Id.*

and those few outsiders who remained interested watched as construction on the pipeline was completed in April 2017. The Lakota prophecy of the Black Snake eventually came true when oil began flowing through the pipeline in May 2017. As predicted, leaks were discovered in five different places along its route by the end of its first year of operation.[105]

Despite the constitutional and statutory guarantees of the free exercise of religion and separation of state from church, indigenous Americans remain largely unable to ensure the continuation of their religious practices by relying on federal laws. The legacy of legal dispossession and destruction of tribal societies left many of the sacred land bases of indigenous peoples beyond the reach of tribal authority and often under the control of the federal government. Also, despite congressional attempts to remedy the yawning gaps in First Amendment jurisprudence for tribal religious claims, courts have been unable or unwilling to prevent federal and private activities that interfere with or even destroy the religious practices of native peoples on federal lands.

As awareness grows out of tribal cultural resources battles like the one at Standing Rock, though, tribes may begin to see increasing recognition by the courts. Also, in this area, unlike others, all cannot be lost at this stage of the law's evolution. This is because, as a matter of constitutional law, tribal members deserve the same legal protections for their religious rights as other Americans. So, despite tribes and their attorneys continuing to bring First Amendment and RFRA claims, many judges hearing those claims are unable to comprehend or are simply ignorant of the cultural and religious values that support them. The result is tribal religious beliefs are treated as lesser than other religious traditions, treatment that is per se unconstitutional.

Also, some glimmers of hope can be seen already. For one, the sincerity of tribal members' religious faith is rarely challenged, and even in devastating opinions like *Lyng*, judges acknowledge the validity of tribal religions, including those based entirely on oral evidence. Moreover, federal judges do understand and acknowledge how various governmental actions desecrate tribal sacred sites and severely impact tribal religions. It may simply be that practitioners advancing these claims in court must refine their legal strategies to avoid the hazards of precedent, and they will begin to see results that more closely adhere to the ideals of religious protection enshrined in the Constitution and federal statutes.[106]

---

[105] Alleen Brown, *Five Spills, Six Months in Operation: Dakota Access Track Record Highlights Unavoidable Reality – Pipelines Leak*, THE INTERCEPT (Jan. 9, 2018, 3:38 PM), https://theintercept.com/2018/01/09/dakota-access-pipeline-leak-energy-transfer-partners.

[106] *See* Monte Mills, *How Will Native Tribes Fight the Dakota Access Pipeline in Court*, THE CONVERSATION (Feb. 14, 2017, 9:03 PM), http://theconversation.com/how-will-native-tribes-fight-the-dakota-access-pipeline-in-court-72839.

4

Clashing Values, the Blackfeet, and a Measure of Success in the Badger-Two Medicine

For thousands of years Badger-Two Medicine has shaped the identity of our people. I have always been told by our elders that our responsibility was to save those lands for our children and all future generations of Pikuni [Blackfeet] People.

— Blackfeet Chief Earl Old Person[1]

The clash of values in indigenous cultural preservation efforts on public lands is readily apparent in the case of the Blackfeet Confederacy and their ceded sacred territory in the Rocky Mountain Front of north central Montana. There, the Rocky Mountains rise from the Great Plains like a snow-covered apparition impossibly hovering above the undulating prairie below. The beauty of these nearly 30,000 square miles of the so-called Crown of the Continent is hard to describe in words, with heavily forested valleys containing wild-flowing rivers, framed by bare alpine peaks on either side. Biologists and ecologists value the Crown because it is home to some of the last great populations of large carnivores, native fish, and untrammeled wilderness, including unbroken natural wildlife corridors spanning hundreds of miles. These corridors are made up of several areas of protected public lands in the United States and Canada, including Glacier National Park; Waterton-Glacier International Peace Park; and the Bob Marshall, Scapegoat, and Great Bear Wilderness areas in addition to several national forests. The area has also been home to the Blackfeet and other indigenous peoples since time immemorial.

Directly in the center of the Rocky Mountain Front lies the Badger-Two Medicine area of the Lewis and Clark National Forest. The almost 130,000 acres that make up the Badger-Two are now wedged between Glacier National Park, two federally managed wilderness areas, and the present-day reservation of the Blackfeet Nation. Historically, however, the area lay in the heart of Blackfeet territory, and members of the Blackfoot Confederacy, who now reside on both sides of the United

---

[1] BLACKFEET NATION, www.badger-twomedicine.org.

FIGURE 4.1 Chief Mountain, Montana
(Abishome/Getty Images)

States–Canada border, relied on the Badger-Two for physical and spiritual sustenance (Figure 4.1).

The Confederacy has defended their lands aggressively since the first contact with trappers and explorers coming up the Missouri River, the latter having recorded many of these encounters in their journals and diaries.[2] Over time, the nonindigenous trappers, miners, settlers, and others had succeeded in taking Blackfeet land and pushing the tribes out of many of the traditional hunting, fishing, and food-gathering areas they originally had relied on, some of which were memorialized in 1855 and 1886 agreements between the Blackfeet and the federal government.[3] By 1895, the federal government forced the Tribe to sell the land it called Mistakis, or "Backbone of the World" to avoid mass starvation.[4] The resulting agreement with the federal government relinquished Blackfeet ownership of the area but reserved the rights of tribal members to continue to access the area for timber and to hunt and fish.[5] Specifically, the agreement reserved the Tribe's right to "go upon any portion of the

[2] Joint Appendix, PPL Montana, LLC v. State of Montana, 2011 WL 3873375 (U.S.), at *253 (U.S. 2011).
[3] Kathryn Sears Ore, *Form and Substance: The National Historic Preservation Act, Badger-Two Medicine, and Meaningful Consultation*, 38 PUB. LAND & RESOURCES L. REV. 205, 225 (2017).
[4] Andrew Schrack, *The Shifting Landscape of Ancestral Lands: Tribal Gathering of Traditional Plants in National Parks*, 9 ARIZ. J. ENVTL. L. & POL'Y 1, 4 (2018).
[5] Act of June 10, 1896, 29 Stat. 321, 354.

lands hereby conveyed so long as the same shall remain public lands of the United States."[6] Part of Mistakis, the Badger-Two is "one of the most cultural and religiously significant areas to the Blackfeet People."[7] According to a 2015 study, "there are 22 sites for vision quests, 13 for offerings or shrines, 9 for group ceremonies, and 7 for paint collecting."[8]

Like many culturally and religiously significant areas, since the ratification of that 1895 agreement, the Badger-Two has been owned by the federal government and managed by federal agencies – the US Forest Service (USFS) and Bureau of Land Management (BLM). The management authority and discretion of these agencies are prescribed by a suite of federal laws that, in many instances, fail to align with or reflect the cultural and spiritual values recognized by indigenous people as inherent in the land. The disjunction between the federal laws governing management and protection of sacred sites and the indigenous cultural connections to those sites often leaves the unique claims of tribes and individual indigenous persons beyond the reach of substantive legal protections. In order to maximize the potential for such protection, however, the clash between the laws governing federal land management and indigenous cultural values demands that those seeking to protect the latter understand how and where they intersect with the former.

This chapter details federal laws like the National Environmental Policy Act (NEPA)[9] and the National Historic Preservation Act (NHPA)[10] that govern the activities of federal agencies like the USFS and BLM, which are often responsible for managing public lands where indigenous people regularly seek to access culturally significant sites. As exemplified by the ongoing 30-year fight to protect the Badger-Two area from oil and gas development, these more general federal laws may offer some procedural avenues for tribes and tribal people to seek protections for those sites but regularly fail to provide lasting substantive safeguards. Similarly, other more generally focused laws, like the Endangered Species Act (ESA)[11] and Clean Water Act (CWA)[12], might provide some substantive protections for particular resources, like the grizzly bear, which is also culturally significant to many indigenous people, but only where those resources are both covered by applicable law and meet the law's culturally ignorant and sometimes exacting standards. If legal challenges are successful, those exacting standards often result in legal protections on a much smaller scope and scale than what a tribe might require for the free and

[6]   Schrack, *supra* note 4, at 4.
[7]   Resolution No. 260-2024, Blackfeet Tribal Business Council (Aug. 20, 2014), http://www.badger-twomedicine.org/pdf/Blackfeet_Tribe_Resolution.pdf.
[8]   JOHN L. WEAVER, VITAL LANDS, SACRED LANDS: INNOVATIVE CONSERVATION OF WILDLIFE AND CULTURAL VALUES, BADGER-TWO MEDICINE AREA, MONTANA 88 (Wildlife Conservation Society, Working Paper No. 44, 2011).
[9]   42 U.S.C. § 4321, *et seq.*
[10]   54 U.S.C. § 300101, *et seq.*
[11]   16 U.S.C. § 1531, *et seq.*
[12]   33 U.S.C. § 1311, *et seq.*

complete exercise of its religion, or other culturally vital activities. Underlying each of these challenges is the inability or unwillingness of these more general federal laws to recognize or align with indigenous cultural values. Indeed, federal law struggles to do so even when specifically focused on protecting such cultures, as demonstrated more deeply in Chapter 5. The remainder of this chapter explores the way in which, notwithstanding the clash of these values, their intersection may still provide important legal avenues for protecting indigenous cultures.

The early 1980s were a heyday for oil and gas leasing and development on federal public lands. Spurred by then-Secretary of the Interior James Watt's zeal for American energy independence, the number of acres of such lands leased for oil and gas development jumped 150 percent in the first year of Watt's tenure.[13] At the time, certain regions of the USFS, housed in the Department of Agriculture, faced a significant backlog of pending oil and gas lease applications. In Montana's Lewis and Clark National Forest, for example, the agency had more than 200 such lease applications by 1981, 85 percent of which were for lands along the Rocky Mountain Front.[14] The combination of mineral development interest and federal desire to authorize such development put a significant amount of pressure on the USFS and the BLM to open up the Badger-Two area and its surroundings to leasing.

Before considering those applications and allowing development, however, the USFS had to at least consider the potential environmental impacts of those leases and the development activity that they would authorize. This general environmental analysis is the bedrock principle at the heart of the NEPA, which was enacted in 1969.[15] NEPA requires that federal agencies identify and consider the potential environmental impacts of any "major Federal actions significantly affecting the quality of the human environment."[16] To determine whether a proposed action will have significant impacts, the agency must assess the potential environmental consequences of that action.[17] If, after such assessment, the agency determines that there will be significant impacts, the agency must prepare a detailed written analysis, called an environmental impact statement (EIS), documenting the likely impacts, any unavoidable environmental consequences, alternatives to the proposed action, and other relevant information.[18] Critically, this stage of the analysis must include a "no-action" alternative, which requires the agency to consider the potential benefits

---

[13] Robert Sangeorge, *Watt: U.S. Moving Closer to Energy Independence*, UPI (Jan. 28, 1983), https://www.upi.com/Archives/1983/01/28/Watt-US-moving-closer-to-energy-independence/9674412578000.

[14] US Department of Agriculture, Forest Service, Lewis and Clark National Forest, Environmental Assessment Oil & Gas Leasing Nonwilderness Lands (Feb. 18, 1981) (Badger-Two Environmental Assessment).

[15] 42 U.S.C. §§4321 *et seq.* (2012).

[16] 42 U.S.C. § 4332(C) (2012).

[17] 40 C.F.R. § 1501.4.

[18] *Id.*

to the environment of denying the proposed action.[19] If, on the other hand, an environmental assessment (EA) determines there are likely no significant impacts, then the agency can issue a finding of no significant impacts (FONSI) with the assessment and move forward with its proposed action.[20]

Thus, while NEPA requires that federal agencies stop to take a hard look at the potential consequences of their actions related to land management, it does not dictate or determine their choices after doing so. NEPA does, however, provide a basis for interested parties to challenge federal agency decisions that fail to comply with its requirements, resulting in delays that sometimes quash the plans entirely if funding or interest wanes over the course of the NEPA process. Importantly, although the regulations implementing NEPA require that the federal government consult with tribes on the same basis as states and other interested parties,[21] nothing in NEPA requires the particular consideration of potential impacts on tribal cultural or treaty uses of lands subject to federal management. Failure to consult a tribe about environmental impacts to one or more cultural resources or sites is a basis for a NEPA lawsuit, though, so NEPA can sometimes assist tribes in pursuing a larger cultural preservation strategy by curtailing a project temporarily.[22]

Like NEPA, the National Historic Preservation Act also requires federal agencies to consider the potential effects of their decisions or activities authorized by those decisions on historic properties, including many tribal sacred sites.[23] Unlike NEPA, however, NHPA expressly requires that federal agencies consult with tribes about cultural impacts, so that the federal agencies "take into account" the effects of their "undertaking[s]" on properties to which an Indian tribe or Native Hawaiian organization "attaches religious and cultural significance."[24] The regulations that implement NHPA further clarify how federal agencies are to engage in such consultations and specifically require that those agencies consider the likelihood that "historic properties of religious and cultural significance are located on ancestral, aboriginal, or ceded lands of Indian tribes and Native Hawaiian organizations."[25] As explored in greater detail in Chapter 5, however, federal agencies often struggle to ensure such consultations adequately live up to those expectations and in many instances, tribal consultation has been anything but meaningful for tribes seeking to halt or stop

---

[19] Union Neighbors United, Inc. v. Jewell, 831 F.3d 564, 575 (D.C. Cir. 2016).

[20] 40 C.F.R. § 1501.4 (2018). Similar requirements were in place in 1981 when the USFS considered the issuance of leases in the Badger-Two. *See* 40 C.F.R. § 1508.12 (1979).

[21] *Id.* at § 1501.2(d)(2).

[22] Matthew J. Rowe et al., *Accountability or Merely "Good Words"? An Analysis of Tribal Consultation under the National Environmental Policy Act and the National Historic Preservation Act*, 8 ARIZ. J. ENVTL. L. & POL'Y 1, 4 (2018).

[23] 54 U.S.C. §§ 300308, 306108 (2012).

[24] Id. at §§ 306108, 302706(b) (2012).

[25] 36 C.F.R. §800.2(c)(2)(ii)(D) (2018).

projects or initiatives that threaten sacred sites and important cultural practices.[26] Courts have also been reluctant to force agencies to consult at a level that tribes would prefer.

Even when a tribe or Native Hawaiian organization, or anyone else, believes that the decision making process of a federal agency failed to comply with NEPA or NHPA, their challenge to the agency's decision must rely on a different federal statute, the Administrative Procedures Act (APA),[27] to bring a lawsuit in federal court. Like NEPA and NHPA, the APA guides agency decisions and prohibits agencies from rendering decisions that are "arbitrary, capricious, an abuse of discretion, or otherwise not in accordance with law" or beyond the agency's delegated statutory authority to make such decisions, among other limitations.[28] Even so, the US Supreme Court has instructed that a court reviewing such claims is "not to substitute its judgment for that of the agency," and the agency need only "examine the relevant data and articulate a satisfactory explanation for its action including a rational connection between the facts found and the choice made."[29] This interpretation of the APA judicial review provisions has created an extraordinary degree of power in federal agencies to make "judgment calls" about critical threshold matters, like what sacred objects might qualify under a statutory term that applies to "objects" of antiquity, among others.

In addition, agency decisions involving interpretation of statutory mandates or decisions that have undergone significant process before becoming final, such as promulgation of final regulations, receive a level of judicial respect when challenged in court nearly guaranteeing that a reviewing court will uphold them in the face of an APA challenge. This principle, known as judicial deference, was initially adopted to protect the sanctity of agency decision making from judicial interference, but has grown over the years to serve as a near carte blanche approval of certain types of agency actions when they are challenged in court. This combination of broad statutory authority and lack of meaningful or searching judicial review has given federal agencies a wide berth to render decisions that suit the agency's goals rather than the tribes impacted by those decisions.

The trifecta of solely procedural requirements of NEPA and the NHPA combined with the APA's high bar for successfully challenging an agency's decision are central to the sufficiency and defensibility of land management decisions made by the USFS and BLM that may affect areas important to indigenous cultural practices or

---

[26] Rowe et al., *supra* note 22, at 4.

[27] 5 U.S.C. §551 *et seq.* (2012).

[28] *Id.* at § 706(2). The APA also is limited to actions against federal agencies, including cabinet Secretaries, but excludes the president. So if the president directly authorizes a federal action that violates a statute like NEPA or the NHPA, the APA cannot be used to challenge that action in federal court.

[29] Motor Vehicle Manufacturers Association v. State Farm Mutual Auto Insurance, 463 U.S. 29, 43 (1983).

beliefs. Importantly, however, the legal framework courts use to evaluate these decisions centers on those procedural standards and the basis for an agency's decision rather than the fundamental substantive need to protect those areas in order to maintain tribal cultural connections. This results in an odd legal truism: by demanding only that agencies *consider* the potential effects of their decisions on the environment or such cultural properties without requiring that those properties and the strong cultural connections to them *actually be protected*, the legal avenues available to challenge such decisions leave room for federal agencies to prioritize other interests or uses of public lands over indigenous cultural or treaty-protected concerns. Indeed, many statutes require that federal agencies prioritize nonindigenous uses over indigenous or other cultural claims. Moreover, the statutes that govern the agencies' management of public lands – the BLM's Federal Land Policy and Management Act (FLPMA) and USFS's Multiple Use and Sustained Yield (MUSY) Act, require the agencies to focus primarily on balancing a handful of individual values, none of which include indigenous values.[30] Even in the rare instance that an agency commits to meaningfully considering indigenous values and making decisions to honor them, the federal bureaucratic and legal framework still weighs strongly against indigenous interests.

Though it would have been hard to predict in 1981, the USFS and BLM officials' review of the potential environmental impacts of oil and gas leasing in the Badger-Two and their subsequent decision to move forward with leasing ignited a nearly 40-year battle that exemplifies the difficulty of relying on this federal legal framework to protect indigenous cultural rights. In February 1981, the USFS released an environmental assessment analyzing the potential environmental impacts of authorizing oil and gas leases on USFS lands across the Rocky Mountain Front, including in the Badger-Two. The assessment included several alternatives, authorizing drilling at various levels. In the record of decision preceding that assessment, the USFS declared its view that the decision to authorize such leases would not "directly result in effects on the environment," because the USFS intended to further analyze subsequent activities conducted on leased lands on a "case-by-case" basis.[31] Therefore, according to the USFS, NEPA did not require the agency to prepare an environmental impact statement.[32]

---

[30] *See, e.g.*, FLPMA, 43 U.S.C. §1701(a)(8) (2012) ("the public lands be managed in a manner that will protect the quality of scientific, scenic, historical, ecological, environmental, air and atmospheric, water resource, and archeological values; that, where appropriate, will preserve and protect certain public lands in their natural condition; that will provide food and habitat for fish and wildlife and domestic animals; and that will provide for outdoor recreation and human occupancy and use."); MUSYA, 16 U.S.C. § 528 (2012) ("the national forests are established and shall be administered for outdoor recreation, range, timber, watershed, and wildlife and fish purposes.")

[31] Badger-Two Environmental Assessment, *supra* note 10.

[32] *Id.*

The USFS's assessment also reflected some of the pressure on the agency to authorize development. Rather than consider an alternative that would prevent leasing entirely, known to NEPA specialists as a "no action alternative," the environmental assessment's alternatives all assumed leasing would proceed. In fact, the EA's most protective alternative called only for not taking action on the lease applications "at this time," but the USFS determined that alternative was "in conflict with National and Regional Forest Service policy" to facilitate the review and approval of backlogged oil and gas leases.[33] In addition, although the agency consulted with the Blackfeet Tribe and "learned that portions of the [area] continue to be of spiritual importance" to the Tribe, the USFS believed that the "Blackfeet people prefer to identify these areas on a project-by-project basis."[34]

Having assessed the potential impacts of its leasing decisions, the USFS authorized the BLM to move forward with issuing leases.[35] As a result, the BLM approved nearly 50 leases in the Badger-Two, including a lease to Sidney Longwell, which was approved in 1982.[36] The following year, Longwell sought approval to begin drilling, which the BLM approved in 1985. But, before any drilling could take place, a number of interested parties, including the Blackfeet Tribe, challenged that approval through an administrative appeal process in the BLM's regulations governing mineral leasing on public lands.[37] Like the USFS's leasing decision, NEPA required BLM to study the environmental impacts of approving the permit to drill and, according to the Blackfeet and others, BLM had failed to adequately consider those impacts. In fact, the Blackfeet specifically alleged that the agency failed to consider the potential impacts that closing certain roads to all but oil- and gas-related traffic would have on the Tribe's treaty reserved rights in the area.[38] The administrative judges considering the appeal agreed that BLM had not complied with NEPA and directed the agency to adequately consider the issues that the Tribe had raised.[39] The BLM then suspended all operations and production on that lease. Two years later, the BLM revived the drilling permit, again was challenged, and withdrew its approval for further consideration.[40] The BLM and USFS then developed a full environmental impact statement analyzing the drilling decision, issued the EIS in 1990, and again approved a drilling permit in 1991.[41] Once more,

---

[33] *Id.* at 31.

[34] *Id.* at 28.

[35] The BLM is the agency responsible for oil and gas leases across all public lands pursuant to the 1920 Mineral Leasing Act, 30 U.S.C. §§ 181–196 (2012). This is part of the agency's broader statutory obligation to manage all of the federal mineral estate, which includes subsurface mineral rights underlying various land categories.

[36] DOI/BLM letter to Solenex 1, 7 (Mar. 17, 2016) (on file with author).

[37] Glacier Two-Medicine Alliance et al., 88 IBLA 133, 136, n. 1 (1985).

[38] *Id.* at 152–53.

[39] *Id.* at 156.

[40] Letter to Solenex, *supra* note 36, at 3.

[41] *Id.*

however, a group of objectors filed an administrative appeal, and BLM again withdrew its approval of that permit.[42]

Finally, after even more BLM study, the Department of Interior's Assistant Secretary of Lands and Mineral Management, who is responsible for overseeing the BLM, again approved the drilling permit in 1993. A group of conservation organizations and Blackfeet religious and cultural leaders immediately filed suit in federal court, alleging that approval of both the drilling permit and the original leasing decision by the USFS and BLM violated NEPA. The suit also alleged that the agencies' failure to adequately consult with tribal leaders about the Blackfeet's cultural connections to the areas impacted by the leases violated the NHPA as well as the American Indian Religious Freedom Act (AIRFA) and the federal government's general trust responsibility to the Blackfeet.[43]

During this time, Congress also began to consider protecting the Badger-Two area. In 1990, for example, Congressman Pat Williams introduced a bill that would have withdrawn the area from further mineral leasing and suspended all surface activities on existing leases for a three-year period.[44] The bill would have required the USFS to work with the Blackfeet Nation to develop a joint management plan for the area, an innovative proposal that sought to ensure "the protection and preservation of areas used by members of the Blackfeet Tribe for cultural or religious purposes."[45] Although that bill did not move forward, in April 1993, Senator Max Baucus introduced the Badger-Two Medicine Protection Act, which would have similarly withdrawn the area from further leasing and suspended surface activities on existing leases.[46] Yet another similar bill was introduced in Congress in 1995.[47]

In light of the 1993 litigation and congressional pressure to protect the Badger-Two, the BLM suspended the lease on an annual basis through 1998. In 1996, however, the BLM also noted that the USFS had determined that, due to the Blackfeet's cultural connections to the region, the Badger-Two might be eligible for protection under the NHPA.[48] In light of the suspension, no drilling activity

---

[42] *Id.* at 4.
[43] National Wildlife Federation et al. v. Robertson et al., CV 93-44 (D. Mont. 1993). The federal trust responsibility is a general duty owed by the federal government to the federally recognized tribes, similar to the duty a trustee owes to a beneficiary in trust law. Breaches of the federal trust responsibility can provide a cause of action in federal court, as in the trust context, though the chances of success are limited and remedies likely include only financial compensation. *See* David H. Getches, Charles F. Wilkinson, Robert A. Williams Jr., Matthew L. M. Fletcher, & Kristen A. Carpenter, Cases and Materials on Federal Indian Law 333 (7th ed. 2017).
[44] H.R. 3873, 101st Cong., 2d Sess.
[45] *Id.* at §1(b).
[46] S. 853, 103d Cong., 1st Sess.
[47] S. 723, 104th Cong., 1st Sess.
[48] BLM Letter to Fina at 1 (June 11, 1996), filed with 1996 Status Report, National Wildlife Federation, *supra* note 43.

could take place, and therefore, the lawsuit was terminated in 1997.[49] In 1998, the BLM suspended the lease until the USFS could complete the necessary NHPA studies and analysis and determine whether the Badger-Two area qualified as a historic property entitled to protection under the NHPA.[50]

By suspending lease operations, the BLM provided more time for the USFS to continue its work to analyze whether the Blackfeet's cultural connections to the Badger-Two were sufficient to protect the area under the NHPA. Coincidentally, Congress amended the NHPA in 1992 to expressly allow the National Register of Historic Places to include properties having traditional religious and cultural importance to federally recognized tribes and Native Hawaiian organizations.[51] Thus, by then, the USFS had statutory authority for considering whether the Badger-Two or some portion of it would be suitable for listing on the National Register. After consultation with the Blackfeet and numerous studies, the USFS recommended, and the keeper of the Historic Register concurred, that a portion of the Badger-Two Medicine was eligible for listing on the National Register as a Traditional Cultural District (TCD) in 2002. The keeper noted that the area "is associated with the significant oral traditions and cultural practices of the Blackfeet people, who have used the lands for traditional purposes for generations and continue to value the area as important to maintaining their community's continuing cultural identity."[52] The Blackfeet then urged the USFS to include the entire Badger-Two area in the boundaries of a TCD and, after further consultation and studies throughout the early 2000s, the keeper concurred with an expanded TCD in 2014.[53]

The inclusion of the entire Badger-Two area on the National Register of Historic Places as a TCD triggered additional requirements under NHPA for the USFS to determine whether the authorization of oil and gas drilling under the long-suspended lease would adversely affect the TCD.[54] Consistent with those requirements, the USFS consulted with the Blackfeet and determined that no mitigation measures could be taken that would avoid adversely affecting the TCD. Therefore, pursuant to the NHPA's regulations, the USFS notified the federal Advisory Council on Historic Preservation (ACHP) and sought the council's input on how best to proceed.[55] Despite the ACHP's involvement, however, the Blackfeet maintained their position

---

[49]   Order of Mar. 10, 1997, National Wildlife Federation, *supra* note 43.
[50]   Letter to Solenex, *supra* note 36, at 4.
[51]   Pub. L. 102-575, 106 Stat. 4754, 4757 (Oct. 30, 1992). A 1990 National Register bulletin also provided guidelines for analyzing and considering traditional cultural properties. GUIDELINES FOR EVALUATING AND DOCUMENTING TRADITIONAL CULTURAL PROPERTIES, NATIONAL REGISTER BULLETIN 38, US DEPARTMENT OF THE INTERIOR, NATIONAL PARK SERVICE, CULTURAL RESOURCES (1990; rev. 1992, 1998), https://www.nps.gov/subjects/nationalregister/publications .htm.
[52]   Letter to Solenex, *supra* note 36, at 5.
[53]   *Id.*
[54]   *See* 54 U.S.C. § 306108 (2012).
[55]   *See* 36 C.F.R. § 800.6 (2018).

that any development in the Badger-Two would desecrate the area and unduly interfere with their cultural uses and access. The Blackfeet then withdrew from further consultation regarding any potential mitigation measures, leaving the ACHP to comment to the Departments of Interior (via BLM) and Agriculture (via USFS) regarding recommendations on how proceed. On September 21, 2015, the ACHP sent letters to the Secretaries of each department noting that, in the ACHP's opinion, development within the Badger-Two "would result in serious and irreparable degradation of the historic values of the TCD that sustain the tribe," and, therefore, the ACHP urged the Secretaries to "terminate the remaining leases in the TCD."[56]

Less than six months after receiving the ACHP's recommendations, the BLM, with the concurrence of the Department of the Interior, canceled the 33-year-old lease to Sidney Longwell, which, by then, had been transferred to his company, Solenex LLC.[57] In doing so, the agency reviewed the entire history of the lease and concluded that the lease was improperly issued in the first place because neither the USFS nor the BLM had adequately complied with NEPA or the NHPA before its issuance. In the BLM's view, the agencies approved the lease after "mistakenly assum[ing] that NEPA and NHPA compliance did not require an analysis of surface disturbance caused by oil and gas activities prior to lease issuance," and that, although those issues had been highlighted throughout the subsequent three and a half decades of conflict over the lease, they had not been resolved.[58] Furthermore, by studying and understanding the Blackfeet's connection to the Badger-Two, the agencies now understood that "surface disturbing activities are incompatible with the irreplaceable natural and cultural resources of the Badger-Two . . . [which] must be safeguarded from all future oil and gas activities."[59] By the end of 2016, the Department of Interior had canceled 15 more leases in the area for the same reasons.[60]

This complicated tale demonstrates how the NEPA and NHPA legal framework and the efforts of administrative agencies within that framework can and do protect indigenous cultural practices and values, even though many federal statutes governing public lands contain mandates that seem to almost inherently conflict with indigenous cultural preservation. After a protracted battle, the Badger-Two area remains free from oil and gas development and Blackfeet tribal members continue

---

[56] COMMENTS OF THE ADVISORY COUNCIL ON HISTORIC PRESERVATION REGARDING THE RELEASE FROM SUSPENSION OF THE PERMIT TO DRILL BY SOLENEX LLC IN LEWIS AND CLARK NATIONAL FOREST, MONTANA at 7 (Sept. 21, 2015), https://www.doi.gov/sites/doi.gov/files/uploads/ACHP%20Rec.%20Letter%20re%20-%20B2M%20Lease.pdf.

[57] Letter from Aden L. Seidlitz, Acting State Director, Montana Dakotas Office, Bureau of Land Management to Solenex LLC (Mar. 17, 2016), https://turtletalk.files.wordpress.com/2016/01/blm-solenex-determination.pdf.

[58] *Id.* at 13.

[59] *Id.*

[60] Lauren Bally and Jason Mast, *Interior Cancels 15 More Oil-Gas Leases in Badger-Two Medicine*, GREAT FALLS TRIBUNE (Nov. 16, 2016), https://www.greatfallstribune.com/story/news/local/2016/11/16/interior-cancels-oil-gas-leases-badger-two-medicine/93961050/.

to exercise their treaty-protected and longstanding rights to access the area for cultural and spiritual purposes. But securing those protections from the BLM and USFS took three and a half decades of committed, dedicated effort, alliances with a variety of conservation and environmental groups, the use of political, legal, moral, and other levers of influence, and the willingness of federal agencies to review their prior work and recognize mistakes and errors of law.

On top of all of those challenges, the final justification for canceling the leases was not the cultural value of the area but, instead, the procedural failures of the federal agencies to adequately study the potential impacts of their decisions. While the numerous studies ultimately demonstrated the "incompatib[ility]" of the agency's leasing decision with Blackfeet cultural values, the bureaucratic process to complete those studies took nearly 15 years. In fact, had the USFS and BLM conducted even cursory analyses of those potential impacts prior to issuing the oil and gas leases in the early 1980s, the discretion to which their decisions would have been entitled if challenged in federal court likely would have resulted in judicial affirmation of their leasing decision. Thus, somewhat ironically, while the outcome at the administrative level eventually aligned with the Blackfeet's cultural values, it did so despite, and not because of, the applicable legal framework in which that outcome was rendered.

Furthermore, even after all of these procedural machinations to reach an outcome that protects Blackfeet cultural values, federal courts may reverse the agencies' decision to cancel the Longwell lease. In September 2018, a judge of the US District Court for the District of Columbia ruled that the government's cancelation of the Longwell lease after more than 30 years of its suspension "constituted an 'arbitrary and capricious' agency action" that was inconsistent with the APA.[61] According to the judge's ruling, because the government had awarded a lease to Mr. Longwell, he was entitled to rely on the rights to develop oil and gas that the lease guaranteed to him without regard to whether the federal government adequately analyzed and awarded the lease in the first place. The ruling focused extensively on the nature of the lease as a contract and the standard expectation that parties to contracts act in good faith, which, in the court's view, the government had failed to do.[62]

This ruling, though subsequently appealed by the United States and other interested parties,[63] further illustrates the challenges of protecting cultural values like the Blackfeet connection to the Badger-Two. Even after a three-decade battle to convince federal land management agencies to overcome the limits of their legal framework and protect those connections from destruction by other interests, the judge reviewing the agencies' decision simply ignored the deeper cultural issues at play in favor of the need to protect the reliance and contractual interests of the

---

[61] Solenex LLC v. Jewell et al., Civ. No. 13-0993 (RJL) Mem. Op. at 15 (D.D.C. Sept. 24, 2018).
[62] *Id.* at 16.
[63] Solenex LLC v. Bernhardt, No. 18-05345 (D.C. Cir. 2019).

lessee, established via a 30-year-old agreement he made with the federal agencies. The irony of this decision, particularly given the Blackfeet's reliance on the Badger-Two area for cultural sustenance since time immemorial and the terms of *their* contracts – the 1855 Treaty with the Blackfeet, and the subsequent 1895 agreement – is profound, bordering on absurd.

The fight over the Badger-Two is emblematic of the larger scale disconnect between the framework, interests, and rights of the American legal system and the values of indigenous cultures. As this example demonstrates, although the procedural standards of the NEPA, NHPA, and APA may govern the manner in which the federal government makes decisions about federal lands to which those cultures are often anchored, those laws allow the agencies to prioritize other interests that may be incompatible with tribal cultural values. Even when the federal government seeks to honor those values, as the USFS ultimately did in studying the Badger-Two as a TCD, the bureaucratic process and effort needed to protect them is complex, cumbersome, and time-consuming. Delays in ensuring such protection create additional concerns, such as the reliance and contract interests recognized by the district court judge in the Badger-Two case.

As the Blackfeet struggle to protect the Badger-Two also demonstrates, overcoming that disconnect to protect indigenous resources and practices requires leveraging the procedural standards of the applicable legal framework, marshaling forces with other allied interests such as environmental and conservation groups, and integrating a variety of tools, such as legislative influence and pressure. In doing so, however, indigenous groups may be forced to cabin their cultural arguments in unfamiliar or seemingly inappropriate terms. For example, the success of getting the Badger-Two oil and gas leases canceled turned on the federal agencies' failure to adhere to NEPA's procedural standards and NHPA's analytical mandates. To pursue those claims, the Blackfeet had to reframe their own interests in order to fit the avenues available for legal challenge.

The need to reframe or refine cultural values in order to support viable legal claims is often the central challenge to protecting indigenous cultures from interference or destruction at the hands of competing public interests. As the Badger-Two saga shows, that challenge is key to protecting important cultural sites, and it also plays a central role in fights to protect culturally important wildlife species. As the Blackfeet's success in convincing the BLM and USFS to cancel the Solenex lease shows, while there is much legal reform needed to fully protect indigenous cultural values and resources on federal public lands, such protections are still possible under existing federal laws, though many challenges remain.

5

Federal Cultural Protection Statutes

Products of the Second Way

Society is like this card game here, cousin. We got dealt our hand before we were even born, and as we grow we have to play as best as we can. We picked our cards up.

—Louise Erdrich[1]

The roots of present-day federal cultural resource protection statutes were planted in the culturally traumatic soils of late-nineteenth-century America. As introduced in Chapter 1, the late 1800s were a period of intense isolation and destruction for indigenous people, their land bases, traditions, and cultures. Federal policies aimed at assimilating indigenous people into so-called mainstream society shattered the integrity of reservations, families, and entire societies, resulting in the loss of millions of acres of tribal lands, generations of tribal and family connections, and ultimately, the abject failure of this draconian federal policy, even by the federal government's own measure.[2]

At the same time that the federal government was intent on destroying indigenous cultures through federal laws and policies, the nonindigenous public was becoming fascinated with the archaeological resources that demonstrated the historic record of those cultures. Beginning in 1879, a number of events coalesced to focus this fascination, including the establishment of the Bureau of Ethnology, first led by Major John Wesley Powell of western river-running fame, and the publication of a new volume of the US Geological Survey's reports on archaeological ruins in Arizona and New Mexico.[3] That year also heralded the founding of the Anthropological Society of Washington and the Archaeological Institute of America, both of

---

[1] LOUISE ERDRICH, LOVE MEDICINE 323 (2016).
[2] See, e.g., INSTITUTE FOR GOVERNMENT RESEARCH, THE PROBLEM OF INDIAN ADMINISTRATION (1928) [also known as the Merriam Report] (documenting the decimation of Indian Country resulting from the federal allotment and assimilation policies of the late 1800s and early 1900s).
[3] Ronald F. Lee, THE STORY OF THE ANTIQUITIES ACT, chap. 1 (electronic version, 2001), https://www.nps.gov/archeology/pubs/lee/Lee_CH1.htm.

which would go on to support numerous expeditions to study the nation's archaeo-logical past, including the heritage of many indigenous nations.[4] The interest generated by those and similar organizations led to an initial legislative proposal to protect those resources in 1882, but that effort eventually failed.[5]

Beyond the start of legislative efforts focused on protecting archaeological and cultural resources, the wave of interest in the artifacts of historic indigenous cultures and more modern cultural materials also had more dire consequences. Widespread looting and "scientific collecting" of these materials, from both uninhabited arch-aeological sites and inhabited tribal communities, further decimated and dimin-ished tribal cultures. At the 1892 Columbian Exhibition in Madrid, Spain, for example, an event held to commemorate the quadricentennial of Christopher Columbus's voyage to the "New World," over a quarter million items were displayed from collections around the world, with most coming from the United States, Spain, and Mexico.[6] Items from collectors and anthropologists working in the United States included "[s]and pictures and altars" demonstrating "the religion and symbol-ism of the Hopi [Tribe]" as well as "a large series of religious paraphernalia."[7] Those presenting various items included private exhibitors as well as federal institutions, like the US Geological Survey, the US Department of Agriculture, and the US Army Medical Museum, as well as various private US museums, anthropological associations, and historical societies.[8] Though the Madrid exhibition was poorly attended,[9] the next year's World's Columbia Exposition in Chicago "excited wide interest," with another enormous showing of indigenous archaeological and cultural resources that had been collected for at least two years.[10] The bulk of the items exhibited in Chicago later became the heart of the famous Field Museum's collec-tion, which opened in 1894.[11]

Despite the lack of any direct connection between the federal laws of the assimilation era and the nation's interest in these exhibitions, both shared an underlying intent and message: indigenous people (and their cultures) were relics of the past to be appreciated only for their scientific, anthropological, and aesthetic value to white America. In these heady decades of American expansionism, the conceit embodied in the widely held value that Native Americans were evidence of a prior evolutionary state and must either be "civilized" or vanish drove both the federal policies aimed at destroying tribal cultures (in the name of civilizing

---

[4] *Id.*

[5] *Id.; see also* 13 Cong. Rec. 3777–3778 (May 10, 1882) (petition for legislation protecting archaeological resources presented, read, and discussed on Senate floor).

[6] Walter Hough, *Columbian Historical Exposition in Madrid*, 6 AMER. ANTHRO. 271 (1893).

[7] *Id.* at 272.

[8] *Id.*

[9] *Id.* at 275.

[10] Lee, *supra* note 3, at chap. 3, https://www.nps.gov/archeology/pubs/lee/Lee_CH3.htm#39.

[11] *Id.; About the Field Museum*, FIELD MUSEUM, https://www.fieldmuseum.org/about (2019).

individuals) and their study by anthropologists and "ethnographers."[12] According to this imperialistic ideal, indigenous people and their cultures were not to be understood and protected on their own terms. Instead, their role was in museums, as relics of scientific or historic interest whose value was in reaffirming and reifying the preeminence and brilliant future of white American civilization.[13]

That conception, represented by the *End of the Trail* sculpture at the Chicago Exposition,[14] and more gruesomely by the 44 skulls stolen from 35 different tribes and displayed in Madrid,[15] was antithetical to the overwhelming evidence of the continuing and successful resistance of tribal people to the immense efforts aimed at their demise. In fact, even at the Chicago Exposition, where many Native Americans were forced to perform throughout the White City built by the fair's organizers in various "ill-conceived ideas of traditionalism," those performers still "resisted in a variety of ways."[16] As reflected elsewhere in the broader story of indigenous resistance and resilience, tribal performers "did not consummately succumb to the disparagement" demanded by the perceived racial and cultural inferiority that motivated the exposition, the study of anthropology, and federal Indian law and policy during that era.[17]

But, although that resistance ensured the survival of indigenous cultures into the twenty-first century, it was in spite of, and not thanks to, the federal laws based on similar-seeming goals. Those laws, like the initial 1882 effort to convince Congress to protect archaeological resources, began from the efforts of anthropologists, archaeologists, and ethnographers and, therefore, implicitly drew on their perspectives regarding cultural protection. The 1906 Antiquities Act is the most direct evidence

---

[12] *See, e.g.,* Mona Domosh, A *"Civilized Commerce: Genter, 'Race', and Empire at the 1893 Chicago Exposition"*, 9 CULTURAL GEOGRAPHIES 181, 185 (2002). Domosh, quoting Philip Deloria, points out that the entire field of ethnography was premised on the idea that native cultures were eternally in a state of "precontact 'ethnographic present' always temporally outside of modernity." *Id.* at 189 (quoting PHILIP DELORIA, PLAYING INDIAN, 106 (1998)). *See also* Vine Deloria JR., CUSTER DIED FOR YOUR SINS: AN INDIAN MANIFESTO 78 (1969) ("Into each life, it is said, some rain must fall. Some people have bad horoscopes, others take tips on the stock market ... . But Indians have been cursed above all other people in history. Indians have anthropologists.").

[13] *See also* Sarah Krakoff, *Public Lands, Conservation, and the Possibility of Justice* 53 HARV. C. R.-C. L. R. 213, 219–20 (2018) ("The story of the Antiquities Act and its era is ... a story of creating a version of the United States that many wanted to be true, and perceived to be at risk. There were steep costs to that project. These included erasing the presence and identities of Native Americans ... and displacing knowledge practices that were incompatible with the scientific aspirations of the emerging social sciences.")

[14] *See* Chapter 1.

[15] Hough, *supra* note 6, at 272.

[16] Melissa Rinehart, *To Hell with the Wigs! Native American Representation and Resistance at the World's Columbian Exposition,* 4 AM. IND. QUARTERLY 403, 423 (2012). Rinehart also noted the irony of the name for the fairgrounds: "Native peoples were ... trophies of scientific racism juxtaposed against the formidable white neoclassical architecture of the massive buildings on the fairgrounds, earning its name the 'White City.'" *Id.* at 405.

[17] *Id.*

of that perspective, although the newer National Historic Preservation Act (NHPA)[18] and Archaeological Resources Protection Act (ARPA)[19] also echo those views. More recently, tribes, Native Hawaiians, and their allies have ensured that tribal voices are better represented with agencies administering federal cultural resource protection statutes, including the NHPA, ARPA, and another statute – the 1990 Native American Graves Protection and Repatriation Act (NAGPRA), which indigenous advocates successfully proposed to and lobbied through Congress.[20] Although NAGPRA was an exciting statutory development on paper, its modern implementation has been hamstrung by the antiquated ideas about tribal cultures that formed the foundations of the White City and a lack of any legal mechanism by which tribes can compel wholesale repatriation of stolen belongings and ancestral remains. Yet, despite the cultural insensitivity, racism, and other forms of discrimination tribes have faced in seeking the protection of NAGPRA, ARPA, the NHPA, and the Antiquities Act, tribes and their advocates have still found ways to overcome the limitations of federal cultural protection statutes and utilize those laws to protect important cultural resources.

This chapter reviews the fundamental federal cultural resource protection statutes – the Antiquities Act, NHPA, ARPA, and NAGPRA – and illustrates the strengths and limitations of each. The chapter concludes with a brief discussion of other federal laws relevant to cultural protection and identifies some developing trends that may predict how federal laws will evolve to better protect cultural resources.

5.1 THE ANTIQUITIES ACT

Motivated by the increasing threats to the nation's archaeological resources – and sometimes, their outright destruction – in the late nineteenth century, representatives from various archaeological and anthropological societies prepared draft legislation focused on protecting sites and objects of "antiquity" they controlled.[21] As originally proposed, their bill would have expressly authorized the president to protect areas of public lands on which "monuments, cliff-dwellings, cemeteries, graves, mounds, forts, or any other work of prehistoric, primitive, or aboriginal man, and also any natural formation of scientific or scenic value of interest, or natural wonder or curiosity" might exist.[22] Almost immediately, however, conflict erupted over the potential breadth of the authority proposed by the legislation, with mostly Western state senators expressing concern over granting the executive branch such

---

[18] 54 U.S.C. § 300301, *et seq.*
[19] 16 U.S.C. §§ 470aa, *et seq.*
[20] David H. Getches, Charles F. Wilkinson, Robert A. Williams Jr., Matthew L. M. Fletcher, & Kristen A. Carpenter, Cases and Materials on Federal Indian Law 758 (7th ed. 2017); 25 U.S.C. §§ 3001–13.
[21] Lee, *supra* note 3, at chap 6, https://www.nps.gov/archeology/pubs/lee/Lee_CH6.htm.
[22] *Id.; see also* H.R. 8066, 56th Cong. (1900) (same language in introduced bill).

broad power to withdraw extensive parcels of land and permanently restrict their use.[23] Those intra-congressional squabbles launched a half decade of debate over the terms of protecting archaeological resources, and though the enactment of the Antiquities Act in 1906 settled that fight in Congress, the conflict over the scope of the executive power authorized by the Act remains unresolved.[24]

Notwithstanding the ongoing conflict over its interpretation, the Antiquities Act that Congress ultimately enacted in 1906 is quite brief, comprising less than one page of text in total.[25] Reflecting a congressional consensus around the archaeological and anthropological interests in protecting historic and prehistoric resources, the law prohibited and criminalized the ongoing unauthorized destruction of historic or prehistoric ruins, "or any object of antiquity" located on lands owned by the federal government.[26] Intended to stem the tide of unauthorized desecration of those resources, the law imposed a criminal penalty of up to 90 days in jail for anyone violating those provisions, although the statute included a permitting authority that allowed the appropriate federal official to approve archaeological and other excavations on lands protected by the law[27]

The Antiquities Act also authorized presidents to issue public proclamations that would declare identified "historic landmarks, historic and prehistoric structures, and other objects of historic or scientific interest that are situated on land owned or controlled by the Federal Government" and surrounding lands as national monuments.[28] Pursuant to this authority, a president could reserve both the object (or objects) and enough surrounding land to ensure the continuing protection of the objects, as long as the declaration was "confined to the smallest area compatible with the proper care and management of the objects to be protected."[29] Over the

---

[23] Mark Squillace, *The Monumental Legacy of the Antiquities Act of 1906*, 37 GA. L. REV. 473, 480–81 (2003).

[24] *See id.* at 485–86; PRESIDENTIAL PROCLAMATION MODIFYING THE BEARS EARS NATIONAL MONUMENT (Dec. 4, 2017) (modifying the size of a national monument established under the Antiquities Act based on the interpretation that "[t]he . . . Act requires that any reservation of land as part of a monument be confined to the smallest area compatible with the proper care and management of the objects of historic or scientific interest to be protected" and that the Act requires consideration of "a number of factors, including the uniqueness and nature of the objects, the nature of the needed protection, and the protection provided by other laws."); Complaint, Hopi Tribe v. Trump, No. 1:17-cv-02590 (D.D.C. filed Dec. 4, 2017) (alleging that the original establishment of the Bears Ears National Monument was appropriate under the Antiquities Act and that subsequent modifications of that monument exceed the authority of the president under the Act).

[25] Pub. L. 59-209, 34 Stat. 225 (June 8, 1906).

[26] *Id.* at § 1; originally codified at 16 U.S.C. § 433 (2012), recodified at 18 U.S.C. § 1866, *see* Pub. L. 113-287, § 3, 128 Stat. 3259 (Dec. 19, 2014).

[27] *Id.*

[28] 16 U.S.C. § 431(a) (2012), recodified at 54 U.S.C. § 320301(a); *see* Pub. L. 113-287, § 3, 128 Stat. 3259 (Dec. 19, 2014).

[29] 16 U.S.C. § 431(b) (2012), recodified at 54 U.S.C. § 320301(b); *see* Pub. L. 113-287, § 3, 128 Stat. 3259 (Dec. 19, 2014).

decades since its enactment, the exercise of presidential authority under the Act has occasionally sparked conflict between the legislative and executive branches as well as between local citizens and units of government who may object to a specific presidential withdrawal of objects and surrounding lands.[30] Nonetheless, a president's authority to create national monuments pursuant to the Antiquities Act is broad and relies only on a determination that an object of "historic" or "scientific" interest warrants protection.[31]

Finally, as noted, the Act also authorized the Secretaries of Interior, Agriculture, and the Army to review and issue permits for the "examination of ruins, the excavation of archaeological sites, and the gathering of objects of antiquity" on lands under their jurisdiction.[32] Importantly, however, the exercise of that authority was limited to activities that would be "undertaken for the benefit of a reputable museum, university, college, or other recognized scientific or educational institution, with a view to increasing the knowledge of the objects," and Congress expressly required that the "gathering shall be made for permanent preservation in a public museum."[33]

The permitting authority and the congressional intent to benefit science, archaeology and nonindigenous museums reflects the interests of the archaeological and anthropological communities who lobbied for the Antiquities Act and, as expected, served only to reinforce their ongoing removal and warehousing of cultural resources from federal lands across the country. While it is theoretically possible that indigenous archaeologists and anthropologists might invoke these provisions to study the homesites, towns, and activities of their ancestors, that is not the type of activity that has occurred pursuant to this statute. Moreover, by allowing, if not encouraging, those activities by nonindigenous scientists and collectors, the Act made clear that it intended to protect historic cultural resources for the purposes of scientific study by nonindigenous Americans interested in treating the objects as museum relics. The Antiquities Act lacks a tribal consultation provision, further compounding the threat of cultural loss that some tribes have faced and will continue to face as a result of the statute's passage. So, while the Antiquities Act did provide an important avenue for reserving federal lands on which historic and prehistoric cultural resources exist, it also established statutory terms on which those resources could be removed for further study—terms that reinforced predominant misconceptions about indigenous cultural inferiority and echoed the days of the Chicago Exposition.

---

[30] *See, e.g.*, Squillace, *supra* note 23, at 495–99, 500 (reviewing conflict over the establishment of Jackson Hole National Monument in Wyoming and noting that, throughout the twentieth century, "[s]ome members of Congress held continuing disdain for the [ ] executive proclamations" under the Antiquities Act).

[31] *Id.* at 475.

[32] Pub. L. 59-209, at § 3, 34 Stat. 225 (June 8, 1906); originally codified at 16 U.S.C. § 432 (2012), recodified at 54 U.S.C. § 320302., *see* Pub. L. 113-287, § 3, 128 Stat. 3259 (Dec. 19, 2014).

[33] *Id.*

Since its enactment, presidents and their advisers have invoked the Antiquities Act under the mantle of protecting important natural and archeological resources but, with regard to the latter, those resources were protected primarily to serve the museum and scientific interests of predominantly nonindigenous communities. For example, in 1907, one year after the statute was passed, President Theodore Roosevelt reserved the lands and resources of Chaco Canyon as a national monument.[34] Now a United Nations World Heritage Site, Chaco Canyon includes multiple thousand-year-old masonry structures that were at the center of one of the richest and most extensive prehistoric Native American communities on the North American continent.[35] Noting that these resources were "of extraordinary interest because of their number and their great size and because of the innumerable and valuable relics of a prehistoric people they contain" Roosevelt issued a proclamation designating them as a national monument.[36] That proclamation did not note, however, the presence of a number of tribes in the area and the continuing importance of Chaco Canyon to those tribes and their members; connections that existed at the time of Roosevelt's proclamation and continue to the present.[37]

Though Roosevelt and his successors used the Act to preserve and protect Chaco Canyon and many other important archaeological sites,[38] those efforts largely retained the same historic and scientific approach in the stated values attached to those sites. In 1949, for instance, President Truman used his authority under the Antiquities Act to establish Effigy Mounds National Monument, an area that was "of great scientific interest" due to the variety of animal and other shaped mounds that, according to Truman, were "illustrative of a significant phase of the mound-building culture of the prehistoric American Indians."[39] For the next few decades, Park Service managers excavated and explored many of the mounds, leading to their

---

[34] 35 Stat. 1094 (Mar. 11, 1907).

[35] Michael Margherita, *The Antiquities Act & National Monuments: Analysis of Geological, Ecological, & Archaeological Resources of the Colorado Plateau*, 30 TUL. ENVTL. L.J. 273, 310 (2017)

[36] *Id.*

[37] *See, e.g.*, Press Release, Navajo Nation Office of the President and Vice President, OPVP Protect Chaco Canyon Region through Collaboration with All Pueblo Council of Governors (Feb. 24, 2017), http://www.navajo-nsn.gov/News%20Releases/OPVP/2017/Feb/OPVP%20PRO TECT%20CHACO%20CANYON%20REGION%20THROUGH%20COLLABORATION% 20WITH%20ALL%20PUEBLO%20COUNCIL%20OF%20GOVERNORS.pdf (quoting Navajo Nation president saying "[w]e are descendants from the Chaco Canyon area. We are connected to these lands spiritually. The voices of our ancestors live in this area . . ."); *see also* Krakoff, *supra* note 13, at 220, 221–27 (describing the use of the Antiquities Act to "Eliminate Indigenous Presence while Saving the Indigenous Past").

[38] *See, e.g., Monuments Protected under the Antiquities Act*, NATIONAL PARKS CONSERVATION ASSOCIATION (Jan. 13, 2017), https://www.npca.org/resources/2658-monuments-protected-under-the-antiquities-act (listing the 157 national monuments proclaimed by 16 presidents, including Chaco Canyon, Montezuma Castle, Gila Cliff Dwellings, Casa Grande Ruins, Yucca House, Aztec Ruins, Hovenweep, and Wupatki national monuments).

[39] 64 Stat. A371 (Oct. 25, 1949).

eventual destruction "as a scientific object of study."[40] According to the Park Service, it was not until the 1980s, nearly a half-century after the Monument was first created, that the Monument managers began to recognize the connections between the area and the cultural beliefs of affiliated tribes and tribal descendants.[41]

Although even more recent executive action under the Antiquities Act still echoes the cultural and scientific divide that animated the passage of the Act and its first century of use, the growing chorus of tribal voices demanding a broader recognition of the cultural values of certain areas and historic resources is shifting how the Antiquities Act is used. President Clinton's 2001 designation of the Kasha-Katuwe Tent Rocks National Monument, for example, noted that, though there was evidence of prehistoric activity and the establishment of ancestral pueblos in historical times, the descendants of those people, the Pueblo of Cochiti, remain in the area and inhabit the region.[42] Though the history of that area, like many areas of cultural importance to indigenous people, resulted in the removal of the Puebloan people from the lands that became the Monument, the recognition of the Pueblo of Cochiti's ongoing connection to this area of historic importance laid the groundwork for the proclamation's command that the Monument be managed in "close cooperation" with the Pueblo.[43]

The subsequent proclamation of Chimney Rock National Monument by President Barack Obama echoed this trend, noting that Chimney Rock "holds deep spiritual significance for modern Pueblo and tribal communities" in addition to its general archaeological, scientific, and historical value.[44] That 2012 proclamation also made clear the continuing cultural value of Chimney Rock, outlining how the "descendants of the Ancestral Pueblo People return to [that] important place of cultural continuity to visit their ancestors and for other spiritual and traditional purposes."[45] The establishment of the national monument recognized its value as a "living landscape" that "brings people together across time," and the importance of indigenous cultural connections as support for protecting it.[46] Though this area is still of value as an archaeological resource, the establishment of Chimney Rock National Monument represented explicit recognition of the Antiquities Act as a vehicle for recognizing and protecting present-day indigenous cultural concerns equally, if not more, meaningfully than those that had historically supported the Act's use.

---

[40] *The Creation and Evolution of Effigy Mounds National Monument*, NATIONAL PARK SERVICE (last updated Jan. 2, 2016), https://www.nps.gov/efmo/learn/historyculture/efmonm.htm.

[41] *Id.*

[42] Proclamation No. 7394, 115 Stat. 2569, 2570 (Jan. 17, 2001).

[43] *Id.* at 2571; *see also* Sandra Lee Pinel & Jacob Pecos, *Generating Co-Management at Kasha Katuwe Tent Rocks National Monument, New Mexico*, 49 ENVTL. MAG. 593 (Mar. 2012).

[44] Proclamation No. 8868, 126 Stat. 2646 (Sept. 21, 2012).

[45] *Id.* at 2647.

[46] *Id.*

FIGURE 5.1 Wolfman petroglyph panel, Butler Wash, Bears Ears National Monument, Comb Ridge, Utah
(Sumiko Scott/Getty Images)

Thanks to the efforts of tribes and their allies across the American Southwest, that reformed vision of the Antiquities Act established firmer roots with President Obama's 2016 proclamation creating Bears Ears National Monument (Figure 5.1). For decades, the Navajo Nation and other tribes in the Four Corners region (where Utah, Colorado, Arizona, and New Mexico meet) had sought to protect an area of southeastern Utah from which the Navajo and others had been historically removed and then mostly excluded by the federal agencies managing what became, after removal, federal public land surrounding two distinctive buttes known to tribes as Bears Ears.[47] After various efforts to pursue legislative protections for the Bears Ears area, the Navajo Nation identified the Antiquities Act as an alternative legal vehicle offering similar protections through the establishment of a national monument.[48] In 2015, a group of five local tribes, the Hopi, Zuni, Navajo Nation, Ute Mountain Ute, and Uintah and Ouray Ute, came together to form the Bears Ears Inter-Tribal Coalition with the specific intent to develop a formal proposal calling for such a proclamation.[49]

---

[47] Bears Ears Inter-Tribal Coalition, Proposal to President Barack Obama for the Consideration of Bears Ears National Monument, 10–12, 14 (2015) [cited as Coalition Proposal].

[48] *Id.* at 14–15; Krakoff, *supra* note 13, at 240–44.

[49] Coalition Proposal, *supra* note 47, at 18; Krakoff, *supra* note 13, at 244.

That proposal, ultimately submitted to President Obama on October 15, 2015, provided a detailed overview of the multitude of tribal connections to the proposed monument and was based on years of work by the Tribes to identify and document the cultural connections that each Tribe held in these lands.[50] Based on the historical and present tribal connections to this place, the proposal requested an ongoing and meaningful management role for the Tribes in the national monument, a role that would step beyond the "close cooperation" required by President Clinton and "offer [ ]a first-ever opportunity to truly infuse Native values into public lands administration by pulling upon both indigenous knowledge and Western science."[51] In doing so, the Inter-Tribal Coalition's proposal presented the opportunity to protect ongoing indigenous cultural values through the proclamation of the national monument and center those values as guiding principles for its future management. The Inter-Tribal Coalition's proposal would, therefore, facilitate an evolution of the Antiquities Act from its dark history into, in the words of Professor Sarah Krakoff, "an instrument for reparations and justice ... [that would allow] public lands [to] become sites of cultural revival rather than solely of pain and trauma."[52]

Though he did not honor the Inter-Tribal Coalition's proposal in its entirety, President Obama's 2016 proclamation of the Bears Ears National Monument went a long way toward making reparations and injecting tribal voices into the monument's management structure. From its opening words, the proclamation recognizes the tribal connection to the region and, though it highlights the area's important archaeological resources, the proclamation focuses on the historic and continuing value of the area to indigenous cultures:

> The area's cultural importance to Native American tribes continues to this day. As they have for generations, these tribes and their members come here for ceremonies and to visit sacred sites. Throughout the region, many landscape features, such as Comb Ridge, the San Juan River, and Cedar Mesa, are closely tied to native stories of creation, danger, protection, and healing. The towering spires in the Valley of the Gods are sacred to the Navajo, representing ancient Navajo warriors frozen in stone. Traditions of hunting, fishing, gathering, and woodcutting are still practiced by tribal members, as is collection of medicinal and ceremonial plants, edible herbs, and materials for crafting items like baskets and footwear. The traditional ecological knowledge amassed by the Native Americans whose ancestors inhabited this region, passed down from generation to generation, offers critical insight into the historic and scientific significance of the area. Such knowledge is, itself, a resource to be protected and used in understanding and managing this landscape sustainably for generations to come.[53]

---

[50] Coalition Proposal, *supra* note 47, at 20–21.
[51] *Id.* at 33.
[52] Krakoff, *supra* note 13, at 254.
[53] Proclamation No. 9558, 82 Fed. Reg. 1139, 1140 (Dec. 28, 2016).

In response to the tribal request for full comanagement authority, the proclamation expressed a compromise of sorts, creating a unique relationship between the federal officials responsible for managing the monument and representatives from the Tribes. Pursuant to that presidential mandate, the federal land managers would be required to "carefully and fully consider" the integration of tribal knowledge and values into the monument's management plan.[54] To do so, the agencies were instructed to consider the recommendations of a commission of tribal representatives and, if recommendations from the commission were not followed, the agencies would have to provide written explanations to the Tribes.[55] While not the comanagement called for by the Inter-Tribal Coalition, this management framework would still ensure a central and important role for tribal values in the day-to-day operations of the monument. Thus, the establishment of Bears Ears National Monument seemingly fulfilled the promise of the Antiquities Act as a federal cultural resource protection statute.

But, like early monument designations, the Bears Ears proclamation sparked controversy and conflict, largely over the question of executive authority that has dogged the Act since its passage. Within a year of President Obama's proclamation establishing the Bears Ears National Monument, President Trump issued a proclamation substantially reducing its size.[56] In his proclamation, President Trump disputed that the Obama monument designation was necessary to protect objects of historic and scientific interest in the area, noting that a suite of other laws, including ARPA and NHPA, already applied to the resources within the Bears Ears area region and afforded adequate protections. Trump also recorded his opinion that the area protected by the original proclamation was not "the smallest area compatible with the proper care and management of the objects of historic or scientific interest to be protected" under the Antiquities Act.[57] Instead, President Trump established two much smaller monument "units," removing more than 90 percent of the lands that President Obama had protected.[58] Much like the monument proclamations during the early 1900s, President Trump's proclamation describes the historical and archaeological resources to be protected, but barely mentions the indigenous cultural values that were at the heart of the monument's original creation. In addition, the subsequent modifications strip the tribal commission of any role in one of the smaller monument units, change the commission's name to a Navajo term for Bears Ears (Shash Jáa), and require the addition of an elected official from San Juan County, Utah to serve on the commission.[59]

Importantly, though President Trump concluded that the original designation of Bears Ears National Monument had not complied with the Antiquities Act, his

---

[54] *Id.* at 1144.

[55] *Id.*

[56] Proclamation No. 9681, 82 Fed. Reg. 58081 (Dec. 8, 2017).

[57] *Id.* at 58081, 58082.

[58] *Id.* at 58085, 58087.

[59] *Id.* at 58086.

proclamation modifying that monument did not specifically challenge President Obama's reliance on indigenous cultural values as a basis for the monument's designation. Similarly, a lawsuit filed by the tribes of the Inter-Tribal Coalition and others challenging President Trump's modifications to the monument focuses almost entirely on the power of a later-elected president to modify or reverse the actions of a prior executive under the Antiquities Act, and the constitutional issues surrounding President Trump's use of the Act to disestablish a predecessor's monument.[60] While the complaint lists many cultural values that tribes hold in the Bears Ears region, the list of legal claims at the heart of the lawsuit focuses on the scope of presidential power under the Antiquities Act, rather than the impacts tribes have suffered as a result of Trump's use of the law to double-down on the pain and trauma they have experienced on these lands.[61] Although President Obama's use of the Antiquities Act inspired hope that this statute could serve as a critical legal tool for protecting tribal cultural landscapes, that hope has been somewhat obscured by political and legal conflicts over presidential power after his successor's proclamations undoing these protections. While the litigation is complex and somewhat legally messy, over the longer arc of history, it is likely that tribes, other indigenous groups, and their advocates can and will again invoke the potential of the Antiquities Act to protect their cultural values.

5.2 ARCHAEOLOGICAL RESOURCES PROTECTION ACT

Like the Antiquities Act, ARPA prioritizes archaeological and cultural resources as objects of scientific study, rather than vital resources that are invaluable to indigenous people and societies. Despite being enacted nearly three-quarters of a century apart, the two acts arise from the same conceptual foundations and, as noted law professor Rebecca Tsosie states, they both "are weighted heavily toward the interest of archaeologists in obtaining knowledge about the past."[62] This weight, in Tsosie's words, leads to the fair conclusion that "the [ARPA] *epitomizes the essential differences in values and beliefs about the past between Native Americans and Euroamericans.*"[63] Those differences are clear from the purposes behind ARPA, which sought to protect archaeological resources as "an accessible and irreplaceable part of the Nation's heritage," so as to "foster increased cooperation and exchange of information between governmental authorities, the professional archaeological community, and private individuals" who have collected archaeological resources prior to

---

[60] Complaint, *supra* note 24, at pp. 52–57 (presenting claims under the Antiquities Act, Separation of Powers doctrine, Property Clause, and Administrative Procedures Act).

[61] *Id.*

[62] Rebecca Tsosie, *Indigenous Rights and Archaeology, in* NATIVE AMERICANS AND ARCHAEOLOGISTS: STEPPING STONES TO COMMON GROUND 69 (Nina Widler, Kurt E. Dongoske, Roger Anyon, & Alan S. Downer eds., 1997).

[63] *Id.* (emphasis added).

ARPA's enactment.[64] Nowhere in ARPA's purposes did Congress consider how those protections might or should connect with, respect, or foster deeper understanding of the indigenous cultures to which these resources belonged.

Like the third section of the Antiquities Act, ARPA's overall structure intended to provide a more detailed review and permitting procedure for authorizing archaeological excavations on federal and tribal lands.[65] ARPA also enhanced the criminal and civil penalties associated with violating the terms of those permits or otherwise damaging archaeological resources (defined as a broad array of materials, including "pottery, basketry, . . . graves [and] human skeletal materials . . . at least 100 years of age,")[66] on federal and tribal lands without the appropriate permit.[67] In both of these ways, therefore, ARPA sought to shore up the Antiquities Act, which had become largely ineffectual in protecting such resources.[68]

But, unlike the Antiquities Act, ARPA at least acknowledged the presence of Indian tribes and Alaska Natives and implicitly acknowledged the cultural connections between these peoples and the objects protected by the statute. With regard to excavations on tribal lands, for example, ARPA exempted from the permitting requirements tribes or tribal members, provided the tribe had developed its own laws for reviewing and permitting those activities.[69] In addition, if the tribe had not developed its own laws and permits were still required under ARPA, no permit could be issued for an excavation on tribal lands without the tribe's consent.[70] Therefore, tribes, including Alaska Native villages and corporations, retained some important regulatory authority under ARPA and could condition the approval of various excavation activities so as to ensure broader protections for their culturally vital resources. In addition, for excavations outside of tribal lands that might harm or destroy "any religious or cultural site, as determined by the Federal land manager . . . [that] manager shall notify any Indian tribe which may consider the site as having religious or cultural importance."[71] But, for these projects, ARPA still prioritized and authorized the excavation and study of those resources. In other words, "the statute does not give a tribe the right to veto excavation on public lands."[72]

That prioritization was further reflected in ARPA's provision regarding the ultimate custody of excavated archaeological resources. According to that provision, the Secretary of the Interior could develop regulations that would "govern the disposition of

---

[64] Pub. L. 95-96, 93 Stat. 721 (Oct. 31, 1979), codified at 16 U.S.C. §§ 470aa, *et seq.* (2012).

[65] *Id.* at § 4.

[66] *Id.* at § 3(1).

[67] *See id.* at §§ 6–8.

[68] *See* Francis P. McManamon, *The Archaeological Resources Protection Act of 1979 (ARPA), in* Archaeological Method and Theory: An Encyclopedia (Linda Ellis ed., 2000), https:// www.nps.gov/archeology/tools/laws/ARPA.htm.

[69] Pub. L. 95-96 *supra* note 64, at §4(g).

[70] *Id.* at § 4(g)(2).

[71] *Id.* at § 4(c).

[72] Tsosie, *supra* note 62, at 69.

archaeological resources removed from public lands and Indian lands."[73] Though those regulations recognized the tribes as the "owners" of such resources removed from their tribal lands,[74] that notion of ownership, particularly as it might apply to human remains and sacred or cultural resources, demonstrated a clear divide between the archaeological or scientific value of such "property," which ARPA prioritized, and the indigenous cultural perspectives, to which the law paid only lip service.[75]

Therefore, while ARPA may reflect a broader tribal presence and role than the Antiquities Act, it does so in the same historically limited context: the treatment of indigenous cultural materials as valuable objects of scientific study rather than essential connections to the daily and ongoing cultural beliefs and practices of modern indigenous peoples. Though ARPA provided a bit more recognition of tribal interests through its notice provisions and in its provisions regarding permitting on tribal lands, it was still premised on, and thereby furthered, the priorities of the archaeological and anthropological communities that pushed for the Antiquities Act's passage almost 75 years earlier.

5.3 THE NATIVE AMERICAN GRAVES PROTECTION AND REPATRIATION ACT

The legacy of the federal government's support for the treatment of indigenous cultural items as objects of antiquity or science, worthy only of study and display for the benefit of reflecting on history in the broader nonindigenous society, persists into the present day. Though the impacts of that legacy and the centuries of removal of cultural objects from indigenous people are multifaceted and deep, the treatment of Native American human remains by nonindigenous society is likely the most traumatic and negative aspect of that legacy. The Native American Graves Protection and Repatriation Act (NAGPRA) provides one important avenue for redressing the cultural trauma inflicted on people whose ancestors were removed from their graves and sold, traded, or given to collectors and museums. But the imprint of centuries of loss remains, as do continuing challenges for federally recognized tribes, Native Hawaiians, tribal members, and other indigenous people working to recover their ancestors and other cultural resources through NAGPRA.[76]

---

[73] *Id.* at § 5.

[74] *See* 49 Fed. Reg. 1028, 1032 (Jan. 6, 1984) (initial ARPA regulations stating that "Archaeological resources excavated or removed from Indian lands remain the property of the Indian or Indian tribe having rights of ownership over such resources."); 43 C.F.R. §7.13 (2018) (retaining same language).

[75] Tsosie, *supra* note 62, at 69. ("ARPA considers research on Indian remains to be 'in the public interest'" and "to the extent that tribes have control over the excavation and disposition of such objects, it is because they are property owners and not because they have recognized interest in their ancestors' remains.").

[76] Jack F. Trope & Walter R. Echo-Hawk, *The Native American Graves Protection and Repatriation Act: Background and Legislative History*, 24 Ariz. St. L.J. 35, 39 (1992).

According to various estimates, by the late twentieth century, at least 100,000 and perhaps as many as 2 million deceased indigenous people "ha[d] been dug up from their graves for storage or, [like the skulls shown at the Columbian Exposition in Madrid,[77]] display by government agencies, museum, universities and tourist attractions."[78] In addition, millions of items buried with the dead were similarly removed, both by archaeologists and anthropologists interested in their scientific value and by private citizens interested in their commercial value.[79] In many cases, the removal of cultural items and violations of the sanctity of the dead were authorized and encouraged by federal law, which, through the Antiquities Act and ARPA, endorsed such treatment by prioritizing excavations and removal of such objects and, in the case of the Antiquities Act, declaring them federal property.[80] But other federal policies went much further. In 1868, for example, the US Surgeon General adopted a directive "direct[ing] army personnel to procure Indian crania and other body parts for the Army Medical Museum."[81] Pursuant to that grotesque policy, the federal government subsequently collected the heads of over 4,000 deceased Native Americans from across the country.[82] Beyond violations of basic human rights and the dignity of the dead respected by societies the world over, these deplorable laws, policies, and practices were also inconsistent with the nation's own common law traditions regarding the treatment of the deceased.[83]

Like the Bears Ears Inter-Tribal Coalition, whose members and affiliates sought to bend the Antiquities Act away from its ignoble roots and toward protecting indigenous cultural connections, by the last quarter of the twentieth century, tribes (including Alaska Natives), Native Hawaiians, and their allies sought to harness the power of federal law to reestablish their connections with generations of lost ancestors and the sacred items and objects buried with them. These efforts began to take shape in the late 1980s with a particular focus on the Smithsonian Institution, which had recently been revealed to be in possession of nearly 20,000 Native American human remains.[84] After a variety of legislative proposals were explored, the first legislation to be enacted carried through on that focus. The National Museum of the American Indian (NMAI) Act, which became law in 1989, set the stage for NAGPRA by codifying an agreement between the Smithsonian and tribal

---

[77] *See* Hough, *supra* note 6.
[78] Trope & Echo-Hawk, *supra* note 76, at 39.
[79] Steven J. Gunn, *The Native American Graves Protection and Repatriation Act at Twenty: Reaching the Limits of Our National Consensus*, 36 WM. MITCHELL L. REV. 503, 509–11 (2010).
[80] *See, e.g.*, Tsosie, *supra* note 62, at 68–69.
[81] Trope & Echo-Hawk, *supra* note 76, at 40; *see also*, Robert E. Bieder, A Brief Historical Survey of the Expropriation of American Indian Remains 36–37 (1990), reprinted in *Hearings on S. 1021 & S. 1980 Before the S. Select Comm. on Indian Affairs*, 278–363, 101st Cong. 2d Sess. (May 14, 1990).
[82] Trope & Echo-Hawk, *supra* note 76, at 40.
[83] *Id.* at 47.
[84] *Id.* at 54.

leaders pursuant to which the Smithsonian would inventory its collection, notify tribes that might have some affiliation with remains or items in that collection and, upon request from a tribe, return affiliated remains and objects to the tribe.[85]

Less than a year after the NMAI Act became law, President George H. W. Bush signed NAGPRA.[86] Like the NMAI Act, NAGPRA focused in part on those institutions warehousing Native American "human remains" and "cultural items," defined to include funerary objects associated and unassociated with human remains, sacred objects and cultural patrimony, and particularly focused on museums and institutions receiving federal financial assistance.[87] NAGPRA required those institutions to, in consultation with tribes (including Native Alaskans) and Native Hawaiian organizations, prepare an inventory of human remains and associated funerary objects and a summary of other remaining cultural items;[88] notify any tribes or Native Hawaiian organization of human remains or associated funerary objects that the institution determines are affiliated with that tribe or organization;[89] consult with and provide requested information to tribes and Native Hawaiian organizations regarding the summary of other cultural items; and, if requested by a tribe or Native Hawaiian organization, "expeditiously return" human remains, associated funerary objects, or cultural items affiliated with that tribe or organization.[90] Importantly, NAGPRA also created an avenue for indigenous descendants, tribes, and Native Hawaiians to assert cultural connections with objects that an institution is unable to affiliate with a particular group through a variety of evidence, including "geographical, kinship, biological, archaeological, anthropological, linguistic, folkloric, oral traditional, historical, or other relevant information or expert opinion."[91] For cultural items, NAGPRA created an inference in favor of repatriation unless the institution can "prove that it has a right of possession to the objects" requested to be repatriated.[92]

NAGPRA also specifically addressed the "ownership" of indigenous cultural items removed from or discovered on federal or tribal lands after its enactment.[93] Rejecting the Antiquities Act description of such items as federal property and going beyond the ARPA's creation of tribal property interests in items coming from tribal lands, NAGPRA established a clear and primary preference for the interests of lineal

---

[85] *Id.* at 56–67; 20 U.S.C §§ 80q-9 (2012).

[86] 25 U.S.C. §§ 3001–13 (2012).

[87] *See* 25 U.S.C. §§ 3001(3)(A)–(D) (defining the categories of "cultural items"); § 3001(8) (defining "museum" as "any institution or State or local government agency (including any institution of higher learning) that receives federal funds and has possession of, or control over, Native American cultural items" but excepting the Smithsonian Institution and federal agencies).

[88] 25 U.S.C. §§ 3003(a), 3004(a).

[89] *Id.* § 3003(d).

[90] *Id.* §§ 3005(a)(1)–(2).

[91] *Id.* § 3005(a)(4).

[92] *Id.* § 3005(c).

[93] *Id.* § 3002.

descendants, and if none could be located, a secondary preference for tribes and Native Hawaiian organizations on whose land the items were found, who are most closely culturally affiliated to those items, or who have aboriginal or traditional connections to those lands.[94] Although properly permitted (under ARPA) excavations could continue, NAGPRA required consultation with or, where on tribal land, consent from an appropriate tribe or Native Hawaiian organization before cultural items could be removed.[95]

According to Rennard Strickland, by rebalancing the interests of those seeking to study or display indigenous cultures and those cultures themselves, NAGPRA marked a new national consensus: "[t]he sacred culture of Native American[s] and Native Hawaiians is a living heritage [and] a vital part of the ongoing lifeways of the United States [that] must be respected, protected, and treated as a living spiritual entity – not as a remnant museum specimen."[96] The tribes and their advocates who secured NAGPRA's passage rejected the use of federal law to continue the desecration and destruction of indigenous cultures and, instead, sought to infuse the law with a more responsible cultural perspective. By opening the system of federal laws to indigenous cultural connections on the terms established by those cultures themselves, NAGPRA began the movement toward a third way for federal cultural resource protection statutes, demonstrating how they might brighten the long shadow of federal cultural destruction. But, as Professor Strickland predicted, "[a]lthough NAGPRA officially dr[ew] culturecide to an end, the tasks of implementing the new policy, particularly with regard to sacred objects and cultural patrimony, w[ould] require much cross-cultural understanding."[97] While NAGPRA's first three decades have included many important and successful accomplishments,[98] the ongoing challenge to secure its full potential highlights the law's shortcomings and the several limits of that understanding.

First, despite its broad reach in other respects, NAGPRA does not address cultural items found on or removed from state or private lands. Similarly, the law does not address private collections of indigenous cultural materials acquired from any source prior to NAGPRA's enactment. While NAGPRA did include provisions criminalizing the trafficking of human remains and cultural items,[99] it stopped short of comprehensively and completely addressing the broad legacy of cultural theft conducted throughout the 1800s and much of the 1900s. Those gaps, combined

[94] *Id.* § 3002(a).
[95] 25 U.S.C. § 3002(c).
[96] Rennard Strickland, *Lone Man, Walking Buffalo, and NAGPRA: Cross-Cultural Understanding and Safeguarding Human Rights, Sacred Objects, and Cultural Patrimony, in* Tonto's Revenge: Reflections on American Indian Culture and Policy 86 (1997).
[97] *Id.* at 87.
[98] *See* Gunn, *supra* note 79, at 521–23 (describing accomplishments under NAGPRA as of 2010, including increased collaboration and cross-cultural understanding).
[99] 18 U.S.C. § 1170 (2012).

with NAGPRA's recognition that properly permitted and authorized excavations could continue, led one commenter to describe NAGPRA as "provid[ing] only limited protection for Native American interests in preventing desecration of ancestral sites," although items removed through that desecration may ultimately be returned to a tribe.[100] Similarly, NAGPRA's complete success has been delayed by the administrative and logistical challenges of the repatriation process, especially with respect to establishing the method by which museums are to fulfill NAGPRA's mandate regarding "culturally unidentifiable human remains," a challenge that delayed directive regulations on that topic until 2010.[101]

At a broader level than the specific gaps left by NAGPRA, however, the law's implementation and interpretation continue to pose challenges for the ongoing conflict between non-Indian perceptions of indigenous cultures as objects of study and indigenous cultural connections. In one famous conflict, a group of scientists sued the US Army Corps of Engineers (USACE) seeking to prevent the USACE from returning the remains of the so-called Kennewick Man to a group of local tribes pursuant to NAGPRA.[102] Also known by those tribes as "the Ancient One," the skeleton had washed out of a riverbank in Washington State and, at first, anthropologists believed it resembled "an early European settler." However, later carbon dating analysis estimated the remains to be approximately 9,000 years old.[103] After the remains were moved to the Smithsonian Institution, scientists wanted to conduct additional studies, but local tribes objected and sought to have the Ancient One returned for reburial.[104]

That conflict led to lengthy litigation over whether NAGPRA recognized the rights of the tribes to have the Ancient One repatriated or whether his remains would be subject to further study and analysis by the anthropological and archaeological community.[105] This included the critical threshold legal question of whether the Ancient One was "Native American," which would invoke NAGPRA. The legal battle ended before the Ninth Circuit Court of Appeals, which ruled that, in order for NAGPRA to apply (and thereby protect the rights of indigenous groups to claim control of their ancestors remains or cultural items), the law requires "human remains to bear some relationship to a presently existing tribe people or culture."[106] The court rejected the oral histories offered on behalf of the tribes as reliable evidence of that relationship and, citing the "limited studies to date," concluded

---

[100] Tsosie, *supra* note 62, at 71.

[101] *See* 43 C.F.R. §10.11 (2018).

[102] Bonnichsen v. United States, 217 F. Supp.2d 1116 (D. Ore. 2002) (cited as Bonnichsen I).

[103] Bonnichsen v. United States, 367 F.3d 864, 868-69 (9th Cir. 2004) (cited as Bonnichsen II).

[104] *Id.* at 870.

[105] *See* Bonnichsen I, *supra* note 102, at 1120–31 (reviewing prelitigation history and issues at hand in federal litigation).

[106] Bonnichsen II, *supra* note 103, at 879.

instead that the remains did not meet that standard, and therefore, were not Native American and did not have to be repatriated to the tribes.[107] That decision frustrated the ability of indigenous peoples to rely on their own cultural traditions to invoke NAGPRA's protections and, worse yet, reaffirmed the heavy weight given to the value of scientific study over those cultural concerns. Despite that 2004 decision, subsequent DNA analysis confirmed the connections between the Ancient One and the Colville Tribes of Washington; the same connections the tribes had originally established through their oral histories.[108] After more than 20 years of conflict and, for the tribal groups involved, inappropriate desecration at the hands of scientists, the Ancient One was finally properly reburied in 2017,[109] but not because of NAGPRA. Instead, to avoid the ongoing legal battle over NAGPRA's interpretation, Congress passed specific legislation directing his repatriation.[110]

Though remarkable, the Ancient One's tortured path under NAGPRA is illustrative of other challenges presented by the ongoing conflict between the legacy of perceived indigenous cultural inferiority so deeply ingrained in the American legal system and the continuing vibrancy of indigenous cultural connections.[111] While a meaningful avenue for asserting the latter, NAGPRA remains unable to entirely overcome the power of the former.

5.4 NATIONAL HISTORIC PRESERVATION ACT

As described in more detail in the preceding and following chapters, the National Historic Preservation Act (NHPA) has been instrumental in providing an avenue through which tribes can assert greater cultural protections, both within federal land management decisions and through their own tribal laws.[112] Because other chapters detail the context and practical application of the NHPA, this section provides an overview of the Act itself, with a particular focus on the challenges of the NHPA's consultation requirements.

---

[107] *Id.* at 879, 881–82. On the role of oral tradition in this case and subsequent developments, *see* Cathay Smith, *Oral Tradition and the Kennewick Man*, 126 YALE L.J. FORUM 216 (2016).

[108] *See* Morten Rasmussen et al., *The Ancestry and Affiliations of Kennewick Man*, 523 NATURE 455–58 (June 23, 2015).

[109] *See* Alene Tchekmedyian, *After Two Decades, the Kennewick Man Is Reburied*, L.A. TIMES (Feb. 20, 2017).

[110] Pub. L. 114-322, 130 Stat. 1628, 1662 (Dec. 16, 2016).

[111] *See, e.g.*, Thorpe v. Borough of Thorpe, 770 F.3d 255 (3d Cir. 2014) (rejecting NAGPRA claim to repatriate the body of Jim Thorpe to his descendants and tribe).

[112] *See* Chapter 4 for a discussion of the use of the NHPA by the Blackfeet Nation to support designation of a sacred area as a Traditional Cultural District and the protections offered by that designation. *See* Chapter 6 for a discussion of how the 1992 NHPA amendments supported the broader exercise of tribal sovereignty through incorporation of Tribal Historic Preservation Officers (THPOs) and the resulting expansion of tribal laws and governmental structures focused on cultural protection.

At the NHPA's core is a commitment of the federal government to "take into account the effect of [any federal undertaking] on any historic property."[113] By broadly applying that requirement to any agency with "direct or indirect jurisdiction of a proposed Federal or federally assisted undertaking" and any agency with authority to license that undertaking, the law sweepingly envelopes almost any activity taking place on federal lands or any activity in which any federal agency might play a role.[114] Importantly, however, "tak[ing] into account" how federal actions may affect historic properties does not secure any particular preservation or protection measures. Instead, even for national historic landmarks, the law contemplates the possibility that federal or federally authorized activities could adversely affect historic properties, and the NHPA's only mandate is the process by which federal agencies identify, consider, and mitigate those potential effects.[115] That process has come to be known as the Section 106 process and it is largely defined by the terms of subsequently adopted regulations that form the basis for federal agency action.[116]

As initially adopted in 1966, the NHPA was silent as to indigenous concerns or cultural values relating to historic properties and their protection.[117] But, as a result of several amendments in 1992, tribes, including Native Hawaiians, now play a critical role in the Section 106 process, regardless of whether a proposed federal undertaking is within the boundaries of a present-day tribal territory.[118] Those amendments authorized "[p]ropert[ies] of traditional religious and cultural importance" to a tribe or Native Hawaiian organization as eligible for inclusion on the National Register of Historic Places and specifically required consultation with tribes and Native Hawaiian organizations in the context of the 106 process.[119] The process for doing so eventually expanded to allow for consideration of Traditional Cultural Properties, a change made in express recognition that such properties "and the beliefs and institutions that give them significance, should be systematically addressed in programs of preservation planning and in the historic

---

[113] 54 U.S.C. § 306108.

[114] *Id.*; 54 U.S.C. § 300320 (defining undertaking broadly).

[115] *See, e.g.*, 54 U.S.C. §§ 306107 (requiring the minimization of harm to national historic landmarks); 306114 (requiring documentation of decisions regarding undertaking that "adversely affect [] any historic property").

[116] *See* 36 C.F.R. Part 800 (2018). Though these regulations were developed by the Advisory Council on Historic Preservation, they provide the baseline standard for Section 106 procedures and are applicable across all federal agencies unless an agency adopts its own regulations that ACHP deems sufficient. 36 C.F.R. § 800.14(a) (2018).

[117] *See* Pub. L. 89-665, 80 Stat. 915 (Oct. 15, 1966).

[118] *See, e.g.*, 54 U.S.C. § 302706 (2016).

[119] *Id.* In addition, as discussed in greater detail in the next chapter, those 1992 amendments also authorized THPOs to assume the primary responsibility for consulting with federal officials regarding projects on tribal lands, responsibilities that would replace the role of the State Historical Preservation Officers (SHPOs) in that process, although SHPOs might still be involved due to the jurisdictional complexities inherent in Indian Country. *See* 54 U.S.C. § 302702 (2016).

preservation components of land use plans.'"[120] That designation, which provided important procedural protections for the Badger-Two Medicine area sacred to the Blackfeet,[121] created a broader basis on which indigenous cultures and their connection to important cultural places can be recognized under federal law. While the process for seeking that designation or inclusion on the National Register still demands that tribal and indigenous cultural connections be presented and defended according to the standards of the "dominant society's legal structure,"[122] they are at least viable avenues for those connections to be considered and, perhaps, even protected. Even then, however, the NHPA offers no substantive protections, instead requiring only that federal agencies consider the potential harm of their undertakings to such properties and document any mitigating measures taken.[123] If they meet those standards, agencies may still proceed to authorize projects or activities that harm historic or culturally important properties.[124]

The 2016 dispute over the Dakota Access Pipeline (DAPL) illustrates the challenges and shortcomings of the Section 106 process. The Tribes of the Sioux Nation, with the Standing Rock Sioux Tribe serving as lead plaintiff, raised extensive NHPA claims related to the approval of DAPL by the US Army Corps of Engineers (USACE). The Tribes initially relied on the NHPA to seek an injunction to stop construction of the DAPL.[125] In their view, construction of the DAPL, and especially its route just north of the Standing Rock's Reservation, which would take it under Lake Oahe and threaten the sacred waters of the Missouri River, would result in significant damage to a number of culturally and historically important sites.[126] Therefore, the Tribes argued that the NHPA and its regulations, required the USACE to involve the tribes in the review of the pipeline permit,[127] seek information from the Tribes about the nature and existence of those properties (while recognizing that the Tribes "may be reluctant to divulge specific information regarding the location, nature, and activities associated with such sites"),[128] work with the Tribes to identify those properties and determine whether the agency's proposed undertaking would adversely affect them,[129] and if so, determine ways to

---

[120] Patricia L. Parker & Thomas F. King, US Department of the Interior, Guidelines for Evaluating and Documenting Traditional Cultural Properties 5 (revised 1998), https://www.nps.gov/nr/publications/bulletins/pdfs/nrb38.pdf.

[121] *See* Chapter 4.

[122] Tsosie, *supra* note 62, at 72.

[123] 54 U.S.C. §§ 306108, 306114 (2016).

[124] *See also* CTIA-Wireless Association v. FCC, 466 F.3d 105, 106-07 (D.C. Cir. 2006) (citing Davis v. Latschar, 202 F.3d 359, 370 (D.C. Cir. 2000)).

[125] Standing Rock Sioux Tribe v. United States Army Corps of Engineers, 205 F. Supp. 3d 4, 7 (D.D.C. 2016).

[126] Monte Mills, *Current Developments in Indian Water Law and Treaty Rights: Old Promises, Recent Challenges, and the Potential for a New Future*, 64 RMMLF-Inst. 9, 9–2 (2018).

[127] 36 C.F.R. § 800.3(f)(2) (2018).

[128] *Id.* at § 800.4(a)(4).

[129] *Id.* at §§ 800.4(b)–(c); 800.5.

mitigate those adverse effects.[130] Unfortunately, however, this process was marked by a number of disagreements, misunderstandings, and miscommunications between the USACE and the Tribes.[131]

Though the precise contours of the consultation required of the USACE by the NHPA were unclear, the DAPL process illustrates a fundamental disconnect between the requirements of the NHPA and indigenous cultural values. While there is certainly room within the consultations required by the Section 106 process for federal agencies to meaningfully and actually consider those interests, the agency retains broad discretion to determine the area in which the federal undertaking may cause potential effects, the method by which the agency will analyze the scope of those potential effects, and the ultimate decision-making authority regarding the scope of undertaking itself. With DAPL, for example, the USACE determined that, because the scope of its authority under other federal statutes was limited to the path of the pipeline construction under Lake Oahe, the agency was required to consider only that specific area during its Section 106 process.[132] In the Tribes' view, because the granting of a permit at that location (and other water crossings) would allow the entire DAPL to proceed, the USACE was required instead to consider the impact of the entire pipeline under Section 106 and engage in consultation regarding the full route of the pipeline. While Dakota Access had conducted cultural surveys along the proposed route, those surveys had been done without consultation with the Tribes, much less substantive input or advice about cultural impacts. Therefore, as the Section 106 process wore on and the USACE sought to consult with the Tribes on its terms, the Tribes demanded a review of the cultural impacts of the entire DAPL and formally requested to be involved in additional surveys of potential cultural sites beyond the immediate area of the Lake Oahe crossing.[133] In the Tribes' view, the USACE's consultation was deficient under NHPA and its regulations, largely because the agency failed to involve them early in the process to help identify important cultural or historic sites, but also because the agency continued to unilaterally narrow the scope of the Section 106 analysis.

In denying the Tribes' request for an injunction to stop DAPL, Judge James Boasberg of the US District Court for the District of Columbia recognized the permissive nature of the NHPA and the broad authority it leaves in the hands of federal agencies:

> Even setting ... aside [the fact that Dakota Access conducted the cultural surveys before the USACE was involved], neither the NHPA nor the Advisory Council regulations require that any cultural surveys be conducted for a federal undertaking.

[130] *Id.* at §800.6.
[131] *See* Standing Rock, *supra* note 125, at 14–24 (detailing the events of the two years leading up to the USACE's granting of a permit for DAPL to be constructed near the Standing Rock Sioux Tribe Reservation).
[132] *Id.* at 30–32.
[133] *Id.* at 26–27.

The regulations instead demand only that the Corps make a "reasonable and good faith effort" to consult on identifying cultural properties, which "may include background research, consultation, oral history interviews, sample field investigations, and field survey."[134]

The judge emphasized that the USACE was not required to honor the Tribes' request for additional involvement and held that the agency had made a sufficient effort to provide the Tribes with "a reasonable and good-faith opportunity to identify sites of importance."[135] As a result, the Tribes were unlikely to prevail on the merits of the NHPA claim and the court denied the Tribes' motion for the requested injunction, which allowed the pipeline construction to be completed.[136]

Though the conflict and movement in support of the tribal concerns over DAPL prompted the Obama administration to temporarily halt the USACE's authorization of the pipeline for additional review,[137] a review that eventually led to the USACE denying an easement for DAPL to pass under Lake Oahe,[138] upon taking office several weeks later, President Trump subsequently directed that the pipeline be constructed, and the USACE again switched course and issued the permit for the easement.[139] Aside from the political winds buffeting these decisions, the flexibility under applicable standards, including the NHPA, allowed the USACE to consider and reconsider its position and, ultimately, approve the construction of DAPL despite the ongoing tribal concerns about its impacts on important cultural sites. Thus, while the NHPA, especially after its 1992 amendments, provides an important avenue for indigenous cultures to engage with federal agencies through the Section 106 process, the meaning and import of that engagement is largely subject to agency discretion and can result in a lack of protection where the agency prioritizes other interests above tribal cultural values and resources.

5.5 OTHER FEDERAL CULTURAL PROTECTION STATUTES

Beyond the Antiquities Act, ARPA, NAGPRA, and the NHPA, all of which focus on cultural sites and materials, tribes and their allies have pushed for federal laws

---

[134] *Id.* at 33 (quoting 36 C.F.R. § 800.4(b)(1)).

[135] *Id.*

[136] *Id.*

[137] *See* Jack Healy & John Schwartz, U.S. Suspends Construction on Part of North Dakota Pipeline, NEW YORK TIMES (Sept. 9, 2016), https://www.nytimes.com/2016/09/10/us/judge-approves-construction-of-oil-pipeline-in-north-dakota.html.

[138] *See* Jack Healy & Nicholas Fandos, Protesters Gain Victory in Fight over Dakota Access Pipeline, NEW YORK TIMES (Dec. 4, 2016), https://www.nytimes.com/2016/12/04/us/federal-officials-to-explore-different-route-for-dakota-pipeline.html.

[139] *See* Juliet Eilperin & Brady Denis, Trump Administration to Approve Final Permit for Dakota Access Pipeline, WASHINGTON POST (Feb. 7, 2017, 6:35 PM), https://www.washingtonpost.com/news/energy-environment/wp/2017/02/07/trump-administration-to-approve-final-permit-for-dakota-access-pipeline./

focused on protecting specific cultural sites or other aspects of indigenous culture as well. When proposals to develop or mine natural resources threaten particular sites of cultural importance, for example, tribes and their conservation allies often lobby the Secretary of Interior or Congress to withdraw or otherwise protect those areas. Recent such efforts have sought to protect areas near the Grand Canyon and Chaco Canyon.[140]

Similarly, Congress has responded to indigenous concerns by enacting federal laws aimed at supporting and protecting other aspects of indigenous culture as well. For example, the Indian Arts and Crafts Act protects Indian artisans by prohibiting non-Indian artists from selling or offering to sell an item that is listed as made by Indians.[141] The Esther Martinez Native American Languages Preservation Act of 2006 focused on reforming existing federal education laws to refocus and revitalize tribal languages and language programs.[142] Indigenous nations have advocated for specific statutory reparations, as well, from apology resolutions to settlement acts distributing payments for treaty violations.[143] These and other efforts on the part of tribes and indigenous allies seek to reshape the landscape of federal laws to go beyond allowing their cultural connections to continue. As this chapter demonstrates, despite centuries of those laws aiming to sever those connections, tribes are now forcing a new reckoning and demanding that future federal cultural protection statutes will reflect and strengthen their own cultural perspectives. This transition marks the beginning of a new era for indigenous cultural protection – a third way forward.

---

[140] *See* Lillian Donahue, *Needed or Misguided? Permanent Ban on Uranium Mining Near Grand Canyon Draws Mixed Reaction*, Cronkite News Arizona PBS (Mar. 1, 2019), https://cronkitenews.azpbs.org/2019/03/01/grand-canyon-uranium-bill; Press Release, Office of Senator Tom Udall, Udall, Heinrich Call for Senate Committee to Move Chaco Protection Legislation Forward (June 14, 2019), https://www.tomudall.senate.gov/news/press-releases/udall-heinrich-call-for-senate-committee-to-move-chaco-protection-legislation-forward.

[141] Pub. L. 101-644, 104 Stat. 4662 (Nov. 29, 1990).

[142] Pub. L. 109-394, 120 Stat. 2705 (Dec. 14, 2006).

[143] *E.g.*, Michigan v. Bay Mills Indian Cemetery, 572 U.S. 782, 786 (2014) (citing Michigan Indian Land Claims Settlement Act, 111 Stat. 2652); Hawaii v. Office of Hawaiian Affairs, 556 U.S. 163, 168 (2009) (reviewing Congress's 1993 Apology Resolution for overthrowing the Hawaiian monarchy); Tom LeGro, *Why the Sioux Are Refusing $1.3 Billion*, PBS NewsHour (Aug. 24, 2011, 3:57 PM), https://www.pbs.org/newshour/arts/north_america-july-dec11-black hills_08-23 (discussing Sioux reasons for declining monies derived from tribal mineral development, sale of tribal lands, and timber harvesting, in violation of Sioux treaties).

6

Tribal Laws

The Embodiment of the Third Way

Tribal laws are necessary to foster conditions under which our modern society and our cultural resources, archaeological resources, and burial items can exist in productive harmony and fulfill the social, economic and other requirements of present and future generations.

— Sisseton-Wapheton Oyate of the Lake Traverse Reservation, Cultural Resources
Protection Act, § 73-01-03(E)

In his seminal 2005 book *Blood Struggle: The Rise of Modern Indian Nations*, Indian law scholar and prolific tribal advocate Charles Wilkinson profiled the remarkable rebirth of tribal sovereignty and political influence in the decades after the dark 1950s termination era.[1] In conjunction with this renaissance, Wilkinson identified the "great irony of the twentieth century . . . that contemporaneously with the rise of Indian entrepreneurship in general and gaming in particular, Indian people experienced a resurgence in traditionalism."[2] The rise of tribal governments and the recognition of their sovereign authority (internally and externally) "released a surge of cultural pride," and energized tribal legal, political, sovereign, and community priorities revolving around cultural identity and protection.[3] Wilkinson explained this connection between culture and sovereign responsibility: "Indian people . . . have their private ways, but there is also a more formal governmental aspect to the cultural revival, tasks that go with the obligations of sovereignty."[4]

Among the most important of those tasks is developing the legal and institutional structures for identifying and protecting cultural resources of value to

---

[1] CHARLES WILKINSON, BLOOD STRUGGLE: THE RISE OF MODERN INDIAN NATIONS 353 (2005).
[2] *Id.*
[3] *Id.* at 352–53. ("The main litigation and legislative initiatives bore directly on culture. Rights to land and hunting and fishing are bathed in ceremony and spirituality. The right to be heard in tribal, rather than state, court means that a controversy will probably come before a judge sensitive to cultural concerns. The sovereign rights to charter and regulate schools and colleges means that tribes can assure culturally appropriate classrooms").
[4] *Id.* at 357.

the people within and beyond the boundaries of tribal or otherwise sovereign lands. This effort, led by tribes building their own laws and regulations, governmental bodies, advisory groups, and more, is complicated by virtue of the weight of historical efforts to decimate tribal governments and cultures and the more recent limitations imposed on inherent tribal authority by the Supreme Court.[5] Beyond those barriers, tribes and indigenous groups face the structural challenges of legal doctrines like federal plenary power and the Doctrine of Discovery, and an inherent disconnect between the laws exercised under those powers and their own cultural norms.[6] Nonetheless, tribes and their allies across the country, including Native Hawaiians, Native Alaskans, and many unrecognized tribes, are innovating and expanding their efforts to assert, maintain, and enforce meaningful protection of their cultures and cultural resources. This chapter focuses on those efforts, beginning with the legal foundations, both inherent and imposed, for tribal laws that aim to protect cultural resources, with a particular focus on natural and archaeological resources. The chapter also highlights examples of how tribes have built new and innovative legal approaches to structuring those laws, including how tribes are now using their own sovereignty to expand their work to protect resources beyond their current reservations. These examples show both the potential and limitations of the tribal legal foundations. But, as tribes and indigenous groups across the country are pushing the boundaries of the current legal structure, the development of their own governments and laws continues to expand the ways in which they maintain and enhance their own cultural and legal sovereignty.

6.1 INHERENT SOVEREIGNTY AND CULTURAL PROTECTION

Since time immemorial, indigenous people have sustained, protected, and evolved their many unique and varied cultures and cultural traditions.[7] Throughout the centuries, these acts of cultural preservation occasionally required an exercise of sovereign authority, be it through governmental, military, or other means; both to defend the underlying values from destruction from outsiders and occasionally to revitalize and expand them within the society itself. Such sovereign exercises are at the core of tribal power and, after centuries of federal approaches alternating between the outright destruction of tribes and their recognition, have resulted in a "measured separatism" between tribal cultures and colonizing external forces.[8] But those distinct cultural identities, their indigenous presence on this continent, and the sovereign powers used to defend them have always posed difficult questions for

---

[5] *See* Chapter 2.
[6] *See* Chapter 4.
[7] *See* Chapter 1.
[8] Charles F. Wilkinson, *American Indians, in* TIME, AND THE LAW: NATIVE SOCIETIES IN A MODERN CONSTITUTIONAL DEMOCRACY 6 (1982).

another sovereign government – that of the United States.[9] Thus the "schizo-phrenic" nature of federal Indian law and policy, as Supreme Court Justice Clarence Thomas has characterized it and as described in more detail in the book's opening chapters,[10] has in large part been the result of the struggle of the American legal system to answer (or, in some instances, deny or ignore) those questions. As a consequence, history and the evolution of American law demonstrates that tribes and indigenous groups have been forced to either conceal their cultures and cultural materials for their own protection or exert sovereignty through the avenues offered within the foreign legal system in order to seek and achieve cultural protections. The tribal effort to protect the Bears Ears region, described in the preceding chapter, illustrates the latter path quite well.

The days of facially intentional efforts to destroy tribal cultures are likely relics of the past, and the future will undoubtedly see tribes and their allies pursuing strategies of expanded tribal sovereignty well beyond the current limitations. However, understanding the force and meaning of that expansion requires recognition of certain historical challenges. Try as they might, tribes simply cannot overthrow centuries of adverse law and devise organic solutions and pathways to cultural protection in a vacuum. For example, tribes prevailing upon the federal government for the return of lands taken from them have met with varying degrees of success, depending on a variety of factors. Most famously, the Taos Pueblo pursued the return of sacred Blue Lake for decades, through federal judicial, legislative, and executive channels, before ultimately succeeding with the passage of federal legislation returning the lake and surrounding lands to Pueblo ownership in 1970.[11] Other tribes similarly succeeded with efforts to reclaim lands excluded from tribal ownership due to inaccurate surveys.[12] These victories largely depended on the tireless advocacy of tribal leaders, tribal members, and their allies, who, as in the case of the Taos Pueblo, dedicated large portions of their lives and careers to pressing the tribal claims through the various halls of federal buildings in Washington, D.C.[13]

Still other tribes were unable to succeed in the return of wrongfully taken lands. The Sioux Nation famously prevailed against the United States in Supreme Court litigation seeking return of the sacred Black Hills;[14] however, due to the limits of the

---

[9] DAVID H. GETCHES, CHARLES F. WILKINSON, ROBERT A. WILLIAMS JR., MATTHEW L. M. FLETCHER, & KRISTEN A. CARPENTER, CASES AND MATERIALS ON FEDERAL INDIAN LAW 28–29 (7th ed. 2017).

[10] *See* United States v. Lara, 541 U.S. 193, 219, (2004) (Thomas, J., concurring); *see also* Chapter 1 and Chapter 2.

[11] WILKINSON, *supra* note 1, at 207–16.

[12] *Id.* at 218–19.

[13] *See, e.g., id.* at 216. Significantly, much of the opposition to these claims was couched in terms of the potential for a resulting cavalcade of tribal claims to return additional lands. Therefore, the unique and compelling facts supporting the Taos Pueblo's assertions and those of tribes seeking to reclaim incorrectly surveyed lands also played a role in their success.

[14] United States v. Sioux Nation of Indians, 448 U.S. 371, 100 S. Ct. 2716 (1980).

federal laws pursuant to which the Sioux were able to bring those claims, the only remedy available was just compensation, not the return of the *Paha Sapa*.[15] Thus, despite the legal validity underlying various assertions of tribal sovereignty to reclaim homelands, the limits of the federal structure in which those assertions were made sometimes prevented the restoration of important cultural lands, which would have offered enhanced cultural protection in the present day.

In other instances, though, assertions of tribal rights through exercise of tribal sovereignty and the federal trust responsibility led to courtroom victories that did spawn additional cultural revivals. The judicial recognition of tribal treaty rights to salmon in the Pacific Northwest carved out space for tribes to both continue their traditional connections to salmon while also taking on important management and regulatory roles. The expansion of sovereign authority exercised by these tribes demanded collaboration among various northwest treaty tribes and, as a result, the Columbia River Intertribal Fish Commission (CRITFC) was born.[16] CRITFC, composed of the four lower Columbia River treaty tribes (Yakama, Umatilla, Warm Springs, and Nez Perce), is now more than 40 years old and has become a national example of successful ecosystem management using an interdisciplinary and cross-cultural approach, combining scientific, technical, and cultural knowledge with intergovernmental regulatory oversight to support healthy Columbia River fisheries and habitat.

By virtue of the imposition of federal laws that prevented broad-scale assertions of tribal sovereignty to promote and preserve cultural traditions, historic tribal efforts to enact laws and build governmental institutions committed to those activities were limited. Those limits were further cemented by the historical legacy and multi-generational trauma of federal efforts to eliminate tribes or to appropriate elements of tribal culture and cultural materials. The Indian Reorganization Act of 1934 illustrates how the history of federal–tribal relations and limits of federal plenary power resulted in barriers to these assertions and manifestations of tribal sover-eignty.[17] After the ravages of the allotment era, the federal government turned to an entirely new approach to Indian affairs. The IRA was the crown jewel of these reforms, and specifically intended to throw congressional authority behind the twin goals of tribal self-determination and economic development.[18] To do so, the Act authorized tribes to organize governments pursuant to constitutions and to incorpor-ate business entities to engage in the corporate structuring and eventual transactions viewed as necessary to spur tribal economic growth. Tribes could choose, through

---

[15] *See generally* Edward Lazarus, Black Hills/White Justice: The Sioux Nation versus the United States, 1775 to the Present (1991).

[16] *The Founding of CRITFC*, Columbia River Inter-Tribal Fish Commission, https://www.critfc.org/about-us/critfcs-founding.

[17] 25 U.S.C. § 5103.

[18] Mescalero Apache Tribe v. Jones, 411 U.S. 145, 152 (1973).

an election conducted by the federal Secretary of the Interior, whether to adopt a constitution pursuant to the IRA, and many tribes did so.[19]

But because both the constitutional option and the form of many of those constitutions were largely dictated and prescribed by federal officials, those constitutions "often perpetuated federal supervisory authority by requiring secretarial approval of [both] the constitutions and other tribal laws."[20] For these tribes, the structure of their governments and manner in which those governments functioned were based in a system of federal oversight, which often did not align with or consider tribal community or cultural concerns.[21] Even tribes who rejected the IRA faced the challenge of building or rebuilding governmental institutions decimated by decades of federal oppression. As a result, although cultural ideals remained at the heart of tribal identity and existence at the individual and community levels, for much of the twentieth century, tribal governments, especially those governments established and recognized by the federal government under the IRA, rarely aligned with or reflected those cultural values within tribal law. Those disconnections were further entrenched by the federal government's devastating effort to terminate tribes throughout the 1950s.

Still, despite the challenges of maintaining cultural values and properties throughout the 1900s, tribes worked to develop cultural resource programs and influence the study of their histories and traditions.[22] The Zuni Pueblo, for example, established a tribal archaeology program in 1975 to monitor and control activities on Pueblo lands that could impact archaeological resources.[23] Through the program, the Pueblo sought to enhance employment, economic opportunity, and technical capacity while also asserting a broader role in protecting its cultural resources.[24] The Navajo Nation developed a similar program, which later evolved to exercise broader regulatory functions.[25] Though the White Mountain Apache tribal government historically reviewed excavation proposals, the Tribe opened a culture center in 1969 in recognition of a need to preserve tribal stories, language, and other cultural resources.[26] Farther to the north, the Confederated Tribes of the Umatilla

---

[19] Felix S. Cohen, COHEN'S HANDBOOK OF FEDERAL INDIAN LAW § 4.04[3][a], at 256–57 n. 16 (Nell Jessup Newton ed., 2012) (77 tribes rejected the IRA option while approximately 180 or more adopted it).

[20] *Id.* at 257.

[21] *Id.*

[22] *See, e.g.,* Roger Anyon & T. J. Ferguson, *Cultural Resources Management at the Pueblo of Zuni, New Mexico, USA,* 69 ANTIQUITY 919–30 (1995).

[23] T. J. FERGUSON, NHPA: *Changing the Role of Native Americans in the Archaeological Study of the Past in* WORKING TOGETHER: NATIVE AMERICANS & ARCHAEOLOGISTS 26 (Kurt E. Dongoske, Mark Aldenderfer, & Karen Doehner eds., 2000).

[24] *Id.*

[25] *Id.*

[26] JOHN R. WELCH, *The White Mountain Apache Tribe Heritage Program: Origins, Operations, and Challenges in* WORKING TOGETHER, NATIVE AMERICANS & ARCHAEOLOGISTS 70 (Kurt E. Dongoske, Mark Aldenderfer, & Karen Doehner eds., 2000).

Indian Reservation (CTUIR) faced similar challenges. There, the Tribal Council recognized as early as 1971 that additional governmental oversight was necessary to protect the reservation's cultural resources from further degradation, but a lack of funding and resources seriously hampered a broad tribal cultural protection effort.[27] Nonetheless, like at White Mountain Apache, the CTUIR began collecting and preserving tribal records, recordings, and histories that were threatened by the failing historic buildings in which they were housed.[28] By 1987, the Tribes established a cultural resources protection program but, echoing earlier eras of federal paternalism, the CTUIR was still somewhat hamstrung by reluctance on the part of the federal Bureau of Indian Affairs to engage or support further cultural protection and preservation efforts.[29] Eventually, as the Tribes' own program grew in stature and built partnerships with other Tribes and agencies, it was able to assume responsibility for on reservation cultural surveys and inventories, projects that "provided the funding [through BIA] and education, training, and employment of tribal members," which in turn enabled the tribes to begin their own cultural work without federal involvement.[30] In this way, CTUIR could better fulfill its goal of developing and managing a program, which, in the Tribes' view, was "specifically driven by the Indian worldview of the Earth and all the resources on the Earth, natural and cultural alike."[31]

But, while these and other tribal efforts were critical steps toward sustaining cultural protections, they were largely programmatic or responsive to crises and not exercises of tribal sovereign authority through constitutional or legal changes. While the tribal governments at Zuni, Navajo, White Mountain, and CTUIR supported these developments, they were also separate from the operation and structure of those affiliated tribal governments. More recently, however, as modern tribal governments have developed additional capacity, resources, and experience, the connections between tribal sovereign power and protecting cultural resources have grown much stronger.

6.2 SELF-DETERMINATION, SOVEREIGNTY, AND CULTURAL REVIVAL

As noted in Chapter 2, the late 1960s and 1970s heralded a shift in federal policy toward tribal self-determination and organic efforts grew in Indian Country. Spurred by the failures of the termination policies of earlier decades and prompted by a growing indigenous rights movement, led by scholars like Vine Deloria, and tribal

---

[27] DARBY C. STAPP & MICHAEL S. BURNEY, TRIBAL CULTURAL RESOURCE MANAGEMENT: THE FULL CIRCLE TO STEWARDSHIP 76 (2002).

[28] *Id.* at 76–77.

[29] *Id.* at 80–81.

[30] *Id.* at 81.

[31] *Id.* at 75 (citation omitted).

activism through organizations like the National Congress of American Indians,[32] tribes prevailed on the Kennedy and Johnson administrations to reform the US approach to its government-to-government relationship with federally recognized tribes. While both administrations took steps in that direction, the effort culminated in President Nixon's 1970 statement to Congress formally repudiating the termination policy and calling for a new era of self-determination, in which tribes would be able to decide for themselves how to govern their people, conduct their daily affairs, and engage in cultural revitalization or preservation efforts.[33]

The shift toward self-determination opened the door for a wealth of new federal laws and opportunities supporting tribes in building their governments and legal institutions. Foremost among these was the Indian Self-Determination and Education Assistance Act (ISDEAA), also known as Public Law 93-638, which authorized and encouraged federal agencies to contract with tribes to shift their governmental programs from federal to tribal oversight.[34] In passing the law, Congress specifically intended to "respond to the strong expression of the Indian people for self-determination by assuring maximum Indian participation in the direction of educational as well as other Federal services ... so as to render such services more responsive to the needs and desires of [Indian] communities."[35] Beyond improving services, however, Public Law 93-638 "provided the legal framework within which tribes [could] jump-start[ ] and develop[ ] the capacity for government-building activities."[36] Tribes soon began taking over programs, services, functions, and activities from the federal government and, with the financial support required by the ISDEAA, running them according to tribal priorities. This process quickly revealed bureaucratic and other barriers to broader tribal success, which tribes addressed by securing amendments to the law in 1988.[37] Though federal agency recalcitrance and bureaucratic hurdles demanded additional judicial[38] and legislative attention,[39] tribes across the country were using Public Law 93-638 to build and expand their sovereign enterprises.

---

[32] *See Seventy Years of NCAI*, NATIONAL CONGRESS OF AMERICAN INDIANS, http://www.ncai.org/about-ncai/mission-history/seventy-years-of-ncai#1960.

[33] *See* Richard Nixon, President Nixon, Special Message on Indian Affairs, PUB. PAPERS at 564–67, 576–76 (July 8, 1970).

[34] 25 U.S.C. §§ 450, *et seq.* (2012).

[35] *Id.* at § 450(a).

[36] Geoffrey D. Strommer & Stephen D. Osborne, *The History, Status, and Future of Tribal Self-Governance Under the Indian Self-Determination and Education Assistance Act*, 39 AM. IND. L. REV. 1, 4 (2015) (Strommer & Osborne, *Tribal Self-Governance*).

[37] *Id.* at 29–32; Indian Self-Determination Amendments of 1987, Pub. L. No. 100-472, § 209, 102 Stat. 2289, 2296-98 (codified at 25 U.S.C. § 450f (1988)), repealed by Tribal Self-Governance Amendments of 2000, Pub. L. No. 106-260, § 10, 114 Stat. 711, 734.

[38] *See* Cherokee Nation v. Leavitt, 543 U.S. 631, 637-38 (2005); *see also* Ramah Navajo School Board v. Salazar, 644 F.3d 1054, 1067 (10th Cir. 2011).

[39] *See, e.g.*, Tribal Self-Governance Amendments of 2000, Pub. L. No. 106-260, § 10, 114 Stat. 711, 734.

That expansion of governmental power coincided with and contributed to a greater role for tribal political influence on the national stage as well. Over the last half-century, Congress responded to tribal concerns with a broad range of federal laws addressing those concerns, including the Indian Child Welfare Act and American Indian Religious Freedom Act, both passed in 1978,[40] amendments to environmental and natural resource management laws, and laws enabling other social and educational benefits for tribes and tribal members.[41] Tribal leaders and advocates also pushed for changes to federal cultural resource laws and, with the 1990 passage of NAGPRA, secured important federal recognition and protection for the ongoing rights of tribes and Native American lineal descendants to recover and, where appropriate, rebury the remains of ancestors that had been taken from them over centuries of looting and theft.[42] Among these important federal legislative changes brought about by tribal initiatives, however, Congress's 1992 amendments to the National Historic Preservation Act (NHPA) may have had the most significant impact in opening the door to a new era of tribal sovereign efforts to develop laws and governmental institutions dedicated to cultural protections. To understand how those changes, when combined with burgeoning tribal governments flexing additional muscle in the self-determination era, catalyzed a revolution in tribal laws focused on cultural issues, it is necessary to briefly review the structure of the NHPA and the historic flaws inherent in federal efforts to acknowledge and address tribal cultural concerns.

As described in detail in Chapters 4 and 5, the NHPA provides a process requiring federal agencies to consider and, where appropriate, mitigate the effects of federal land management decisions on historic properties. As a result of the 1992 amendments to NHPA, tribal cultural properties that could qualify as Traditional Cultural Districts must be taken into account in this analysis and tribes with relevant cultural knowledge and information must be consulted on both the possible existence of culturally important areas and the potential impacts of federally authorized activities in those areas.[43] Tribes pushed for those amendments as a remedy for the lack of tribal consultation or involvement in cultural resource management throughout the 1970s and 1980s.[44] With those changes, federal agencies were required to meet minimum standards of outreach and bilateral consultation with tribes, Native Hawaiians, and other indigenous groups who may attach cultural import to particular areas over which the federal government had authority. Because of that

---

[40] Indian Child Welfare Act of 1978, Pub. L. 95-608, 92 Stat. 3069 (codified at 25 U.S.C. §§ 1901–63); American Indian Religious Freedom Act, Pub. L. 95-341, 92 Stat. 469 (codified at 42 U.S.C. § 1996).

[41] *See* WILKINSON, *supra* note 1, at 261–63.

[42] Native American Graves Protection and Repatriation Act, Pub. L. 101-601, 104 Stat. 3048 (codified at 25 U.S.C. §§ 3001 *et seq.*).

[43] *Id.*

[44] STAPP & BURNEY, *supra* note 27, at 48.

requirement, however, the 1992 NHPA amendments also challenged tribes with the additional responsibilities of responding to those requests, which paradoxically created the opportunity for tribes to consider how to develop a sustainable and effective governmental institution to engage in that process. These changes to the NHPA were one critical part of the reframing of cultural resource preservation with an eye toward tribal primacy, but another focus of the 1992 amendments was central to sparking further change.

Since its original enactment in 1966, the NHPA focused on the protection of historic properties through consultation and partnership with states, including authorizing federal grants to the states to support the preparation of historic surveys.[45] The federal initiative to localize historic preservation through state governments spawned the growth of State Historic Preservation Offices (SHPOs), which, with federal funding and support, could survey and identify the state's historical resources, engage with federal agencies to ensure their protection, and if eligible, obtain formal listing of those resources on the National Register of Historic Places.[46] The NHPA also authorized grants to states to purchase or acquire historic properties to ensure their protection.[47] In addition to spurring the growth of state authority over such historic preservation, the NHPA's acknowledgment of the unique value of these areas and grants to states and local communities also prompted "unexpected economic forces behind preservation."[48] By empowering states and local communities to assume responsibility (and federal funding) for surveying and acquiring historic properties, the NHPA also ensured that state and local governments would have an ongoing role in the protection of historic properties and provided support for them to create the infrastructure necessary to maintain that engagement. Therefore, for much of the late 1990s, SHPOs played a primary role in the NHPA consultation process authorized by Section 106 and, with federal support as a catalyst, state historic preservation programs expanded to address other state historic and cultural priorities.

By 1992 tribes and their allies recognized that they had been excluded from the formal procedural protections of the NHPA and sought to ensure at least equal footing with the states in the Section 106 process. Such parallel treatment of tribes and states under federal law had found favor with Congress in the late 1980s and early 1990s in amendments to the nation's foundational environmental protection statutes that authorized a tribal role similar to that of states in the environmental

---

[45] Historic Properties; preservation program, Pub. L. 89-665, 80 Stat. 915 (Oct. 15, 1966).

[46] Charles Rennick, *The National Historic Preservation Act: San Carlos Apache Tribe v. United States and the Administrative Roadblock to Preserving Native American Culture*, 41 NEW ENG. L. REV. 67, 76 (2006).

[47] Pub. L. 89-665 at § 101(b)(2).

[48] *National Historic Preservation Act*, National Park Service (last updated Dec. 2, 2018), https://www.nps.gov/subjects/historicpreservation/national-historic-preservation-act.htm.

federalism structure of those laws.[49] Under those laws, this "treatment as [a] state" or "tribes as states" (TAS) concept permitted tribes to adopt their own water quality standards pursuant to the Clean Water Act, to assume primacy under the Clean Air Act, and to protect water resources under the Safe Drinking Water Act.[50] As a result, tribes could set their own environmental regulatory standards and, if they sought and received EPA's approval, enforce those standards, potentially even beyond a reservation's boundaries.[51] However, the potential for such standards also demanded that tribes develop the scientific, regulatory, and legal structures necessary to take advantage of and implement that authority. Like the ongoing expansion of tribal governmental authority spurred by the ISDEAA, the TAS provisions of the environmental laws provided important support for tribes to take on greater sovereign responsibilities and authority. That same concept found purchase in the 1992 changes to the NHPA.

To invigorate the requirement that tribes, Native Hawaiians, and their cultural concerns be included in the Section 106 process and to provide support for the review and development of TCD designations, the 1992 NHPA amendments included an option for tribes to pursue designation and certification of their own Tribal Historic Preservation Offices (THPOs).[52] Under those amendments, once a tribe's THPO application is approved by the Secretary of Interior, that THPO would act essentially on the same basis as SHPOs and could assume responsibility for all of the duties on tribal lands (defined as on-reservation) that a SHPO would otherwise carry out.[53] To receive approval, tribes are required to develop a plan establishing how those activities would be conducted, demonstrate that "the tribal preservation program is fully capable of carrying out" those functions, and acknowledge that the SHPO may still have certain responsibilities, particularly where such activities would be carried out on properties owned by non-Indians.[54] If approved, a THPO could then contract with the Secretary to assist in broader protection activities, including the assessment of historic and cultural properties for potential listing on

---

[49] *See, e.g.,* 33 U.S.C. § 1377 (Clean Water Act); 42 U.S.C. § 300j-11(a) (Safe Drinking Water Act); 42 U.S.C § 7601(d)(2)(B) (Clean Air Act); *see also* Hillary Hoffmann, *Congressional Plenary Power and Indigenous Environmental Stewardship: The Limits of Environmental Federalism,* 97 OR. L. REV. 353, 383 (2019).

[50] Hoffmann, *supra* note 49, at 383. The federal EPA has interpreted additional environmental laws to authorize similar tribal participation. *See Tribal Assumption of Federal Laws – Treatment As a State (TAS),* UNITED STATES ENVIRONMENTAL PROTECTION AGENCY, https://www.epa.gov/tribal/tribal-assumption-federal-laws-treatment-state-tas.

[51] *See id.,* at 389; City of Albuquerque v. Browner, 97 F.3d 415 (10th Cir. 1996) (holding that upstream, nontribal municipal wastewater facility had to comply with water quality standards adopted by downstream Pueblo of Isleta).

[52] Reclamation Projects Authorization and Adjustment Act of 1992, Pub. L. 102-575 § 4006, 106 Stat. 4753, 4755 (Oct. 30, 1992).

[53] *Id.*

[54] *See* 54 U.S.C. § 302702 (2014).

the National Historic Register and the maintenance of databases on those properties.[55] Tribes could also enter into agreements with the Advisory Council on Historic
Preservation (ACHP), which was created by the original NHPA in 1966, to replace
the ACHP's regulations with their own tribal regulations delineating the process of
reviewing federal activities on tribal lands for potential threats to cultural resources
of value to the tribe.[56] Finally, to support these additional tribal responsibilities and
activities, the 1992 NHPA amendments also loosened the federal purse strings by
including tribes in the pool of noncompetitive grants that had previously been
available to states for historic preservation activities.[57]

Tribes quickly recognized the value and opportunity presented by THPOs;
15 tribes created THPOs and received certification in the first five years after the
amendments were passed.[58] As of April 1, 2019, 185 tribes had federally recognized
THPOs, with authority covering more than 50 million acres in 30 states.[59] That
explosion of THPOs corresponded with a significant growth in federal funds flowing
to tribes to support those initiatives. In fiscal year 1996, the first year that funding
was available for THPO activities, 12 tribes applied for and received almost
$2 million in federal financial support, for an average of about $80,000 per tribe.[60]
More broadly available grant funding from the National Park Service (NPS) provided nearly $9 million to 170 tribes between 1990 and 1997.[61] By 2019, that
figure had risen to nearly $12 million annually, but because of the growth in the
number of THPOs, the average share for each tribe dropped to just over $60,000.[62]
These funds are allocated based on an NPS formula that accounts for equity and
tribal land base and, given the explosion in THPOs across Indian Country, each
share is now insufficient to make a significant impact for any individual tribe.[63]
Tribes, Alaskan Native corporations, and Native Hawaiians are also eligible for

---

[55] *Id.* §§ 320704; 302304.
[56] *Id.* § 302705 (provided the tribal regulations would provide "equivalent" protection to the
ACHP's regulations).
[57] *Id.* § 302703 (2014).
[58] Ferguson, *supra* note 23, at 27.
[59] *Find a THPO*, National Association of Tribal Historic Preservation Officers, http://
www.nathpo.org/thpos/find-a-thpo. By comparison, the environmental program with the
greatest number of tribes opting in is under the Clean Water Act, with EPA documenting
60 tribes that have received approval to administer their own water quality standards. Hoffmann, *supra* note 49, at 387.
[60] *What Is the History of THPO Funding?*, National Association of Tribal Historic Preservation Officers, http://www.nathpo.org/thpos/history-of-funding.
[61] Ferguson, *supra* note 23, at 28.
[62] *THPO Funding History*, National Association of Tribal Historic Preservation
Officers (Feb. 14, 2019), http://www.nathpo.org/wp-content/uploads/2019/03/THPO-HPF-
Funding-2020-google.pdf.
[63] *See THPO Grants*, National Park Service, https://www.nps.gov/thpo/grants/index.html;
Tribal Historic Preservation Program: 2017 Annual Report 16 National Park Service,
https://www.nps.gov/articles/upload/997-066-Tribal_Preservation_Program_jm4-1.pdf.

additional grant funding through the NPS's Tribal Heritage Grant program, which, in 2018, totaled nearly a million dollars.[64]

From the beginning of these efforts, however, tribes were linking the expanded authority of a THPO under federal law to broader exercises of their own sovereign authority under tribal law. For example, nearly half of the NPS grants that tribes sought and received in the early years of THPO development (1995–1996) were for "research, the *development of tribal ordinances* governing historic preservation, or other historic preservation *regulatory activities*."[65] While many tribes may have already had cultural resource programs or historic preservation offices prior to 1992, the THPO designation and corresponding responsibilities under federal law motivated a number of tribes to expand on their existing practices and develop their own legal and governmental avenues for the protection of cultural resources. As noted by a recent annual report of the Confederated Salish and Kootenai Tribes, one of the first tribes to receive a THPO designation in 1996, "[a] key difference between" the Tribal Historic Preservation Department, which operates pursuant to a 1995 Tribal Ordinance,[66] and the Tribes' preexisting advisory cultural committees, "lies in the federally delegated authority vested in the department to regulate undertakings subject to compliance with [NHPA]" and other applicable tribal and federal laws.[67] With the contemporaneous growth in tribal governments sparked by the self-determination era, this expansion of tribal sovereignty resulted in a significant increase in tribal laws focused on cultural resources.

These assertions of sovereignty take a variety of forms, each of which reflect the desire of a particular tribe to exert greater governmental authority over cultural resources. The Rosebud Sioux adopted its Cultural Resources Management Code in 2006 in order to "[p]rotect[ ] and provide[ ] guardianship of cultural resources, traditions, and the independent cultural sovereignty" of the Tribe while also making sure that "future Tribal developmental practices [would] adhere to th[e] Code and other jurisprudence as developed in the course of Tribal expansion."[68] The Tribe's THPO holds primary authority to oversee and regulate these functions and is tasked with a broad range of responsibilities,[69] including enforcement of the code's

---

[64] News Release, National Park Service, National Park Service Awards Historic Preservation Grants to American Indian Tribes, Alaskan Natives, and Native Hawaiian Organizations (Sept. 7, 2018), https://www.nps.gov/orgs/1207/national-park-service-awards-historic-preserva tion-grants-to-american-indian-tribes-alaskan-natives-and-native-hawaiian-organizations.htm.

[65] FERGUSON, *supra* note 23, at 28.

[66] *Annual Report 2014–15: Success and Wellness* 11 CONFEDERATED SALISH & KOOTENAI TRIBES OF THE FLATHEAD RESERVATION, http://www.csktribes.org/government/annual-reports.

[67] *Annual Report 2018–19: Growing Health Populations* 16–17, CONFEDERATED SALISH & KOO- TENAI TRIBES OF THE FLATHEAD RESERVATION, http://www.csktribes.org/government/annual- reports.

[68] Rosebud Sioux Tribe Cultural Resources Management Code of 2006, Title 18, Chapter 26, § 103, https://www.narf.org/nill/codes/rosebudcode/title18chapter26.pdf.

[69] *See id.* at § 202.

requirements through the tribal judiciary.[70] The code also applies across a range of resources, including cultural plants,[71] sites,[72] remains,[73] and records.[74] But, with regard to records, the code still relies on a cultural advisory board, consisting of volunteers and charged with the responsibility of assisting the THPO in reviewing and maintaining important tribal cultural records and also working with the public and other partners.[75]

While broad in scope, especially with the specific inclusion of cultural plants and the requirement that the THPO develop, analyze, and protect an inventory of those plants,[76] the Rosebud Cultural Resources Management Code reflects a fairly straightforward tribal implementation of the THPO and cultural resources management framework. Like Rosebud, many tribes have followed the guidance provided by the NPS to apply for THPO certification, which sets forth the functions to be assumed by THPOs, the suggested role of a cultural advisory board, and related details necessary to incorporate the THPO program, including the jurisdictional acknowledgment required by the NHPA.[77] With this framework as a general structure, many tribes have built cultural resource codes that provide their own unique regulatory and advisory bodies, procedures for identifying and listing cultural or historic properties on their own tribal historic registers, permitting processes for on-reservation activities that may affect cultural resources and judicial review and enforcement mechanisms.[78] Though the specifics of each of these approaches vary, many include a central role for the THPO and incorporate the important assumed responsibilities for that position as authorized by the NHPA.[79] Consistent with the growth of other tribal governmental structures and operations resulting from the ISDEAA, these codes reflect how tribes have sought to assume greater responsibility

---

[70] *Id.* at §§ 801–1001.

[71] *Id.* at § 301.

[72] *Id.* at § 401.

[73] *Id.* at § 501.

[74] *Id.* at § 601.

[75] *Id.*

[76] *Id.* at §§ 301(D)-(I).

[77] See *Tribal Historic Preservation Program Tribal Historic Preservation Officer Application*, National Park Service (last updated Sept. 11, 2019), https://www.nps.gov/articles/thppapps .htm.

[78] See, e.g., Confederated Tribes of the Umatilla Indian Reservation Historic Preservation Code, http://ctuir.org/system/files/FINAL%20Historic%20Preservation%20Code_effective%202001-25-16.pdf; Mille Lacs Band of Chippewa Tribal Code, Cultural Resources, Title 10, https://millelacsband.com/content/3-government/17-statutes-policies/statutestitle10.pdf; Colville Tribal Code, Cultural Resources Protection, Title 4, Chapter 4, https://static1.squarespace.com/static/572d09c54c2f85ddda868946/t/5824973637c58111093b0c19/1478793015067/4-4-culturalresource sprotection.pdf; Poarch Band of Creek Indians Tribal Code, Tribal Historic Preservation, Title 39, https://library.municode.com/tribes_and_tribal_nations/poarch_band_of_creek_indians/codes/code_of_ordinances?nodeId=TIT39TRHIPR; Lummi Code of Laws, Cultural Resources Preservation Code, Title 40, https://narf.org/nill/codes/lummi/40Cultural_Resources.pdf.

[79] See, e.g. Confederated Tribes of the Umatilla Indian Reservation Historic Preservation Code, § 4.01; Poarch Band of Creek Indians Code § 39-2-2.

FIGURE 6.1 Wild Horse, Mount Hood, Warm Springs Reservation, Oregon
(Cameron MacPhail/Aurora Photos/Getty Images)

under the NHPA while molding those functions to fit a tribe-specific view of government, culture, and sovereignty.

Some tribes have taken even greater leaps beyond that general structure to incorporate additional expressions of and protections for their cultural sovereignty. The Confederated Tribes of the Warm Springs in Oregon, for example, developed a comprehensive code addressing archaeological, historical, and cultural resources (Figure 6.1).[80] Though these Tribes were also among the first to have a federally certified THPO,[81] their code does not specifically establish the THPO or provide for the THPO's responsibilities. Instead, according to the Tribes' broad definition of culture and cultural resources, the code is intended to fulfill the tribal government's trust responsibilities to manage, protect, and preserve those resources across the entirety of the Tribes' traditional territory, extending even beyond the current reservation boundaries. To accomplish this goal, the code broadly defines protected lands, sites, and objects, as well as "Cultural Materials," which include "such things as eagle feathers, fish, game, roots, berries, cedar bark, Indian medicines and water having special significance," whether obtained within or outside of the reservation.[82]

---

[80] *See* Warm Springs Tribal Code, Protection and Management of Archaeological, Historical, and Cultural Resources, Chapter 490, https://warmsprings-nsn.gov/government/tribal-code/?pid=1064.

[81] *Tribal Historic Preservation Program, supra* note 63, at 2.

[82] *Id.* at § 490.010(5).

The code further designates a nonexhaustive list of 48 items as cultural materials and prohibits tribal members from gathering, collecting, possessing, selling, bartering, exchanging, purchasing, offering to sell, purchase or exchange, or transporting any of those materials in violation of either tribal laws or tribal traditions or customs.[83] In addition to other legal sanctions, punishment for violating those prohibitions could include traditional sanctions determined by the Tribes' Culture and Heritage Committee.[84] These provisions provide an important legal tool for enforcing the uniquely cultural value of those materials and incorporate the terms of tribal tradition and culture directly into the Tribes' governmental and legal structures.

Similarly, the Warm Springs Code commits the Tribes to protect the religious freedom of its members and other Indians on the reservation through express incorporation of the American Indian Religious Freedom Act and the recognition of "traditional Indian religious leaders" as the arbiters of religious practices on the reservation. The code requires the Tribal Council to protect sacred sites identified by these leaders and establishes the "prerogative and the duty of the Tribal Council ... to define traditional Indian religious practices insofar as they relate to the exercise of tribal Treaty rights" after consulting with those leaders.[85]

Those treaty rights are also an important priority within the Tribes' code. Despite the potential for interjurisdictional complications, the Warm Springs Code specifically incorporates the terms of the Tribes' 1855 Treaty and expressly provides for the protection of tribal members' off-reservation activities through tribal permitting procedures and other provisions encouraging intergovernmental cooperation and reporting of off-reservation activities that may interfere with those treaty rights.[86]

Like the Warm Springs Tribes, the Yurok Tribe of California was one of the first THPO-certified tribes.[87] For the Yurok, the establishment of a THPO followed closely upon the heels of the Tribe's 1993 Constitution, which from its first words, recognizes and revolves around the Tribe's cultural identity, history, and traditions.[88] The Tribe adopted the 1993 Constitution to "[p]reserve and promote [the Tribe's] culture, language, and religious beliefs and practices, and pass them on to [the Tribe's] children ... grandchildren, and to their children and grandchildren on, forever," among other priorities.[89] In exercise of that authority, the Tribe adopted the Cultural Resources Protection Code that, like other tribal codes,

---

[83] *Id.* at §§ 490.510-520.

[84] *Id.* at § 490.520.

[85] *Id.* at §§ 490.400-430.

[86] *Id.* at §§ 490.300-350.

[87] *Tribal Historic Preservation Program*, supra note 63, at 2.

[88] Yurok Tribe Const. pmbl., https://yurok.tribal.codes/Constitution ("Our people have always lived on this sacred and wondrous land along the Pacific Coast and inland on the Klamath River, since the Spirit People, Wo-ge', made things ready for us and the Creator, Ko-won-no-ekc-on Ne-ka-nup-ceo, placed us here. From the beginning, we have followed all the laws of the Creator, which became the whole fabric of our tribal sovereignty").

[89] *Id.*

establishes a permitting, enforcement, and penalty scheme while defining the roles and responsibilities of the Tribe's THPO and related cultural advisory committees.[90] But the Yurok Tribal Code goes further by protecting tribal artisans through a Yurok Cultural Arts Code[91] and specifically protecting "Traditional cultural items," such as baskets, regalia, jewelry, and ceremonial items used for cultural purposes by prohibiting their alienation and providing for both civil penalties and injunctive relief.[92] Finally, in order to protect important aspects of tribal culture that may be intellectual property, otherwise unable to be protected by state or federal laws,[93] the Yurok Code's Culture chapter ends with the Copyright Protection Title establishing an organic system for protecting original tribal works through registration and penalties.[94] Those provisions recognize that "certain specific symbols and basket designs" are not subject to the code because those designs are recognized as "sacred [ ] gifts from the Creator to the Yurok people," although they may be protected as part of a larger work or in the name of the Tribe as a whole.[95]

As these tribal laws demonstrate, for the Yurok, the Warm Springs, and other tribes, tribal laws provide important legal protections for cultural resources and serve as sovereign reflections of unique cultural values. And, although many tribes have developed provisions that follow a "standard" structure for implementing permitting, penalties, and advisory bodies that complement THPO authority under the NHPA, the Yurok, Warm Springs, and others have expanded their sovereign authority beyond those procedural and largely federal structures to weave cultural protections together with tribal governmental authority. As the innovative codes of the Warm Springs and Yurok demonstrate, these purely tribal expressions of cultural sovereignty serve to protect important cultural values while invigorating tribal laws with those same values. In so doing, tribes are now making their laws and sovereignty part of their cultural heritage, bringing new meaning to both culture and the rule and power of law. These culturally oriented tribal legal reforms reflect the broader renaissance of tribal sovereignty taking place across Indian Country because of and, in many instances, despite, the limits of the federal government's self-determination policies and in the case of cultural protection, the inherent limitations of the NHPA.

As described earlier, one of these limitations lies in the 1992 amendments to the NHPA, which may have seemingly opened the door for tribes to further develop their existing cultural resource programs and connect those efforts to exercises of their governmental sovereignty, but the federal government has since proven to be

---

[90] Yurok Tribal Code, Cultural Resources Protection, Chapter 14.10, https://yurok.tribal.codes/YTC/14.10.

[91] *Id.* at chap. 14.05.

[92] *Id.* at chap. 14.15.

[93] *See* Chapter 8.

[94] Yurok Tribal Code, Copyright Protection, Chapter 14.20, https://yurok.tribal.codes/YTC/14.20.

[95] *Id.* at § 14.20.010(a).

woefully unprepared to support the explosion of THPOs prompted by those amendments. The funding that was critical to developing THPOs during the 1990s has increased only slightly, while the number of THPOs has grown rapidly, resulting in significantly less per capita funding for ongoing THPO operations. Thus, tribes interested in building on the development of a THPO to enhance and expand the legal protections available under tribal law must identify additional sources of funding to supplement those federal funds.

In addition, the jurisdictional limitations on tribal authority, described in more detail in Chapter 2 and flowing from the adverse decisions of the US Supreme Court in the 1980s, 1990s, and early 2000s, depend on the status of an individual as an "Indian" and, in civil matters, may also depend on the ownership status of the land on which a tribe seeks to exert that authority. These restrictions further limit tribal efforts to enact effective legal protections for their cultural activities, resources, and materials. While the permitting procedures established by the majority of tribal cultural resource protection codes provide a basis from which each tribe could assert civil authority under the Supreme Court's consensual relations requirement,[96] the lack of tribal criminal authority over non-Indians limits tribal power to arrest, prosecute, and potentially incarcerate non-Indians who may severely threaten or interfere with important aspects of tribal culture, further restricting the legal avenues for cultural protection available to tribes.[97] But, as demonstrated by the provisions of the Warm Springs Tribal Code, tribes may authorize the removal or exclusion of certain individuals from their reservations, although those procedures also present some additional legal risk.[98]

Finally, as described in the opening chapter of this book, tribes seeking to enact tribal laws that protect their own cultural values, places, practices, and objects also face the broader challenge of overcoming the historical oppression of federal laws and priorities. As demonstrated by the need for the 1992 amendments to the NHPA,

---

[96] *See* Montana v. United States, 450 U.S. at 566. Arguably, the second so-called *Montana* exception, recognizing tribal authority over the conduct of non-members that "threatens or has some effect on the political integrity, the economic security, or the health or welfare of the tribe," could also justify tribal regulatory authority over cultural interference; however, federal courts have been largely unwilling to recognize tribal jurisdiction under this exception. *Compare, e.g.*, Attorney's Process and Investigation Services, Inc. v. Sac & Fox Tribe of Mississippi in Iowa, 609 F.3d 927, 939 (8th Cir. 2010) (recognizing tribal jurisdiction under *Montana*'s second exception where defendant "organiz[ed] a physical attack by thirty or more outsiders armed with batons and at least one firearm against the Tribe's facilities and the tribal members inside, including the duly elected council") with Plains Commerce Bank v. Long Family Land and Cattle Co., 554 U.S. 316, 341 (2008) (denying tribal jurisdiction and suggesting that the second exception contemplates "'catastrophic consequences'" (citation omitted)).

[97] Oliphant v. Suquamish Indian Tribe, 435 U.S. 191, 195 (1978).

[98] Poodry v. Tonawanda Band of Seneca Indians, 85 F.3d 874, 884 (2nd Cir. 1996) (discussing potential for banished members to seek habeas corpus relief in federal court). The Warm Springs Tribal Code recognizes limits on this power by excluding from removal residents of the reservation, tribal and federal employees; Warm Springs Tribal Code, § 490.130.

those federal laws and priorities typically do not align with tribal perspectives and it takes significant effort to open additional avenues through which tribes can build authority to protect their own sovereign and cultural priorities. These cultural protection efforts follow on and align with the broader tribal self-determination movement of the last half century, and tribes have capitalized on both to rebuild and reshape their constitutions, laws, and governments to better reflect their own priorities. But, like the imposition of the IRA form of government that has stubbornly persisted across Indian Country, overcoming that legacy of federal oppression takes time, reflection, and effort. Even then, tribal efforts to exercise broader self-determination can be hamstrung by a lack of federal funding or support for innovative tribal efforts where those efforts do not take advantage of existing federal programs. Ironically, for some tribes, opting into these systems of federalism may be seen as an act of sovereign subjugation, and they may prefer to use their inherent sovereignty to develop organic preservation laws that arise more directly from their own cultural values. For others, it may be easier to just "play by the federal rules," obtain the necessary federal financial assistance, and seek what protective measures they can under the foreign system.

As this chapter demonstrates, over the last quarter century, tribes across the country have melded cultural values and tribal laws to create new and revolutionary approaches to cultural preservation, while also building critical legal and governmental structures to protect those cultures. Those new legal and governmental structures may benefit tribes in other, unexpected ways; as tribe builds infrastructure to pursue one initiative, it may find that the increased infrastructure allows it to undertake other social, economic, or cultural programs of interest and value to tribal members. Many of those legal and governmental structures were sparked by the THPO revolution of the 1990s and 2000s, but a number of tribes are now changing them to better fit their own cultural and other priorities instead of simply taking advantage of the authority offered by the NHPA and federal law. As these efforts continue, it is not hard to imagine a time in the near future when tribal laws focusing on cultural protections are providing the basis from which the federal government works to recognize and respect tribal culture, rather than the other way around.

As a short postscript to this chapter, it is necessary to acknowledge that only tribes with which the federal government has a formally acknowledged, government-to-government relationship may opt in to federalism structures like that contained in the NHPA. Similarly, only those tribes (and a subset of them, at that) have a common, independent land base over which to assert their sovereign authority. There are estimates that more than 100 tribes, indigenous communities, and bands of existing tribes are culturally separate communities and yet lack any recognized sovereignty or political authority in the eyes of the federal government. This often leaves such tribes unable to participate in federal programs for which the distribution of funds is attached to a label of "Indian," or "federally recognized tribe." They may be recognized at the state level, but not at the federal level, and this would allow some measure of participation in state-funded cultural preservation programs and initiatives, but as will be discussed in the next chapter, these opportunities are quite limited or nonexistent in many states. A full discussion of the consequences of the historical and current federal policy of recognizing some tribes, but not others, is beyond the scope of this book, but for tribes deprived of this federal status, cultural preservation remains a real and daily struggle.

7

Both Ends of the Spectrum and Everything in Between

State and Local Governments and Indigenous Cultures

He ali'i ka 'āina; he kauwā ke Kānaka.[1]

Hawaii and Vermont illustrate many of the themes surrounding indigenous peoples' relationships with the states in which they reside, sometimes dating back long before the ratification of the US Constitution. Vermont was the fourteenth state admitted to the Union, and by 1791, the year of its admission, the lands within its boundaries had been home to indigenous peoples since as early as 11,000 CE and perhaps before.[2] The state keeps no historical records about indigenous populations, language groups, or virtually any other information that might assist a tribal historian to piece together the history of one or more of the local indigenous people, which complicates the matter of recounting the state's historic relationship with indigenous cultures. As of the twenty-first century, there are approximately 2,000 people living in Vermont who identify as indigenous on census surveys, and these are mostly members of different bands of Abenaki in the northern part of the state.

More than 150 years after Vermont was admitted to the Union, the various islands formerly constituting the Kingdom of Hawaii became the most recent state. Those islands have been home to descendants of Polynesian peoples who migrated to the island chain in 300–600 CE.[3] Today, they identify themselves using the Hawaiian term for "the people," or *kānaka maoli*.[4] Twenty-first-century Hawaii is home to nearly 350,000 *kānaka maoli*, nearly half of the total population of the state of

---

[1] The approximate translation is "the land is chief and humans are its servants." Elena Bryant, *Innovation or Degradation?: An Analysis of Hawai'i's Cultural Impact Assessment Process As a Vehicle of Environmental Justice for Kānaka Maoli*, 13 ASIAN-PAC. L. & POL'Y J. 230, 231 (2011).

[2] Vermont Commission on Native American Affairs, *State Recognized Tribes*, STATE OF VERMONT, https://vcnaa.vermont.gov/recognition/recognized-tribes.

[3] Jon M. Van Dyke & Melody K. MacKenzie, *An Introduction to the Rights of the Native Hawaiian People*, 10 HAW. B.J. 63, 63 (2006).

[4] *Id.*

Vermont.[5] Between these two dramatically different states situated at the eastern and western edges of the country, there are hundreds of other indigenous nations living within the present-day boundaries of states that, at times, have posed hostile threats to their very existence. Like Georgia's historical perspective on the Cherokee Nation, described in Chapter 2, states have traditionally viewed tribal governments and indigenous nations as threats to their own sovereignty.[6] In many instances, this hostility permeated the relationship between states and indigenous peoples over time and in many cases has informed the development of each state's laws around cultural preservation, which vary accordingly.

In Vermont, the state's relationship with indigenous peoples has been consistently antagonistic and is only recently showing signs of improvement, but it is still nowhere near offering a level of affirmative legal protections for indigenous culture. This history dates back thousands of years, and the modern relationship has largely grown out of state officials misunderstanding or ignoring it altogether. Archaeological records show evidence of indigenous villages around the shores of *Pitawbagok*, as the Abenaki-language speakers referred to Lake Champlain, and scattered throughout the lake region of the northeastern part of the state in prehistoric times, many thousands of years before any evidence of Europeans in the region.[7] Contact was first documented in 1609, when the French explorer Samuel de Champlain noted the presence of "savages" living along the shores of Lake Champlain and in the Champlain islands in the northern part of the lake.[8] These people were likely Wabanaki, or Abenaki (the terms are often used interchangeably in historical records), or possibly Haudenosaunee (historically referred to as "Iroquois"); members of these two confederacies had lived in this region before Champlain arrived and began scouting the area for the French in the early seventeenth century. Champlain's journals do not contain much detail about the indigenous peoples he saw, other than the fact that they "withdraw as deep into the land as possible" when his company passed through their territory.[9]

For the next century after Champlain's first visit, Europeans documented their presence in Vermont, but they did not jot down lasting notes about the indigenous peoples they likely encountered.[10] The Europeans seem to have used the region

[5]   LINDSAY HIXSON, BRADFORD B. HEPLER, & MYOUNG OUK KIM, THE NATIVE HAWAIIAN AND OTHER PACIFIC ISLANDER POPULATION: 2010, 7, U.S. CENSUS BUREAU (May 2012), https://www.census.gov/content/dam/Census/library/publications/2012/dec/c2010br-12.pdf.

[6]   *See, e.g.*, United States v. Kagama, 118 U.S. 375, 384 (1886) ("Because of the local ill feeling, the people of the states where the[tribes] are found are often their deadliest enemies.")

[7]   GORDON M. DAY, *"Abenakis in the Lake Champlain Valley,"* in LAKE CHAMPLAIN: REFLECTIONS ON OUR PAST, 277 (Jennie G. Versteeg, ed. 1987).

[8]   *Id.*

[9]   *Id.* at 279. Some anthropologists have concluded that by the time Champlain arrived, the Haudenosaunee had abandoned Lake Champlain for the lake region of what is now New York State, and the sole indigenous residents recorded by Europeans were Wabanaki, or Abenaki, people, based on their observed habits and settlement patterns.

[10] *Vermont History*, NATIONAL PARK SERVICE, US DEPARTMENT OF THE INTERIOR, https://www.nps.gov/nr/travel/centralvermont/vhistory1.htm.

FIGURE 7.1 Lake Champlain, Vermont
(Dominic Labbe/Getty Images)

around Lake Champlain mostly as a safe travel route between French settlements to the north and British to the south, which avoided having to clear routes through heavily forested mountain ranges on either side of the lake basin.[11] The primary indigenous residents of this region were at that time the Wabanaki, or "Dawn Land People," a confederacy of five indigenous nations that spoke related languages.[12] Their history was not well documented by the Europeans, but archaeologists have noted that some of their villages were permanent settlements, containing timber-framed long houses similar to those used by the Haudenosaunee to the west.[13] Abenaki culture was rooted in a creation story closely tied to natural features in what became the state of Vermont. For instance, Ojihozo was a powerful figure who formed the earth, creating prominent features like Lake Champlain (Figure 7.1).[14] After his work was finished, he turned himself to stone and installed himself as a rocky feature protruding from the eastern part of the lake near the modern town of Shelburne.[15] According to Abenaki historians, lesser mythological figures like Bedegwajoiz and Azeban lived and worked magic in the regions surrounding the modern towns of Middlebury and Swanton, at the far southern and far northern edges of Lake Champlain, respectively.[16]

The Dawn Land People hunted, fished, and farmed in the Green Mountains and lowlands surrounding the lake, and they appear to have tried mightily to avoid the constant armed conflicts between the Haudenosaunee to the west and the indigenous nations to the north in Quebec, then later between the British and French occupiers and their allies from other tribes.[17] When the battles and then wars broke

---

[11] DAY, *supra* note 7, at 279; BRUCE HYDE & JOHN CHARLES HUDEN, INDIAN PLACE NAMES OF NEW ENGLAND (1962).

[12] Day, *supra* note 7, at 279.

[13] *Id.* at 285.

[14] *Id.* at 288.

[15] *Id.*

[16] *Id.*

[17] *Id.* at 280, 286.

out, they would abandon their villages and retreat to the densely forested Green Mountain and White Mountain ranges; a survival strategy they would repeat for nearly one hundred years.[18] It was not until approximately 1815 that armed conflict in Vermont ceased, well after the Revolutionary War ended.[19]

This postwar period brought further destabilization for the Wabanaki Confederacy, however, because the signing of the Treaty of Paris created a new international boundary between Canada and the United States, cutting their sacred lake and surrounding homelands in half.[20] Abenaki living north of the border continued to be subject to decisions made by the British Crown and were eventually made Canadian citizens while Abenaki to the south became subject to decisions made by US officials in Washington, D.C. and, much later, became US citizens. Yet, despite this severing of nations and the creation of international boundaries that divided Canadian Abenaki from Vermont Abenaki, Abenaki people never left the state of Vermont.[21]

Up until 1823, when Chief Justice Marshall issued his opinion adapting the Doctrine of Discovery, British colonial authorities, and then Americans, had tried to establish as widespread a presence in Vermont as possible.[22] This matters for the Abenaki of the twenty-first century because the British occupiers of Vermont wrote "the official history" of the region. These historical whitewashed accounts often omitted any reference to Vermont's indigenous peoples but would later create legal arguments for state officials in court proceedings in which the Abenaki sought formal recognition from the state.

Despite the whitewashing, there was evidence of the Abenaki presence in the state dating back to the colonial period. This came in the form of British land records, which revealed the product of negotiations around Abenaki settlements, producing maps containing carve-outs for Abenaki communities and lands.[23] Indeed, the British colonial governor of Vermont encouraged British settlers to lease lands of the Missisquoi Abenaki in the mid-1760s,[24] and "[i]n 1765 the Governor of Lower Canada refused to grant title of 2000 acres on the Missisquoi River because it was found to be Abenaki land."[25] In 1775, 400–500 Abenaki were documented as living in Missisquoi village.[26]

---

[18] *Id.* at 285.

[19] *Id.*

[20] *Id.* at 286.

[21] *Id.* at 288.

[22] Gene Bergman, *Defying Precedent: Can Abenaki Aboriginal Title Be Extinguished by the "Weight of History"*, 18 AM. INDIAN L. REV. 447, 461 (1993).

[23] *Id.* at 472 ("Actual settlement practice left the Abenaki in control of their historic homelands").

[24] *Id.*

[25] *Id.*

[26] *Id.* (citing William A. Haviland & Marjory W. Power, The Original Vermonters: Native Inhabitants, Past & Present 38 (1981) & Colin G. Calloway, The Western Abenakis of Vermont, 1600–1800 (1990)).

The Vermont territorial legislature subsequently organized the state as an independent republic, ratifying the Vermont Constitution in 1777, which created the first formalized European nation-state in New England. This early constitution was remarkable in several respects; it prohibited slavery and provided for universal male suffrage, giving the right to vote to all "adult males," whether they owned land or not, both progressive principles for their day.[27] Along with Pennsylvania, Vermont was in a tiny minority of states to grant constitutional freedom of the press and freedom of speech rights to its citizens.[28] Yet, as with the constitutions of many states at that time and later, these constitutional protections and the values they enshrined did not reach indigenous peoples. They did not confer suffrage on adult Abenaki males, who also were not considered citizens or residents of the state, and unlike the US Constitution, the Vermont Constitution was entirely silent about their presence in the state.

Many scholars have noted the historic and collective attempts to ignore, or even erase, the Abenaki from Vermont's historical records since 1777.[29] This started with the Vermont Constitution and later came in the form of omitting reference to Abenaki people in early censuses, statutes passed by the state legislature, and other local laws and records. At times, it was more overt – starting in the early 1930s and continuing through 1957, Vermont pursued one of the most aggressive state-sanctioned forced sterilization programs in the nation, initiated by the Vermont legislature and facilitated by multitudes of physicians licensed in the state.[30] The Abenaki were one group targeted by this law, which on its face applied to those deemed to be "idiots, imbeciles, feeble-minded or insane" and was aimed at preventing them from having children, but in effect was used as a tool to implement European American notions of racial purity throughout the state.[31] During the time of this state-sanctioned eugenics policy, the Abenaki (and others having with indigenous heritage) hid from white Vermonters, as they did in Champlain's day, sometimes literally and sometimes by changing their names and their racial identification in census surveys.[32]

One anthropologist has described the Abenaki as having a "perilous persistence" in the state, teetering at times on the edge of being completely erased from historical records, fighting misrepresentation by state government officials, and defending against claims by nonindigenous Vermonters that they have vanished, fled, or been

[27] Peter R. Teachout, *"Trustees and Servants": Government Accountability in Early Vermont*, 31 Vt. L. Rev. 857, 866 (2007).

[28] *Id.* at 866.

[29] *E.g.* Bergman, *supra* note 22, at 461.

[30] Lutz Kaelber, *Eugenics: Compulsory Sterilization in 50 American States*, University of Vermont (2012), http://www.uvm.edu/~lkaelber/eugenics.

[31] Angela Evancie, *What Is the Status of the Abenaki Native Americans in Vermont Today?"* Vermont Public Radio (Nov. 4, 2016), https://www.vpr.org/post/what-status-abenaki-native-americans-vermont-today#stream/o.

[32] *Id.*

"assimilated" into mainstream society. The tension between Abenaki historians and non-Abenaki historians over Abenaki history in Vermont came to a head in the late 1980s, when the Abenaki sought federal recognition and began to assert aboriginal fishing rights on waters regulated by the state. When thirty-six Abenaki staged a "fish-in" on the Missisquoi River, fishing without state licenses, they were criminally charged.[33] As a defense, they asserted aboriginal title to the river, and the lower court in at least one case ruled in their favor.[34] On appeal to the Vermont Supreme Court, the state argued that the Abenaki had not satisfied one of the legal requirements to assert aboriginal title, which was proof of a continuous presence in the region. The state's reasoning was that the Abenaki were absent from the historical record during the period 1763–1791. The court agreed, finding that the "extinguishment of Abenaki aboriginal title was complete by 1791, when Vermont became the fourteenth state," due to the British Crown's "sanctioning of dominion over the area" and the British and American settlement patterns throughout.[35]

Although the Vermont Supreme Court's opinion in this case, *State* v. *Elliott*, issued in 1992, is not remarkable in the substantive result it reached – many state and federal courts have declined to find in favor of tribes on aboriginal title claims – it is somewhat shocking in the reasoning that was used to reach this conclusion.[36] For one, the court determined that the evidence of "white settlement," well documented by the settlers themselves, was enough to extinguish Abenaki title.[37] Moreover, the court concluded that "claims that the Abenakis never voluntarily abandoned the area and that they were never completely removed have no effect on a finding of an intent to assert complete control over the area in a manner adverse to the Abenakis." In other words, the Abenaki could be divested of title to their lands even while continuously occupying those lands, provided there was sufficient evidence of "white settlement."[38] The court also seemed to completely disregard extensive contemporaneous evidence of the British carve-outs for Abenaki lands reflected in the accounts of town clerks documenting the settlement patterns on the ground, and Abenaki historians' accounts of indigenous settlements and presence in Vermont during the contentious period.[39] It also disregarded historical records like Champlain's, which indicated that the reason Abenaki people were not visible at many times during the postcontact era was because they were trying to avoid being killed.

The supreme court of Vermont was not alone in its hostility to the state's first occupants, though. Starting in the 1970s, the Abenaki sought recognition from the federal and state governments, and their efforts were strenuously opposed by

[33]   State v. Elliott, 616 A.2d 210, 215 (1992).
[34]   *Id.* at 218.
[35]   *Id.* at 218.
[36]   *Id.* at 219.
[37]   Bergman, *supra* note 22, at 474.
[38]   Elliott, *supra* note 33, at 219.
[39]   *Id.*

governors, state legislators, and many other notable Vermonters.[40] Governor Thomas Salmon granted the Abenaki a form of state recognition by executive order in 1976, which was overturned by his successor, Governor Richard Snelling, only one year later. One of Vermont's most famous politicians, former Governor Howard Dean, vocally opposed Abenaki recognition and directed his attorney general, William Sorrell, to fight the Tribe's attempts to gain state or federal recognition in the 1990s by arguing that the Abenaki had not maintained a continuous presence over time, including during the eugenics era of the early twentieth century.[41] The *Elliott* decision only served to further these arguments.

It was not until 2011 that the Abenaki began to secure recognition of their present legal status as tribes in the state. That year, the Vermont legislature passed the first of two statutes recognizing four Abenaki bands, although this statute, like those of many other states, did not confer any rights along with the formal recognition.[42] In the preamble to one statute, the legislature recognized that "the Missisquoi and Cowasuck Abenaki were indigenous to and farmed the river floodplains of Vermont at least as far back as the 1100s A.D."[43] This was a significant departure from the prior stance of state officials, who had consistently denied any continuing Abenaki presence. The 2011 and 2012 statutes therefore marked the first moments in the state's history that the legislature enacted statutes that, at least in part, acknowledged Abenaki people and began the process of recognizing their contributions to the state's history.[44] However, the statutes did not go so far as to provide the Abenaki with rights that would facilitate cultural preservation, such as fishing, hunting or land repatriation. The legislature also did not acknowledge or apologize for the eugenics policy and forced sterilizations. And in those aspects, Vermont is hardly alone. Many other states have either consciously or unconsciously erased, minimized, or mischaracterized the history of indigenous peoples within their borders.

The picture is not so bleak in some states, though. Like many states that have embraced their indigenous residents, visitors to the state of Alaska's department of commerce website are greeted in Dena'ina, an indigenous language spoken in the region surrounding Tikahtnu, otherwise known as Cook Inlet.[45] If a visitor clicks on the greeting, she is taken to the University of Alaska's website and a map of the state

---

[40] Maryann Ullmann, *Vermont Finally Recognizes the Abenaki*, Cultural Survival Quarterly Magazine (Sept. 2006), https://www.culturalsurvival.org/publications/cultural-survival-quar terly/vermont-finally-recognizes-abenaki.

[41] David Mace, *Abenaki Chief Slams Dean Record*, Rutland Times Argus (Nov. 20, 2003), https://www.timesargus.com/news/abenaki-chief-slams-dean-record/article_279e20b1-94b8-5559-bd40-7193135774be.html.

[42] Vt. Stat. Ann. tit. 1, § 851.

[43] *Id.*

[44] *Id.* § 852.

[45] *Alaska Native Language Preservation & Advisory Council, The Great State of Alaska*, https://www.commerce.alaska.gov/web/dcra/AKNativeLanguagePreservationAdvisoryCouncil/Languages.aspx.

depicting all of the major indigenous language groups, with labels for geographic features, towns, and cities in the respective indigenous languages.[46] Reflecting this deeper commitment to respect and protect indigenous cultures, Alaska's legislature has enacted a statute declaring "The policy of the state to preserve and protect the historic, prehistoric, and archeological resources of Alaska from loss, desecration, and destruction so that the scientific, historic, and cultural heritage embodied in these resources may pass undiminished to future generations."[47] Statutes like these, mirroring the federal laws discussed in Chapter 5, have been passed in many states, including versions of the Archaeological Resources Protection Act,[48] the Antiquities Act,[49] and the Native American Graves Protection and Repatriation Act (NAGPRA). Some states have modified versions of NAGPRA, either requiring a form of repatriation,[50] even if it does not reach that of the federal law, or not requiring repatriation but instead recommending or authorizing consultation with tribes asserting a cultural affiliation with the discovered remains or burial objects.[51]

North Carolina's version of the Antiquities Act reflects its unique prehistoric indigenous heritage, including a culture that constructed cities and towns distinctive for their only surviving features, which are earthen "mounds" up to one thousand feet long by several hundred feet wide.[52] The North Carolina legislature recognized the so-called 'mound builders' contributions to the state's cultural history by statute in 1973. This law prohibits private owners of lands containing "Indian relics, artifacts, mounds or burial grounds" from "the excavation or destruction thereof and to forbid such conduct by others, without the cooperation of the director of the State Museum and the Secretary of Natural and Cultural Resources or without the assistance or supervision of some person designated by either as qualified to make scientific archaeological explorations."[53]

Many states have established commissions on Indian affairs to guide state officials, agencies, and educational institutions in preserving tribal cultures and educating the

---

[46] *Id.*

[47] Alaska Stat. Ann. § 41.35.010 (West).

[48] Alaska Stat. Ann. § 41.35.070; Ark. Code Ann. § 13-6-307 (prohibiting individuals from "knowingly remov[ing] an artifact from the private land of the owner without first obtaining the owner's permission."); Del. Code Ann. tit. 7, § 5303; N.C. Gen. Stat. Ann. § 70-10.

[49] N.C. Gen. Stat. Ann. § 70-1.

[50] *E.g.*, Alaska Stat. Ann. § 41.35.100 (preventing excavation of "archaeological remains."); Ariz. Rev. Stat. Ann. § 41-844; Ark. Code Ann. § 13-6-404 (requiring repatriation of exhumed remains "a Native American tribal group recognized by the United States Government who can provide written or scientific documentation of such descent"); Cal. Health & Safety Code § 8014; Colo. Rev. Stat. Ann. § 24-80-1302; Ga. Code Ann. § 44-12-262.

[51] *E.g.*, Conn. Gen. Stat. Ann. § 10-389 (West); Del. Code Ann. tit. 7, § 5406; Fla. Stat. Ann. § 872.05; N.C. Gen. Stat. Ann. § 70-10.

[52] N.C. Gen. Stat. Ann. § 70-10; Amber Veverka, *Excavated Rubbish at N.C.'s Town Creek Indian Mound Casts New Light on Pre-Columbian Village*, Charlotte Observer (updated Nov. 16, 2014, 1:18 PM), https://www.charlotteobserver.com/news/science-technology/article9231188.html.

[53] N.C. Gen. Stat. Ann. § 70-1.

nonindigenous citizenry about indigenous history in the state and modern cultural items or practice of significance. The scope of these commissions varies widely, however.[54] Maryland's Commission on Indian Affairs has a mission to "(1) initiate, direct, and coordinate projects that further the understanding of Indian history and culture; (2) survey historic buildings, sites, artifacts, archives, and repositories and publish and disseminate the results; (3) make a comprehensive study of the influence of indigenous Indian tribes and their influence on Maryland history and culture, including as subjects of the study" of certain statutorily listed federally recognized tribes.[55] The Maryland commission is also charged with studying "all Indian communities in the State" and assisting them with obtaining federal recognition; analyzing the "economic and social needs of Indians in the State" and generating recommendations to address those needs; and finally, with locating, preserving, and distributing information to the public "about significant buildings and sites relating to Indian history and culture."[56] In a similar vein to the state commissions, many states mark a certain official day, week, or month to recognize indigenous peoples.[57]

Some states have native education programs, authorized and funded by the state legislature. Alaska has a Native Alaskan language education program, requiring each school board in the state to establish a "local Native language curriculum advisory board" if "a majority of the students are Alaska Natives" and authorizing a native language advisory board for *any* school district with Alaska Native students in its district.[58] Alaska also has legislatively authorized and funded Native arts and crafts competitions.[59] The cultural contributions that Native Alaskan artisans make to their own cultures and to the broader culture of the state as a whole is recognized by Alaska state agencies, and Alaska's consumer protection agency maintains a website that allows anyone to submit a claim involving fraudulent native arts and crafts.[60]

Alaska's state-level cultural resource preservation initiatives have been funded largely through the leasing of mineral development rights on lands formerly occupied by Native Alaskans, which hold some of the richest oil and natural gas deposits in the country. So, somewhat ironically, the lands taken by the federal government from Alaska Natives and given to the state upon its admission to the Union in 1959, have

---

[54] Membership in the state commissions is often mandated by statute and it is worth noting that many states require both indigenous and nonindigenous members on Native affairs commissions. *See, e.g.,* Alaska Stat. Ann. § 41.35.310 (West) (creating historical commission and requiring one person appointed to represent "indigenous ethnic groups").

[55] Md. Code Ann., State Gov't § 9.5-307.

[56] *Id.* § 9.5-307.

[57] Ark. Code Ann. § 1-5-113; Del. Code Ann. tit. 1, § 603; Maryland General Prov. § 7-506; 1 Vt. Stat. Ann. § 371.

[58] Alaska Stat. Ann. § 14.30.420. North Carolina has a much less comprehensive state mandate to provide for "American Indian education." N.C. Gen. Stat. Ann. § 115C-210.4

[59] Alaska Stat. Ann. § 44.33.501 ("The competitions shall be held each summer to select outstanding examples of Alaskan Native arts and crafts").

[60] *See* Alaska Department of Law Consumer Protection Unit, *Alaska Native Art*, THE GREAT STATE OF ALASKA, http://www.law.alaska.gov/department/civil/consumer/Nativeart.html.

served to fund state-level initiatives involving indigenous cultural preservation, along with other state social programs. In addition to these specific initiatives, Alaska Natives also benefit financially from the oil and gas revenue raised from their former lands. Alaska Natives, like other Alaska residents, receive a dividend check every year from the Alaska Permanent Fund, which is a state-administered program available to every individual in the state, including children, allowing them to receive a portion of the state's oil and gas royalties.[61] The permanent fund pays out approximately $1,000 per year per person, on average, and has since the state started the fund in 1982.[62]

In addition, Native Alaskans also sometimes benefit, culturally or financially, or both, from the congressional compromise that resulted in Alaska's admission into the Union.[63] To avoid the mass of aboriginal land claims by Native Alaskans who had occupied the state long prior to its purchase by the US government, Congress essentially bought out the claims, passing a statute that authorized a lump sum payment in exchange for Native Alaskans ceding their lands and forever waiving their legal right to challenge the seizure of those lands in court.[64] This statute, the Alaska Native Claims Settlement Act (ANCSA), divided the state into 12 regions and established a corporate governance structure over these regions, making each person defined as an eligible Native a shareholder of the regional corporation for the region in which the Native is enrolled.[65] In addition, the majority of Alaska Natives are also shareholders of a village corporation, which is a subsidiary entity existing under the umbrella of the regional corporation. Native Alaskans not residing in or enrolled in a village corporation can also be "at-large" shareholders of the regional corporations.[66]

Although ANCSA is a federal law, the structure it established operates primarily under state law. Both regional and village corporations are formed and operate under the corporate laws of the state of Alaska.[67] Village corporations can be for-profit or nonprofit, but thus far all village corporations have elected to be organized for profit.[68] Pursuant to ANCSA, all regional corporations must be for-profit.[69] ANCSA infused the village corporations with a $1 billion monetary settlement at their inception, but the village and regional corporations have since operated with mixed financial success rates.[70] Some have struggled to comply with state laws

---

[61] Christopher L. Griffin Jr., *The Alaska Permanent Fund Dividend and Membership in the State's Political Community*, 29 ALASKA L. REV. 79, 80 (2012).

[62] *Id.*

[63] Kathryn A. Black, *et al.*, *When Worlds Collide: Alaska Native Corporations and the Bankruptcy Code*, 6 ALASKA L. REV. 73, 75–76 (1989).

[64] *Id.*

[65] *Id.* (citing 43 U.S.C. §§ 1604(a) & (b)) A thirteenth region was created for Alaskan Natives living outside of the state.

[66] *Id.*

[67] *Id.*

[68] *Id.*

[69] *Id.*

[70] *Id.* at 81, n. 33.

requiring periodic financial reports and other corporate filings, and some have made investments in business ventures that ultimately failed, placing them at risk of, or in, bankruptcy, despite the initial infusion of ANCSA funds.[71]

Many of the Native village corporations have dedicated part of their corporate mission to cultural preservation, though, which is often reflected on their websites.[72] Cook Inlet Region, Inc. (CIRI) states that its mission is "to promote the economic and social well-being and Alaska Native heritage of our shareholders, now and into the future, through prudent stewardship of the company's resources, while furthering self-sufficiency among CIRI shareholders and their families."[73] Arctic Slope Regional Corporation's website states that the corporation's mission is to "actively manage our businesses, our lands and resources, our investments, and our relationships to enhance Iñupiaq cultural and economic freedom – with continuity, responsibility, and integrity."[74] Many Native village corporations have prioritized job creation and some have sought to "provide special financial assistance for elderly members of their communities."[75]

Moreover, since ANCSA was enacted, the Alaska Native leaders who negotiated the initial legislation and formed the Native corporations also created nonprofit organizations focusing on cultural, educational, and community health objectives.[76] As a result, "[e]very regional corporation and some of the village corporations now have corresponding non-profits that provide health and social services."[77] The regional Native corporations also formed nonprofits, and they provide millions of dollars in annual funding for these entities.[78] The same tension that underlay ANCSA's passage remains under the state-law structure, though, which is that the corporate status selected by all of the native corporations thus far, requires them to operate with the purpose of making profits to distribute to shareholders. For some, this often means developing valuable natural resources on lands controlled by the villages and regional corporations, including oil, natural gas, and timber, to generate capital with which to fund the cultural preservation efforts.[79]

Alaska's laws are quite unique, though, and most states have nowhere near that level of legal recognition of indigenous cultures, much less legal or financial support for them. A few states have passed unique and very specific, but isolated cultural protection laws, such as those exempting practitioners of indigenous medicine or healing from generally applicable state laws regulating healthcare practitioners.

---

[71] *Id.*
[72] William Robinson, *The Benefits of a Benefit Corporation Statute for Alaska Native Corporations*, 33 ALASKA L. REV. 329, 335–36 (2016).
[73] *Id.*
[74] *Id.*
[75] *Id.*
[76] *Id.* at 336.
[77] *Id.*
[78] *Id.*
[79] *Id.* at 349.

In Alabama, for instance, the legislature passed a statute exempting "Native American healers using traditional healing practices" from licensure requirements otherwise applicable to practitioners of alternative medicine.[80] Arizona has a statutory provision that protects "Traditional Native American religious practitioners ... perform[ing] prayers and religious services" for Native American inmates under special arrangements."[81]

In recognition of the importance that hunting, fishing, and food gathering have to many indigenous cultures, several states have taken measures to protect those essential practices, as defined by tribes. California, for one, has a state statute allowing subsistence fishing and food gathering on state lands, allowing "every Indian" to "gather acorns, berries, mushrooms, fruits, insects, seaweed, fish, and other natural foods, materials for regalia and ceremonial purposes and for traditional Indian activities such as making baskets, boatmaking, stoneworking, woodworking, and making of nets, such as roots, reeds, bark, wood, skins, feathers, shells, seeds, nuts, grasses, stones, bones, dyestuffs, plants, sticks, and leaves."[82] For one tribe, the Round Valley Indian Tribe, the state has passed a statute that authorizes state and tribal co-management of fishing in the "boundary streams of the historic 1873 Round Valley Indian Reservation." In the statute, the legislature recognized that "To California Indian tribes, control over their minerals, lands, water, wildlife, and other resources is crucial to their economic self-sufficiency and the preservation of their heritage."[83] California's protection of indigenous resources also reaches the local level, with many municipalities, cities, and towns prohibiting development activities that might harm prehistoric sites of significance to the state's many tribes.[84]

California has more general statutes on its books relating to indigenous cultural preservation, as well. In its Native American Historic Resource Protection Act, California specially recognizes the religious rights of its indigenous peoples.[85] This state law prohibits any public agency or any private party using or occupying public property pursuant to a license, permit, grant, lease, or other contract from interfering with "the free expression or exercise of Native American religion as provided in the United States Constitution and the California Constitution."[86] Further, the law prohibits any agency or private party from causing "severe or irreparable damage to any Native American sanctified cemetery, place of worship, religious or ceremonial site, or sacred shrine located on public property, except on a clear and convincing showing that the public interest and necessity so require."[87] Additionally,

---

[80]   Ala. Code § 34-43-5.
[81]   Ariz. Rev. Stat. Ann. § 31-206.
[82]   Cal. Gov't Code § 186.
[83]   Cal. Fish & Game Code § 16000.
[84]   *See e.g.,* Alpine County Zoning Ord. § 18.68.060; City of Petaluma Zoning Ord. § 15.060.
[85]   Cal. Pub. Res. Code § 5097.9.
[86]   *Id.*
[87]   *Id.*

California's state version of the National Environmental Policy Act, the California Environmental Quality Act (CEQA), requires projects to undergo a cultural resources impact analysis in the context of the broader environmental study.[88] "Cultural resources" are defined by the CEQA as "Sites, features, places, cultural landscapes, sacred places, and objects with cultural value to a California Native American tribe if they have been designated as federal or state historical sites or are of cultural significance to the tribe."[89] If a project has an effect "that may cause a substantial adverse charge in the significance of a tribal cultural resource," it is a project that triggers a full CEQA analysis, including the equivalent of an environmental impact statement under NEPA.[90]

Washington is another state that is leading the charge to recognize the importance of considering tribal cultural practices and tribal cultural values in decisions by state agencies. In May 2019, Washington Attorney General Bob Ferguson announced a new policy requiring the state to obtain "free, prior, and informed consent (FPIC)" before starting a program or approving a project that could impact tribes, tribal rights, tribal lands, or sacred sites.[91] The policy makes Washington the first state "to fully recognize a Tribal Nation's right to simply say 'Yes' or 'No!' to proposals that directly and tangibly impact their lands, rights, and sacred sites," according to attorney for the Quinault Nation, Matthew Randazzo, who was a primary author of the policy.[92] Modeled after the UN Declaration on the Rights of Indigenous Peoples (UNDRIP), which the UN General Assembly adopted in 2007 to guide nations around the world in implementing human rights for indigenous peoples, Washington's policy is the first of its kind in the United States. It is notable that the state policy followed the UNDRIP recommendations even though the United States initially opposed UNDRIP and has since indicated its approval of the resolution only to the extent that it does not recognize indigenous sovereignty in a manner that would conflict with the various jurisdictional rules outlined in Chapter 2.[93] Although the federal government has faced extensive criticism from indigenous communities, it has remained steadfast in its refusal to recognize legal protections and rights according to UNDRIP. However, Washington has set a precedent for states to bypass the federal government's position and directly implement the resolution under state law. The jurisdictional limits of this approach are that it applies only to state projects or projects approved or funded by the state, but it signals a new way of recognizing tribal cultural rights.

---

[88] *Id.* § 21080.3.2.

[89] *Id.* § 21074.

[90] 8 Cal. Real Est. § 26:1 (4th ed.).

[91] *Historic Tribal Consultation Policy Announced in Washington State*, NATIVE DAILY NEWS (May 10, 2019), http://www.nativedailynetwork.com/2019/05/aglandmarkconsulttribes.

[92] *Id.*

[93] *UN Declaration on the Rights of Indigenous Peoples*, UNITED NATIONS (adopted Sept. 13, 2007), https://www.un.org/development/desa/indigenouspeoples/declaration-on-the-rights-of-indigenous-peoples.html.

The state of Washington has been somewhat of a reluctant cultural innovator in another respect, though, under a federal statute that allows tribes to negotiate gaming compacts with states, facilitating the development of tribal gaming operations. Gaming is big business in Indian Country, according to the National Indian Gaming Commission (NIGC), which reported a total of $32.4 billion in revenue for tribal gaming operations in 2017 alone.[94] Washington is one of the five states with the most tribal gaming facilities in the nation, along with Oklahoma, California, Minnesota, and Wisconsin.[95] It is home to 32 tribal casinos, owned by 25 tribes, and reporting $5 billion in revenue in 2014, while employing almost 34,000 people.[96] Tribal gaming data, including details about revenue to tribes and tribal per capita distributions, are confidential, and therefore, it is not possible to determine the direct impacts of gaming on cultural preservation efforts unless the tribes share that information voluntarily, but the generally available figures speak volumes about the potential for increasing cultural protections through tribal gaming.[97]

The federal statute that provides the framework for tribal gaming is the Indian Gaming Regulatory Act, which authorizes gaming on "Indian lands" in states where gaming is allowed pursuant to state law and only pursuant to the terms of a gaming compact negotiated with the state in which the Indian lands are located.[98] IGRA authorizes three categories of gaming: Class I, which includes traditional tribal forms of gaming, and which is regulated solely by the tribes; Class II, which includes bingo, pull-tabs, scratch tickets, and other forms of lower-stakes gaming, which is regulated by the tribes and the NIGC pursuant to certain conditions in IGRA; and Class III gaming, which is high-stakes gaming involving betting against a "house," and which is regulated by tribes and the NIGC and is subject to the terms of the relevant tribal–state gaming compact.[99] When states, like Washington, which allows non-Indian gaming, stall over compact negotiations or attempt to stymie them by negotiating in bad faith, tribes can file an action under IGRA and seek judicial intervention,[100] although the US Supreme Court has substantially undercut that remedy in favor of upholding state sovereign immunity.[101] After a compact has been negotiated, states and tribes can also seek relief in court if one party breaches the terms of the agreement.

[94] National Indian Gaming Commission, *2017 Indian Gaming Revenues Increase 3.9% to $32.4 Billion*, Cision PR Newswire (June 26, 2018, 2:52 AM), https://www.prnewswire.com/news-releases/2017-indian-gaming-revenues-increase-3-9-to-32-4-billion-300672663.html.

[95] Alan Meister, The Economic Impact of Tribal Gaming: A State by State Analysis, American Gaming Association, 5 (Sept. 2017), https://www.americangaming.org/sites/default/files/Economic%20Impact%20of%20Indian%20Gaming%20in%20the%20U.S.%20September%202017.pdf.

[96] *Id.*

[97] *Id.* at 3.

[98] IGRA was passed in 1988 and applies to federally recognized tribes only; 25 U.S.C. § 2501-2513.

[99] *See* United States v. Spokane Tribe of Indians, 139 F.3d 1297, 1299 (9th Cir. 1998).

[100] *Id.*

[101] *See* Seminole Tribe of Florida v. Florida, 517 U.S. 44, 72-73 (1996).

Tribes in Washington and elsewhere have pushed the limits of IGRA, opening casinos without finalized state compacts and sometimes creating intertribal pressure to negotiate compacts so as to be the first to corner the lucrative gaming market within a state.[102] The compact negotiation process has also given states some measure of control over that intertribal race, with favored tribes sometimes receiving compacts ahead of others, which serves to deepen the animus between tribes that may have held no historical ill will toward one another.[103] Gaming has also sometimes divides members of the same tribe, with some fearful of the social ills that large-scale gaming, and the revenue it generates, brings to tribal communities, and others enthusiastic about economic prosperity and the prospects of funding critical tribal programs.[104] Washington State has attempted to address some of the concerns about tribal gaming facilities through its compacts, by requiring tribes to donate a percentage of their gaming revenue to charitable organizations.[105] Under this program, Washington tribes have donated millions of dollars annually to programs advancing various social causes, including cultural preservation, both on and off reservation.[106]

Although Hawaii does not receive any gaming revenue from any tribes, the state is still developing unique forms of cultural preservation. There, the state has developed multilayered legal protections for the *kānaka maoli* and their culture. This protection starts at the constitutional level; the Hawaiian Constitution in Article XII, section 7, provides that "[t]he State reaffirms and shall protect all rights, customarily and traditionally exercised for subsistence, cultural and religious purposes and possessed by ahupua'a tenants who are descendants of native Hawai'ians who inhabited the Hawaiian Islands prior to 1778, subject to the right of the State to regulate such rights."[107] In a relatively recent development, this provision has been interpreted by the Hawaiian Supreme Court as guaranteeing due process rights for Native Hawaiians who object to state regulation of their cultural rights, including allegations that state-approved projects violate the rights of Native Hawaiians to engage in traditional religious and cultural practices.[108] Native Hawaiians refer to their homelands as *'āina*. According to Hawaiian history, *'āina* is the progenitor of

---

[102] Michigan v. Bay Mills Indian Community, 572 U.S. 782, 791 (2014).

[103] David Rogers, *The New Indian Wars in Washington*, POLITICO (Oct. 30, 2015, 5:18 AM), https://www.politico.com/story/2015/10/new-indian-wars-washington-215208.

[104] *Id.*

[105] Richard Walker, *Tribes Contribute Millions of Dollars to Washington Communities, Non-profits*, INDIAN COUNTRY TODAY (Feb. 19, 2016), https://newsmaven.io/indiancountrytoday/archive/tribes-contribute-millions-of-dollars-to-washington-communities-non-profits-e6EUomApDUavXGfpFJhsGg.

[106] *Id.* (In addition to the revenue they generate for tribes, tribal casinos have also provided many tribes with an opportunity to showcase tribal art, language, and other cultural features.).

[107] Haw. Const. art. XII, § 7.

[108] Mauna Kea Anaina Hou v. Board of Land & Natural Res., 363 P.3d 224, 239 (2015).

the human race.[109] Also according to Hawaiian belief, 'Aina have no real need for humans, . . . but humans, or kanaka, need 'āina to survive."[110] There is, therefore, a notion of stewardship in the Hawaiian language known as *malama 'āina*, which translates roughly to "to serve and care for the land."[111] To many Native Hawaiians, the dormant volcano Mauna Kea, looming nearly 14,000 feet above sea level on the island of Hawaii, is wahi pana, or a most sacred type of 'āina.[112] Measured from its actual base depth at the floor of the Pacific Ocean, Mauna Kea is the tallest mountain on Earth, surpassing Mount Everest by nearly a mile.[113] It comes as no surprise, therefore, that the mountain is incredibly important to the kānaka maoli and their culture: "[I]t's where the heaven and the earth come together, where all life forms originated from . . . It is a temple, but one not made by man but for man, so that man could learn the ways of the heavens and the laws of this earth, which mean how do we live with each other; how do we live in relationship to the earth; how do we live in relationship to the heaven."[114]

When the University of Hawaii at Hilo applied for a permit to build a 30-meter telescope and observatory atop Mauna Kea, many kānaka maoli objected, arguing that the construction and telescope would desecrate their sacred mountain (Figure 7.2).[115] The Hawaii Board of Land and Natural Resources approved the permit, then scheduled a contested case hearing to more fully vet the competing arguments between those in favor of, and against, the permit.[116] In a 63-page decision, the Hawaiian Supreme Court held in 2015 that the board's vote to grant the permit before holding the full contested case hearing violated the due process rights of the Native Hawaiians who objected to the permit.[117] After the board again considered the arguments of both sides, it granted the permit in 2019, removing any remaining legal barriers to construction commencing,[118] but the supreme court's decision was an important step in the direction of advancing indigenous constitutional rights at the state level. Protests against the telescope continued throughout 2019 and, in December of that year, Hawaii governor David Ige announced a halt to planned construction activities on Mauna Kea.[119]

---

[109] *Id.*

[110] *Id.*

[111] Teri Māhealani Wright, *Demolition of Native Rights and Self Determination: Act 55's Devastating Impact through the Development of Hawaii's Public Lands*, 35 U. Haw. L. Rev. 297, 302 (2013).

[112] Mauna Kea, *supra* note 108, at 234 ; Wright, *supra* note 111, at 299.

[113] Remy Melina, *Which Mountain Is the Tallest in the World?* Live Science (May 17, 2010), https://www.livescience.com/32594-which-mountain-is-the-tallest-in-the-world.html.

[114] Mauna Kea, *supra* note 108, at 234.

[115] *Id.* at 227–28.

[116] *Id.* at 228.

[117] *Id.*

[118] Daniel Clery, *Divisive Giant Telescope Cleared for Construction on Hawaiian Peak*, Science (June 25, 2019, 9:00 AM), https://www.sciencemag.org/news/2019/06/divisive-giant-telescope-cleared-construction-hawaiian-peak.

[119] *Id.*

FIGURE 7.2 Telescopes on Mauna Kea, Hawaii
(Christopher Chan/Getty)

Hawaii has a multitude of legal tools for cultural protection, including several state statutes. State laws protect Native Hawaiian cultural practices;[120] education in the Hawaiian language;[121] Hawaiian arts and crafts; and access rights connected to traditional cultural practices, including hunting, gathering, and subsistence fishing rights.[122] One provision requires the establishment of a "state cultural public market" in Honolulu, with a statutory directive to the community development authority charged with establishing and running the market to "[e]nsure that the Hawaiian culture is the featured culture in the cultural public market."[123] A provision of the state's coastal management law provides that "[i]n all state small boat harbors, the department shall accommodate the mooring of native Hawaiian canoes owned or leased by a nonprofit corporation, association, organization, or other duly chartered entity that operates native Hawaiian canoes for educational purposes."[124]

Another manner in which Hawaii differs from most states is that it has a state agency dedicated specifically to issues of concern to the kānaka maoli – the Office of Hawai'ian Affairs (OHA). Created at the state's 1978 Constitutional Convention, the

---

[120] Haw. Rev. Stat. Ann. § 205-17; 201B-7.
[121] *Id.* § 302H-1.
[122] *Id.* §§ 7-1; 200-12.5; 188-22.6.
[123] *Id.* § 206E-34.
[124] *Id.* § 200-12.5.

OHA, unlike many other state agencies, draws its authority directly from the state constitution.[125] One of its purposes is "To acquire in any lawful manner any property, real, personal, or mixed, tangible or intangible, or any interest therein; to hold, maintain, use, and operate the same; and to sell, lease, or otherwise dispose of the same at such time, in such manner and to the extent necessary or appropriate to carry out its purpose."[126] The property obligation this provision refers to are the roughly 1 million acres within the so-called 5(f) trust lands that were ceded to the United States by the Kingdom of Hawaii prior to Hawaii's admission as a state.[127] In exchange for the cession, Congress mandated that the lands be held in trust and managed for the benefit of the kānaka maoli.[128] In the words of the enabling Act, this was to "enable native Hawaiians to return to their lands in order to fully support self-sufficiency for native Hawaiians and the self-determination of native Hawaiians in the administration of this Act, and the preservation of the values, traditions, and culture of native Hawaiians."[129] Although the OHA's history of land management and other decisions have sparked controversy and received much criticism over the years, it has served as an important symbol of the rights of Native Hawaiians in their traditional homelands.

Hawaii's depth of laws relating to native cultural practices, places, and objects is also notable because many of them use Hawaiian terms. The constitution, statutes, and cases are replete with words like *ahupua'a, mahele,* and *Wao Kele o Puna,* and these terms have legal meaning for the state and federal courts resolving issues surrounding Native Hawaiian cultural rights. Hawaii is also unique in that the federal government has not recognized Native Hawaiians in the same manner as mainland Indian tribes, but their cultural rights remain protected at multiple levels. Hawaii's unique history supports this differential treatment and calls remain for the restoration of the sovereign Kingdom of Hawaii, separate and apart from the trappings of federal Indian law or control by the state government.[130]

Many states, like Vermont, have a long way to go to catch up with states like Washington, Alaska, and Hawaii. In 2018, the Vermont legislature finally passed its second law relating to the protection of indigenous cultures, eliminating the state recognition of Columbus Day in favor of Indigenous Peoples' Day.[131] In the bill, the legislature stated its hope that the law "will aid in the cultural development of Vermont's recognized tribes, while enabling all indigenous peoples in Vermont

---

[125] Troy J. H. Andrade, *Legacy in Paradise: Analyzing the Obama Administration's Efforts of Reconciliation with Native Hawaiians,* 22 MICH. J. RACE & L. 273, 278 (2017).

[126] Haw. Rev. Stat. Ann. § 10-4.

[127] Wright, *supra* note 111, at 306.

[128] *Id.*

[129] Haw. Homes Commission Act, § 101.

[130] *See, e.g.,* Noelani Goodyear-Ka'ōpua, *"Now We Know": Resurgences of Hawaiian Independence,* 6(3) POLITICS, GROUPS, AND IDENTITIES, 453–65 (2018).

[131] Katie Mettler, *Vermont Passes Bill Abolishing Columbus Day in Favor of Indigenous People's Day,* WASH. POST, Apr. 20, 2019.

and elsewhere to move forward and formulate positive outcomes, from the history of colonization."[132] From the perspective of Rich Holschuh, representing the Elnu Abenaki on the Vermont Commission on Native American Affairs, "[t]he degree of disinformation and lack of understanding around the situation of native people in Vermont, as a microcosm of the national situation, is totally exemplified in the way that Columbus has been celebrated and the native people ignored."[133] Recognizing Indigenous Peoples' Day, Holschuh says, is "not trivial" and "opens up an opportunity for that story to begin to change,"[134] even if that change may still be a long time in the making.

[132] *Id.*
[133] *Id.*
[134] *Id.*

8

Indigenous Cultures and Intellectual Property

The theft of culture is part of the one-way transfer of property from indigenous to non-indigenous hands seen in colonies and settler states around the world – it includes not only the taking of land, natural resources, personal property, but even the heritage of indigenous peoples and their very identities, plucking them as clean as a Safeway chicken.

—Walter Echohawk[1]

Nonindigenous American society has oscillated over the past two centuries between degrading indigenous cultures and appropriating them for pecuniary gain, whether as fashion statements or musical trends or perhaps to satisfy some broader twenty-first-century cultural yearning to resurrect the myth of the "Noble Savage," deeply and purely connected to nature and immune from the toxins of modern daily life.[2] Whatever or however it is labeled, this yearning remains an obsession; one rooted in the myths of American identity and at the same time inherently contradictory. On the one hand, nonindigenous society still derogates indigenous cultures the same way it did in the nation's founding document[3] or in legal opinions like *Johnson* v. *M'Intosh*.[4] But, on the other hand, an element of non-indigenous society is simultaneously attracted to and collectively in awe of certain other aspects of indigenous culture. This attraction is reflected in the mass theft, looting, and general appropriation of indigenous imagery, music, religious practices and icons, ceramics, jewelry, totem poles, and regalia on a scale that is so

---

[1] WALTER R. ECHOHAWK, IN THE LIGHT OF JUSTICE: THE RISE OF HUMAN RIGHTS IN NATIVE AMERICA AND THE U.N. DECLARATION ON THE RIGHTS OF INDIGENOUS PEOPLES 198 (2013).

[2] Helen Gardner, *Explainer: The Myth of the Noble Savage*, THE CONVERSATION (Feb. 24, 2016, 8:59 PM), http://theconversation.com/explainer-the-myth-of-the-noble-savage-55316.

[3] *See* Declaration of Independence (using the term "merciless Indian savages").

[4] The 45th president of the United States, Donald J. Trump, has often used the name *Pocahontas* in a derogatory manner to refer to one of the Democratic presidential candidates, Senator Elizabeth Warren, who claims Cherokee ancestry.

vast it can be difficult to comprehend.[5] The depth of the cultural assault on indigenous people has in many ways become so imbedded within American culture and the popular psyche that few nonindigenous citizens even notice it. Though similarly hidden, that cultural assault can be seen in rules of law as well.

Sports mascots and the laws surrounding them are one area where cultural appropriation is obvious to most. Sports teams, from the elementary to college level and in semi-professional and professional leagues, have appropriated indigenous words and images for mascots, sometimes rendering them almost cartoon-like in appearance. Until the end of the 2018 season, the Cleveland Major League Baseball franchise used a mascot named Chief Wahoo, which was depicted on uniforms and advertising materials as a caricatured indigenous man, with a red face, enlarged teeth, a gaping grin, and a feather poking out from behind his head.[6] Fans of the team would bring feathers and face paint to games, to dress and look like Chief Wahoo as they cheered for their team in the stands. Other fans, and many in the general public, protested the use of this racist mascot, sometimes burning an effigy of Chief Wahoo on the season's opening day.[7] The public outcry eventually grew so great that in 2018, the team's owner announced that the mascot would be phased out at the end of the season, replaced with a large red C in 2019. But the team name remains "the Indians."

Appropriation does not stop with sports, though. Traditional tribal music has been recorded, then sold or given away to musicians, who copyright the music or lyrics and sell them for profit, sometimes winning awards for their "creativity."[8] Popular bands like OutKast and No Doubt have co-opted indigenous music and lyrics and produced music videos depicting themselves as indigenous peoples, wearing modified versions of traditional regalia, dancing around tepees.[9] Halloween costumes styled as a form of traditional tribal regalia or everyday dress are still sold every year by most of the major costume retailers and department stores throughout the United States. Images of tepees, dream catchers, and feather-laden warbonnets are printed on T-shirts and sold by major US retailers like Old Navy, Target, Urban Outfitters, and the Gap.[10] Nonindigenous spiritual gurus have appropriated indigenous

---

[5] See Tanya Ballard Brown, *Totem Pole Stolen 84 Years Ago by Actor John Barrymore Goes Home*, NATIONAL PUBLIC RADIO (Oct. 23, 2015, 7:04 AM), https://www.npr.org/sections/thetwo-way/2015/10/23/451069354/totem-pole-stolen-84-years-ago-by-actor-john-barrymore-goes-home.

[6] Jacob Bogage, *The Cleveland Indians' Season Is over – And so Is Chief Wahoo's 71-Year Run*, WASHINGTON POST (Oct. 10, 2018), https://www.adn.com/sports/national-sports/2018/10/10/the-cleveland-indians-season-is-over-and-so-is-mascot-chief-wahoos-71-year-run.

[7] *Id.*

[8] Angela R. Riley, *"Straight Stealing": Towards an Indigenous System of Cultural Property Protection*, 80 WASH. L. REV. 69, 70 (2005) (describing the use of traditional music and other cultural property by the band OutKast at the 2004 Grammy Awards).

[9] *Id.*; Priya Elan, *No Doubt's Native American Video: Why It Wasn't Looking Hot* THE GUARDIAN (Nov. 5, 2012, 12:01 AM), https://www.theguardian.com/music/shortcuts/2012/nov/05/no-doubt-looking-hot-video.

[10] Navajo Nation v. Urban Outfitters, Inc., 935 F. Supp. 2d 1147, 1152 (D.N.M. 2013).

religious ceremonial practices like sweat lodges, selling access to them as part of package retreat weekends designed to improve spiritual and mental health.[11] Elementary schoolchildren in some parts of the United States still learn the fictionalized version of the Thanksgiving story and reenact scenes and storylines crafted entirely from fiction, depicting hostile and sometimes violent indigenous people attacking peaceful colonial settlers in the New World, before the colonialists pacify them, after which they all sit down to have a meal together.[12]

These examples demonstrate how far nonindigenous society has to go to recognize and respect the indigenous cultures that are part of American society. In this area of intangible cultural property, the law works against tribes in some ways and in their favor in others. Developing a legal strategy to defend against an act of cultural appropriation or to seek positive legal protections for a cultural innovation might therefore require using a combination of legal strategies. But unlike some other areas of the law, there are various legal tools available to protect indigenous peoples against theft of their cultural property, including music, religious works, iconography, imagery, and to protect them from derogatory or offensive depictions. The most well-known legal mechanisms in the area of intellectual property law are patent protections, copyrights, trade secrets, and trademarks.[13] Whichever option or combination of options a tribe chooses, there are particular and sometimes onerous requirements for invoking these protections, which will be explored in some depth in this chapter. This chapter focuses on federal and state laws because the majority of acts of cultural appropriation take place outside of tribal lands and therefore, unfortunately, largely outside of the jurisdictional purview of tribal laws and tribal courts.[14]

Outlining a general legal strategy to protect against cultural property theft or assault is complicated given the numerous methods employed by those who appropriate indigenous cultural property and the vast array of items, images, and elements that constitute cultural property. It may even be difficult to recognize an aspect of tribal history, religion, or traditional ceremonies as cultural property until it is stolen,

---

[11] Some of these efforts have disastrous consequences. In 2009, three people died in a sweat lodge run by the self-help guru James Arthur Ray after he encouraged them to remain in an excessively heated sweat lodge that reached temperatures their bodies were unable to withstand. Jason Kravarik & Sara Sidner, *Sweat Lodge Guru's Attempted Comeback Angers Victims,* CNN (Dec. 8, 2016, 2:04 PM), https://www.cnn.com/2016/12/01/us/sweat-lodge-james-arthur-ray-victims/index.html.

[12] One of the authors experienced this through her kindergarten-aged children, who, while enrolled in public school in a small New England town, were asked to dress as Indians and act out a dramatized, entirely fictional Thanksgiving play. *See* Philip Deloria, *The Invention of Thanksgiving: Massacres, Myths and the Making of the Great November Holiday,* THE NEW YORKER (Nov. 18, 2019), https://www.newyorker.com/magazine/2019/11/25/the-invention-of-thanksgiving.

[13] JESSE DUKEMINIER ET AL., PROPERTY 64 (7th ed. 2010).

[14] *See, e.g.,* Hornell Brewing Co. v. Rosebud Sioux Tribal Court, 133 F.3d 1087, 1093-94 (8th Cir. 1998).

demeaned, or degraded. As scholar of indigenous law and professor Rebecca Tsosie explains, there are a multitude of "indigenous rights in cultural production, which is a process that involves many different dynamics, including social media, the entertainment industry, the art industry, the marketplace, the laws that govern the rights of individuals to their creations (intellectual property law), and the laws that govern the rights of tribal governments to their cultures (Federal Indian law)."[15] The body of laws explaining tribal sovereign rights is explained in Chapter 2 and will not be revisited here, except for this brief reminder that the sovereign status of federally recognized tribal governments can play a central role in any legal battle to protect tribal culture. Sometimes intellectual property rights might be integral to a tribe's legal argument for treaty enforcement, for instance, and in that situation the tribal government must play a central role in asserting the treaty right to advance the cultural protection objective.[16]

As far as the intellectual property legal strategies, there are several, and although intellectual property is a somewhat complex area of law, the general principle is straightforward enough: intellectual property rights grant "limited monopolies over protected material," which can be tangible or intangible.[17] There are three categories of intellectual property rights under federal law: trademark, patent, and copyright,[18] and one category under state law, generally known as proprietary interests or trade secrets.[19] The theory behind creating legal rights in works of art, literature, music, images, and even scientific processes and experiments, is a very European and individualistic one: if the originators put effort into creating the original work, they should be given legal rights in the work, protecting them from interlopers copying it and reaping the financial benefit that is legally due the originators.[20] The American legal system disfavors long-term monopolies on ideas, expressions, or other artistic and scientific works, so there are limits on the duration of intellectual property rights.[21] According to property law professor Jesse Dukeminier, these limits are designed to encourage competition on some level, preventing individuals from locking up a corner of the artistic, scientific, or business market and obtaining a monopoly, while also simultaneously serving as an incentive for creators

---

[15] Rebecca Tsosie, *Just Governance or Just War?: Native Artists, Cultural Production, and the Challenge of "Super-Diversity"*, 6 Cybaris An Intell. Prop. L. Rev. 56, 65–66 (2015).

[16] Amanda Raster & Christina Gish Hill, *The Dispute over Wild Rice: An Investigation of Treaty Agreements and Ojibwe Food Sovereignty*, 34 Agric. & Hum. Values 3–4 (2016).

[17] Dukeminier et al., *supra* note 13, at 64.

[18] *Id.*

[19] *See e.g.* Cal. Civ. Code § 3426.1 (West) (defining "trade secret" under California law as "information, including a formula, pattern, compilation, program, device, method, technique or process that (1) Derives independent economic value, actual or potential, from not being generally known to the public or to other persons who can obtain economic value from its disclosure or use; and (2) Is the subject of efforts that are reasonable under the circumstances to maintain its secrecy").

[20] Dukeminier et al., *supra* note 13, at 64.

[21] *Id.*

to push the boundaries of creativity to the absolute maximum levels, driving individuals to actively create new ideas, concepts, and works and deterring them from one-off or half-hearted creative attempts.[22]

8.1 PATENTS

Perhaps the most straightforward intellectual property right is a patent. Patent protection stems directly from the Constitution, which provides that "The Congress shall have power ... To promote the progress of science and the useful arts, by securing for limited times to authors and inventors the exclusive rights to their respective writings and discoveries."[23] The first patent act was passed in 1790[24] and has been amended several times. The current federal statute governing patents is the 1952 Utility and Patent Act, which provides that "[w]hoever invents or discovers any new and useful process, machine, manufacture, or composition of matter, or any new and useful improvement thereof, may obtain a patent therefor, subject to the conditions and requirements of this title."[25] Embedded in this relatively straightforward provision is an implicit requirement of human involvement, ensuring that no one can patent entirely natural events, processes, or occurrences, although this has been stretched to the bounds of the imagination by recent developments in genotyping and genetic modification techniques.[26] Securing a patent from the US patent office requires the applicant to demonstrate that her process or product is "novel, useful, and nonobvious."[27] Obvious processes or products, such as the laws of nature, physical phenomena, or abstract ideas lacking practical application cannot be patented.[28] Novelty, as construed by the Supreme Court, relates to "whether the invention or discovery was known or used," and utility is concerned with whether the invention or discovery has some readily apparent" usefulness to society.[29]

Once issued, patents last for 20 years from the date of the original patent application (which might be some time before the patent is granted).[30] Patents are not renewable, so when they expire, the process or product involved becomes part of the public domain, free to all to manufacture, sell, or use.[31] According to the Supreme Court, the objective behind intellectual property laws is to "promote the Progress of Science and useful Arts."[32] Issuing patents promotes this goal by offering an

---

[22] *Id.*
[23] U.S. Const., Art. I, § 8.
[24] Richard A. Guest, *Intellectual Property Rights and Native American Tribes*, 20 Am. Indian L. Rev. 111, 117 (1996).
[25] 35 U.S.C. § 101.
[26] Dukeminier et al., *supra* note 13, at 64.
[27] *Id.* at 64.
[28] *Id.*
[29] Guest, *supra* note 24, at 118.
[30] *Id.*
[31] *Id.*
[32] Kewanee Oil Co. v. Bicron Corp., 416 U.S. 470, 480–81 (1974).

exclusive right, for a limited period, to the inventor of an original, innovative process or product, while protecting the inventor's investment of sometimes enormous creative costs in terms of time, research, and development.[33] To secure patent protections, applications must satisfy various statutory criteria, including a description of the process or invention that contains enough detail to enable others skilled in the art to make it (eventually, once it becomes part of the public domain), otherwise referred to as the "enablement" requirement.[34] In the Supreme Court's view, the productive effort fostered in pursuit of the patented process or invention "will have [a] positive effect on society through the introduction of new products and processes of manufacture into the economy and the emanations by way of increased employment and better lives for our citizens."[35]

Patents might have limited use for protecting tribal intellectual and cultural property and cultural values because some tribal cultural knowledge and cultural expressions that might qualify as "works" are quite old, originating before patent laws were developed. This form of cultural property, sometimes referred to as traditional knowledge, or TK in international law, is not protected under US law.[36] However, tribal culture is not static and tribal innovations in certain areas might benefit from patent protection, which is possible even without formal recognition of TK under US law. For example, agriculture is part of the cultural fabric of many indigenous cultures throughout different regions of the United States.[37] In a section of the general Patent Act of 1952, called the Plant Patent Act, Congress provided patent protections for cultivated plants and seedlings, to recognize and protect the value of the practice of horticulture.[38] The Plant Patent Act protects only cultivated plants, not gathered ones, though, and is limited to asexually reproduced species.[39] Under this Act, individuals who create new plant species by grafting, budding, cutting, layering, and division can seek patents, while those who harvest and plant seeds cannot.[40] Tuber-propagated plants are not eligible for plant patents either, so by definition, this statute excludes many species of plants that might be traditional food

---

[33] *Id.*

[34] Deepa Varadarajan, *A Trade Secret Approach to Protecting Traditional Knowledge*, 36 YALE J. INT'L L. 371, 383 (2011).

[35] Kewanee Oil, *supra* note 32, at 481.

[36] Dalindyebo Bafana Shabalala, *Intellectual Property, Traditional Knowledge, and Traditional Cultural Expressions in Native American Tribal Codes*, 51 AKRON L. REV. 1125, 1129 (2017) (discussing international pressure to recognize indigenous rights in TK before the United Nations).

[37] Harry W. Lawton, Philip J. Wilke, Mary DeDecker, & William M. Mason, *Agriculture among the Paiute of Owens Valley*, 3 J. CAL. ANTHROPOLOGY 13–14 (1976), https://escholarship.org/uc/item/0595h88m.

[38] 35 U.S.C. § 161.

[39] Yoder Bros., Inc. v. California – Florida Plant Corp., 537 F.2d 1347, 1377 (5th Cir.1976).

[40] Imazio Nursery, Inc. v. Dania Greenhouses, 69 F.3d 1560, 1566 (Fed. Cir. 1995) (citing S. Rep. No. 315, 71st Cong., 2d Sess. 3 (1930)).

sources for tribes in various regions of the country.[41] Under a similar statute, the Plant Variety Protection Act, though, Congress extended patent protection to any individual who "invents or discovers and asexually reproduces any distinct and new variety of plant."[42] This statute allows plant breeders using seeds to secure a patent on any new plant varieties they create through intentional breeding processes.

These plant patent statutes might appear enticing to indigenous cultures that have cultivated plants for food, medicinal, and spiritual purposes, especially if they sought to breed new plant varieties or otherwise modify aspects of plant biology. However, as courts have interpreted the plant patent statute, there are several requirements that are incongruous with many indigenous practices and values in traditional plant cultivation, which would be worth evaluating when approaching a patent application of this nature –namely, there must be a single "inventor" or "discoverer" of the plant and the plant must be "distinct and new."[43] By definition, then, it would be impossible to patent plant cultivation processes that have been practiced by indigenous nations for hundreds or thousands of years, as they do not qualify. The plants that have been cultivated by many tribes since time immemorial are likely distinct species, but obviously not new, and their cultivation is the work of generations of tribal members. Assigning legal rights to one tribal member who cultivates the plants might also disrupt a collective cultural tradition attached to the process. Thus, despite the tremendous benefits that society might reap from the preservation of traditional plants, seeds, and cultivation techniques, the current patent laws do not quite reach them. However, if tribal corporations or tribal members seek to create new plant varieties using the traditional seeds, those processes would be eligible for protection under the patent laws.[44]

Also, the limitations of patent laws have not stopped indigenous nations from dedicating significant resources in recent years to the revitalization of traditional cultural practices associated with seeds, plants, and agriculture. From Alaska to New Mexico and from Minnesota to the northeastern region of the United States, many organizations and tribal members have begun a process of "rematriation" of traditional seeds.[45] Facilitated by nonprofit organizations that research and identify seeds

---

[41] 35 U.S.C. §§ 101, 161.

[42] *Id.* § 161.

[43] Guest, *supra* note 24, at 121.

[44] This might benefit tribes that have begun cannabis operations, which is an emerging source of economic development in Indian Country. Richard Walker, *Many Tribes Say Billion Dollar Cannabis Business Is a Gateway to Economic Development*, INDIAN COUNTRY TODAY (Feb. 25, 2019), https://newsmaven.io/indiancountrytoday/news/many-tribes-say-billion-dollar-cannabis-business-is-a-gateway-to-economic-development-2mDYegq8vo2VmO-7SzjyQg.

[45] Liz Susman Karp, *How Seed Saving Is Repairing a Painful Past for Native Americans*, MODERN FARMER (May 20, 2019), https://modernfarmer.com/2019/05/how-seed-saving-is-repairing-a-painful-past-for-native-americans; *see* SEED SAVERS EXCHANGE, http://blog.seedsavers.org/blog/seed-rematriation.

in remote seed banks, museums, and universities that were once used by indigenous communities, the rematriation process has helped indigenous communities reconnect with a fundamental cultural value that for many, was lost during the removal and reservation period discussed in earlier chapters. Returning seeds to these tribes to enable them to restore these traditional practices, even if far from their aboriginal homelands, and has been an essential aspect of cultural revitalization for some tribes in recent years.[46]

Some tribes have also begun the process of defending their traditional food sources and agricultural products from patents sought by non-members.[47] One example of this is the Ojibwe and their battle against wild rice patent 5955.648.[48] For the Ojibwe, wild rice, or manoomin, and the activities associated with harvesting and consuming it are core cultural resources. Famed Ojibwe scholar and economist Winona LaDuke explains it this way: "The wild rice harvest of the Anishinaabeg [of which the Ojibwe are part] not only feeds the body, it feeds the soul, continuing a tradition which is generations old for these people of the lakes and rivers of the north."[49] To those who gather wild rice, known to the tribe as ricers, the season of Wild Ricing Moon-Manoominikegiizis, "is the season of a harvest, a ceremony, and a way of life."[50] According to one ricer, it is a chance to reconnect with other members of the Anishinaabe culture every year; "I grew up doing that ... You get to visit people you haven't seen for a whole year, because just about everyone goes ricing."[51]

The tradition of ricing is so integral to the Ojibwe that it was secured by treaty when the nation ceded much of its aboriginal lands to the federal government in the White Pine Treaty of 1837.[52] To the Ojibwe, it was essential to preserve the cultural practice of ricing because it was fundamental to Ojibwe spiritual integrity and fulfilling a duty of stewardship owed by the people to the rice beds. Ojibwe history holds that, wild rice was the lure that pulled the people from the deep waters of the east, to the shallow lakes and rivers in the west, "to the place where food grows on the water."[53] When the people arrived in the west, they received the manoomin from a figure named Wenabozhoo, as a gift and signal that they had arrived in the place that would feed them for generations to come.[54] Part of the obligation passed down from generation to generation ever since this migration was a duty to protect the manoomin. This required the people to steward the environment in which the

---

[46] Karp, *supra* note 45.
[47] Winona LaDuke, *Wild Rice: Maps, Genes, and Patents*, INSTITUTE FOR AGRICULTURE & TRADE POLICY (Sept. 7, 2001); Raster & Hill, *supra* note 16, at 3.
[48] Raster & Hill, *supra* note 16, at 6.
[49] LaDuke, *supra* note 47, at 1.
[50] *Id.* at 10.
[51] *Id.*
[52] Raster & Hill, *supra* note 16, at 3.
[53] *Id.* at 9.
[54] *Id.*

manoomin grows, and over time, the Ojibwe developed specific practices around this cultural obligation. These involved weeding competing plants out of rice beds, monitoring water levels in the beds, harvesting a certain limited amount of manoomin every year, and trapping animals that eat the manoomin, such as muskrats.[55] These acts proved over time that the Ojibwe could harvest a sufficient crop each year to sustain the various communities throughout what is now northern Minnesota.[56] Over the years, the Ojibwe have also effectively "bred" wild rice into strains through selective harvesting methods that were passed down from generation to generation.[57]

In 1999, a California corporation, Nor-Cal, obtained a patent for a process it used to breed male sterility into a species of wild rice harvested by the Ojibwe.[58] This method – cytoplasmic-genetic male sterility (CGMS) – ensures that the reproductive process of the plant can be controlled in a laboratory, allowing companies that grow, mechanically harvest, and sell wild rice to eliminate genetic defects and ensure a specific annual crop yield.[59] Nor-Cal's patent gives it legal property rights in the CGMS process, allowing it to control the use and implementation of this technology, which also allows the company to control somewhat the natural evolution of the wild rice itself.[60] In 2000, researchers from the University of Minnesota succeeded in mapping the wild rice genome, opening the door to new breeds of genetically modified "wild" rice.[61] Although the Ojibwe strongly object to the Nor-Cal patent and to the genetic mapping efforts of the University of Minnesota, they have not yet taken these objections to court to try to protect the naturally growing manoomin in northern Minnesota from contamination or cross-pollination. In part, this is because of a cultural belief of the Ojibwe people that no one owns, or should own, wild rice. Participating in legal action to challenge the patent or the genetic mapping efforts of the University of Minnesota would potentially place the Ojibwe in a position of claiming some type of property ownership interest or rights, and thus the tribe has chosen to use political pressure and other means of influence to attempt to protect the wild-growing manoomin.[62] This example illustrates well the cultural complexity of patents as a tool of cultural protection.

8.2 TRADE SECRETS

In addition to challenging patents, another option for indigenous nations like the Ojibwe, should they wish to pursue formal legal protections for a traditional practice

[55] *Id.* at 9–10.
[56] *Id.* at 4.
[57] *Id.* at 5.
[58] *Id.* at 22.
[59] *Id.*
[60] *Id.* at 22.
[61] *Id.*
[62] *Id.* at 25–26.

like ricing, could be under state law in the area of trade secrets. Trade secret protections vary from state to state, but in general, they apply to formulas, patterns, compilations, computer programs, devices, methods, techniques, and financial processes and plans that have "independent economic value, actual or potential, from not being generally known to, and not being readily ascertainable by proper means by, other persons who can obtain economic value from its disclosure or use," and which have been kept secret by the creator.[63] Trade secret protections are potentially perpetual, as long as the subject of the trade secret is not publicly disclosed, which makes this an attractive option for protecting traditional knowledge and practices.[64]

Several scholars have advocated the use of trade secrets to protect traditional cultural knowledge, practices, and information of indigenous peoples.[65] For the Ojibwe, the traditional method of cultivating wild rice would be eligible for protection as a trade secret, as it is a protectable process or technique under Minnesota law. Courts have historically interpreted trade secrets quite generously.[66] Unlike copyright and patent requirements, the process or subject of trade secrets protections does not have to be novel or nonobvious.[67] There are also few formal requirements to secure trade secrets protections; unlike patents, copyrights, or trademarks, there is no formal application process and no need to identify one author or inventor.[68]

The limitation of trade secrets is that legal protections can be invoked only when there has been an unlawful attempt to access, use, or disseminate the formula, process, or technique.[69] So if a non-member corporation were to sell the Ojibwe ricing technique, the Ojibwe could invoke trade secrets protections by filing a lawsuit in state court against the corporation. However, the tribe could invoke this legal mechanism only if the knowledge of the ricing process has been kept secret and not released into the public domain.[70] This includes the "release" by academics who have studied the process and published articles about it, and of course any disclosure by tribal members themselves, at any point in time.[71] Typically, trade secret conflicts arise out of contract arrangements, in which the parties have agreed that certain information should be kept confidential and one party either errs or breaches the contract and discloses the proprietary material. Tribes entering into contracts with non-member corporations would therefore want to exercise caution if those contracts involved critical processes, techniques, or practices that the tribe would not want released into the general public or appropriated by outsiders.

---

[63] *See* Georgia Code Ann. § 10-1-761; Minn. Stat. Ann. § 325C.01(5).
[64] 20A1 Minn. Prac., Business Law Deskbook § 18:15.
[65] Varadarajan, *supra* note 34, at 396.
[66] *Id.*
[67] *Id.* at 397.
[68] *Id.*
[69] *Id.*
[70] *Id.* at 398.
[71] *Id.*

These limitations render trade secrets one of the least effective protections within intellectual property laws.

8.3 COPYRIGHT

Indigenous cultures in the United States have faced a long history of cultural appropriation by outside artists, academics, musicians, corporations, and isolated individuals. The hazards of cultural appropriation of imagery are illustrated well by the story of a young up-and-coming photographer from Wisconsin who opened a studio and gallery in Seattle, Washington, in the 1890s.[72] Initially, he earned a modest living taking photographs of society ladies, but in 1895, he took a photograph of a young indigenous woman named Angeline, a photograph that would change the course of his life, and to some degree, history. Angeline was the youngest daughter of Chief Si'ahl (or Seattle, as he was known in English) of the Suquamish and Duwamish Nations, and the photographer was Edward S. Curtis. Curtis liked photographing Angeline; she sat for several sessions, he paid her a dollar for each pose, and although they did not speak the same language, Curtis interpreted Angeline's gestures and hand signals to mean that she enjoyed sitting for the photographs.[73]

Taking Angeline's photograph would launch Curtis on a path that he never expected; for in the coming years, Curtis discovered that he had a passion for taking photographs of indigenous peoples. In Curtis's view at the time, he was capturing and documenting a moment in time for each tribe he visited – sealing the historical record of "how tribes were" as they faced the culturally devastating processes of removal, reservations, allotment, and assimilation. Yet, Curtis's desire to capture these images on film drove him to lengths that proved controversial. For one, to make his photographs as "accurate" as possible, Curtis staged many of his scenes, asking his models to wear certain clothing, even braided wigs, adopt specific poses, and appear on location, always posed and directed by Curtis.[74] Curtis sometimes used the same prop in photographs of individuals from different tribes, and he used the editing process to eliminate objects that he did not deem culturally appropriate – such as a modern clock on the floor of a tribal residence.[75] For another, he was backed by the financial resources of John Pierpont Morgan, whose railroads brought so much cultural and literal destruction for tribes like those at Fort Peck.

---

[72] Gilbert King, *Edward Curtis's Epic Project to Photograph Native Americans*, SMITHSONIAN MAGAZINE (Mar. 12, 2012), https://www.smithsonianmag.com/history/edward-curtis-epic-pro ject-to-photograph-native-americans-162523282.

[73] *Id.*

[74] Kevin Noble Maillard, *The Pocahontas Exception: The Exemption of American Indian Ancestry from Racial Purity Law*, 12 MICH. J. RACE & L. 351, 386 (2007).

[75] Andy Grundberg, *More Than Meets the Eye*, NEW YORK TIMES (Sept. 5, 1982), https://www .nytimes.com/1982/09/05/books/more-than-meets-the-eye.html.

Curtis eventually compiled a 20-volume collection, containing over 40,000 individual images of members of more than 80 tribes, and representing nearly 30 years' work in the field.[76] At the time, and in later years, he had a great number of defenders, including among indigenous communities, who recognized him for the artistic attributes of his work, and for his efforts to capture aspects of indigenous history and preserve it on film, sometimes right before that history was forever altered in devastating ways.[77]

One of the little-discussed aspects of the artist whom Navajo subjects nicknamed the "Shadow Catcher" is the intellectual property rights that attached to his work, and the greater story about cultural appropriation those rights tell in a modern context. During Curtis's era, and still today, copyright protection is a matter of federal law. The modern federal statute governing the acquisition of copyright protections is the Copyright Act of 1976.[78] To obtain legal protection for a "work" under the Copyright Act, it must be original, authorship must be determinable, and the work must be "fixed in any tangible medium of expression, now known or later developed," from which it can be "perceived, reproduced, or otherwise communicated, either directly or with the aid of a machine or device."[79] Although products of the twentieth-century Congress, these requirements reflect European values surrounding art and artists, and the corresponding value of artwork in European society – values that crystallized during the Romantic period of the late eighteenth century.[80] The Romantic movement, which consumed European society at the time, prized individual creativity over collectivism, novelty of an individual's work over works derived from previous creators, and if an artist were even to dabble in a style developed by a predecessor, the successor artist was strongly encouraged to reform, restyle, and otherwise make the work as original as possible. This would create works that were individualized, rather than collective, and ever changing, rather than static.

The European Romantic inspiration to create and produce original works of art, music, literature, and theater quickly took root in the United States.[81] Over the subsequent evolution and development of copyright law in the years since the nation's founding, this area has been the subject of continual academic criticism, whether it be for being too restrictive or not restrictive enough, depending on one's perspective, but none of these critiques have motivated Congress or the courts to forge a new path away from the European values underpinning the laws. Thus,

---

[76] King, *supra* note 72.

[77] Meghan Saar, *The Shadow Catcher Endures: Why Everyone Loves/Hates the Edward Curtis Indians*, TRUE WEST MAGAZINE (June 18, 2018), https://truewestmagazine.com/shadow-catcher-edward-curtis.

[78] 17 U.S.C. § 102(a).

[79] *Id.*

[80] Angela R. Riley, *Recovering Collectivity: Group Rights to Intellectual Property in Indigenous Communities*, 18 CARDOZO ARTS & ENT. L.J. 175, 181 (2000).

[81] *Id.* at 182.

copyright law in the United States remains much the same in the twenty-first century as it was in Curtis's day.

Copyright law is incredibly rigid, and the rigidity starts with the concept of "authorship," which is almost inherently problematic for tribal "works," such as traditional songs, stories, prayers, or other depictions or representations of interest to the nonindigenous world, and particularly for images or depictions of indigenous peoples or aspects of their culture. Authorship is problematic for indigenous cultures because their works, as the legal world defines them, are collective by nature. Consider the example of the Hopi kachina from Chapter 3. An individual Hopi artisan could theoretically copyright an original rendering of a kachina, but in doing so, the artisan would have exclusive legal rights to that image. This would potentially prevent other Hopi from legally reproducing it unless the copyright holder assigned rights to it and could take a collective object of critical religious importance to Hopi people and make its representation legally the property of a single Hopi artisan. In this way, seeking copyright protections for indigenous "art" could threaten the cultural integrity of the tribe, rather than fostering or protecting it.

The kachina example raises another critical point about the incongruity of copyright laws with indigenous cultural values, which is that what nonindigenous people, like Edward Curtis, might see as "art" may actually be part of an act of prayer or religious devotion. Items like kachina, prayer bundles, totem poles, jewelry, baskets, and other objects are often displayed in museums or sold to nonindigenous buyers as art, when these objects were not created for the purpose of entertainment or aesthetic pleasure. Although there are certainly objects that indigenous peoples create for artistic purposes, some objects and other works are critical components of religious or other ceremonies. They may also be necessary to ensure continuing tribal health, cultural longevity, or serve as a tribe's historical record.

For some indigenous cultures, therefore, it may be a matter of necessity to preserve the oral histories, songs, or other traditional practices intact, as they had existed for centuries prior, rather than creatively adapting them to suit modern legal frameworks. The history and traditions passed down from generation to generation, through stories, ceremonies, sacred objects, imagery and other practices may date back to time immemorial. What makes them sacred to the tribes who continue them is that they have no single human author, only human vessels, who carry the traditions forward, from one generation to the next. Thus the legal concept of authorship under federal copyright law is not only foreign to many indigenous cultures, but could even be antithetical to the value system of a tribe. Altering these traditions to obtain legal protection in the form of a copyright could be seen as a cultural affront or threat to a tribe's cultural integrity.[82] On the other hand, some collective cultural images, depictions, or other cultural property may change over

---

[82] If copyright law allowed for an entire tribe to be an author, it might be possible for tribes to attempt to copyright some of these stories, songs, and traditions because most tribal members

time and seeking copyright protections might be advantageous because others would be prohibited from reproducing them without the consent of the tribal author or creator.[83]

Another important point about copyright protections is that federal law also requires that works be original to qualify.[84] Specific works covered by the federal statute are only those that fit into one of the following categories delineated by Congress: literary works; musical works, including any accompanying words; dramatic works, including any accompanying music; pantomimes and choreographic works; pictorial, graphic, and sculptural works; motion pictures and other audio-visual works; sound recordings; and architectural works.[85] While these statutory categories easily encompass a portrait of a member of the Rockefeller family by John Singer Sargent, a petroglyph carved in a canyon wall in Grand Gulch, near the Bears Ears in Utah, might be harder to place within the framework (see Figure 5.1). However, preserving the petroglyph and guarding against its modification or destruction could be arguably more integral to the modern Pueblo tribal cultures than the Sargent painting is to European American society, if one were to compare these items side by side to evaluate their relative cultural value.

Perhaps even more important than seeking copyright protections for tribal works is the need for indigenous peoples to guard against exactly what happened during the Curtis era: the use and appropriation of tribal members and tribal cultural elements *as* artwork or *in* artwork to secure financial gain for the copyright holder. That is to say, under federal copyright laws, Curtis, J. P. Morgan, or their assignees held the copyrights to 40,000 photographs of hundreds, if not thousands of other tribal members, during the lifetimes of those subjects and likely, for many years after.[86] Neither the subjects of Curtis's photographs nor their tribes had any legal rights to the individual images, which is especially ironic, given that Curtis claimed to have set about on his documentation project for the purpose of capturing and preserving tribal history and culture. Moreover, the purpose of the copyright protection is to protect the copyright holder's financial investment in the work, allowing Curtis, Morgan, and their assignees to sell the rights to reproduce these images and profit from them. At the time, and for

would likely agree that the tribe should be the primary repository of the cultural property. However, federal copyright law requires an individual, identifiable author – and only one.
[83] Varadarajan, *supra* note 34, at 379.
[84] 17 U.S.C. § 102(a).
[85] *Id.*
[86] The length of a copyright is somewhat technical and beyond the scope of this book, but in general, a copyright in a work created after January 1, 1978, exists from the date of creation and lasts for a term of 70 years beyond the life of the author; 17 U.S.C. § 302(a). Anonymous works, pseudonymous works, or contract works are copyrighted for 95 years from the date of first publication or 120 years from the date of creation, whichever expires first. U.S.C. § 302(c). Copyright in a work created before January 1, 1978, but not part of the public domain or copyrighted, has a creation date of January 1, 1978, and endures for the term provided by section 302; but this is subject to certain caveats related to the public domain status of the work (published or unpublished) and the date of the author's death.

the duration of the copyright, the Navajo Nation (or any other tribe seeking to use the Curtis photographs as part of a cultural repatriation effort) would have to purchase the Curtis photos of its members from a collector, and purchase the copyrights associated with print reproduction, to gain control of the original images and prevent their distribution, sale, or use by those outside the tribe. Through this structure, US copyright laws have served to enable and even promote the appropriation and use of indigenous culture by non-indigenous people for their own financial gain.

8.4 TRADEMARK LAW

Another legal tool, perhaps of more limited use, for indigenous nations seeking to protect their cultural property is trademark law. Trademarking theoretically offers one of the strongest forms of protection for intangible cultural property, although its application to indigenous intangible property can be complex.[87] In general, a trademark is a "symbol used by an individual or a company in commerce to serve as a source identifier."[88] Federal trademark protections are governed by the Lanham Act, which protects any "juristic person," including any "firm, corporation, union, association, or other organization capable of suing and being sued in a court of law."[89] Indian tribes are juristic entities for purposes of the Lanham Act and other statutes, meaning that, like other sovereigns, tribes may sue and be sued, although, given their sovereign immunity, they may be sued only with their or Congress's express consent.[90]

   Although federal law regulates aspects of their use, it does not create trademarks.[91] Trademarks and their precursors have ancient origins, and trademarks were protected at common law and in equity dating back to the late eighteenth century. Trademarks are distinct from copyrights and patents in that they offer general protections to the holder – they do not incentivize creativity and do not "depend upon novelty, invention, [or] discovery."[92] Rather, they employ a form of first-come, first-served vesting under which the first to use a distinctive "mark" in commerce can obtain a trademark for it.[93] This is accomplished by "registering" the mark with the US Patent and Trademark Office (USPTO).[94] The principle underlying trademark protection is that distinctive marks – words, names, symbols, and the like – can help distinguish a particular author, creator or artisan's goods from those of another.[95]

---

[87] Chante Westmoreland, *An Analysis of the Lack of Protection for Intangible Tribal Cultural Property in the Digital Age*, 106 CAL. L. REV. 959, 975 (2018).

[88] *Id.*

[89] 15 U.S.C. § 22.

[90] Paula M. Yost, Ian R. Barker, & Sara Dutschke Setshwaelo, *Branding the Band: Protecting Tribal Identities through Trademark Law*, 61 FED. LAW. 48, 50 (2014).

[91] Matal v. Tam, 137 S. Ct. 1744, 1751 (2017).

[92] Westmoreland, *supra* note 87, at 975.

[93] *Id.*

[94] *Id.*

[95] Matal, *supra* note 91, at 1751.

The purpose of the Lanham Act was to organize and regulate the system for registering and protecting trademarks. But more broadly, the statute was designed to "protect the public so it may be confident that, in purchasing a product bearing a particular trademark which it favorably knows, it will get the product which it asks for and wants to get."[96] This law protects trademark owners from misappropriation by so-called free riders. In other words, "by applying a trademark to goods produced by one other than the trademark's owner, the infringer deprives the owner of the goodwill which he spent energy, time, and money to obtain. At the same time, the infringer deprives consumers of their ability to distinguish among the goods of competing manufacturers."[97]

Prior to 2017, the Lanham Act prohibited trademarking content that "[c]onsist[ed] of or comprise[d] immoral, deceptive, or scandalous matter; or matter which may disparage or falsely suggest a connection with persons, living or dead, institutions, beliefs, or national symbols, or bring them into contempt, or disrepute."[98] This provision was the basis of several lawsuits filed against the owners of the trademark for the professional football team from Washington, DC, which is one of five professional sports teams that, to this day, use a trademarked name that is racist and derogatory toward indigenous peoples.[99]

The Washington team's name was first used by a professional football team in 1933, when owner George Preston Marshall selected it for his newly launched franchise, then based in Boston.[100] Marshall chose the name to distinguish the team from the Major League Baseball team then called the Boston Braves.[101] The US.-Patent and Trademark Office approved registration of the first mark in 1967.[102] After 1967, the organization registered several other marks, including the derogatory team name and various images of indigenous men in profile, wearing stereotypical tribal clothing.[103] In addition, the organization sought and received a trademark incorporating the derogatory team name followed by "-ettes" to be used for the cheerleaders accompanying the football team to its games and doing various promotional appearances on the team's behalf.[104]

As early as 1971, the organization faced challenges from individuals based on the derogatory nature of the trademarked team name, which was a term that arose as a

[96] Gary Myers, *Trademarks & the First Amendment after Matal v. Tam*, 26 J. INTELL. PROP. L. 67, 69 (2019).
[97] *Id.*
[98] Lanham Act, 15 U.S.C. § 1052.
[99] Pro-Football, Inc. v. Harjo, 415 F.3d 44, 47 (D.C. Cir. 2005); *A Public Accommodations Challenge to the Use of Indian Team Names and Mascots in Professional Sports*, 112 HARV. L. REV. 904 (1999).
[100] Pro-Football, Inc. v. Blackhorse, 112 F. Supp. 3d 439, 448 (E.D. Va. 2015), *vacated by* 709 F. App'x 182 (4th Cir. 2018).
[101] *Id.*
[102] *Id.*
[103] *Id.*
[104] *Id.*

racial slur at a time when there was a value on the commercial market for the scalps of murdered "Indians."[105] According to lawsuits filed by various tribal members over the years, the use of this term has the same effect on indigenous people – and society more broadly – as the use of other slurs used to express animus toward marginalized groups. In the words of the Native American Bar Association, which filed a brief supporting the plaintiffs in the most recent lawsuit challenging the trademark of the Washington team, "'r[******]s' conveys animus and hatred toward Native Americans. It is to Native Americans what 'n[****]r' is to African Americans."[106]

Yet, despite the undisputedly racist and offensive nature of this trademark, challenges to it under the Lanham Act have been unsuccessful, most recently because the Supreme Court determined in 2017 that the disparagement prohibition in the Lanham Act was unconstitutional.[107] In the case that decided this issue, *Matal v. Tam*, the Court faced a question involving a trademark sought by a pop music group called The Slants.[108] The group, led by singer Simon Tam, "chose this moniker in order to 'reclaim' and 'take ownership' of stereotypes about people of Asian ethnicity."[109] Tam sought to trademark the band's name, and the US Patent and Trademark Office denied his application based on the disparagement clause. Tam appealed, and on appeal, the Supreme Court ultimately determined that it was unconstitutional for Congress to regulate the contents of private speech, which is how the Court characterized the Lanham Act's disparagement clause.[110] More specifically, the Court found that the provision allowed the Patent and Trademark Office to engage in unconstitutional viewpoint discrimination because it could approve some marks containing offensive words or images, but deny others.[111] In an even more recent case, the Court held that a neighboring provision of the Lanham Act, which prohibited the registration of marks that contained "immoral" or "scandalous" material, was also unconstitutional, for the same reasons.[112]

After these opinions, it is an uphill battle for tribes challenging culturally offensive trademarks or trademarks that result in derogatory cultural appropriation.[113] Beyond statutory trademark protections, the Washington football team likely holds a common law trademark right even if the US Patent and Trademark Office were to cancel the statutory patent.[114] Under the first use rule, common law trademark

---

[105] Brief of Amici Curiae Fred T. Korematsu Center for Law and Equality, et al., in Pro-Football, Inc. v. Blackhorse, 2016 WL 613926, at *8 (filed Feb. 11, 2016).

[106] *Id.* at 8–9.

[107] Matal, *supra* note 91, at 1751.

[108] *Id.* at 1754.

[109] *Id.*

[110] *Id.*

[111] *Id.* at 1763.

[112] Iancu v. Brunetti, No. 18-302, slip op. at 6 (June 24, 2019).

[113] Mark Conrad, *Matal v. Tam–A Victory for the Slants, a Touchdown for the Redskins, but an Ambiguous Journey for the First Amendment and Trademark Law*, 36 CARDOZO ARTS & ENT. L.J. 83, 126 (2018).

[114] *Id.*

rights vest if the individual or corporation holding the trademark can show that it was the first to use the mark in commerce.[115] However, at least one scholar has identified a way to challenge sports trademarks that disparage indigenous Americans and other people of color, who have been damaged by the registration of that mark.[116] The potential grounds for the challenge lies in a USPTO rule that allows a mark to be challenged if it is "deceptive," "misdescriptive," or "bring[s] an individual into disrepute."[117] This would allow for a challenge to a mark representing a mascot that brought indigenous individuals into disrepute, at least in theory. Potential challenges also can be brought for marks based on "likelihood of confusion, deception or mistake."[118] Under this rule, if the sports team were holding out the trademark as a respectful or unoffensive image, it could be challenged by showing evidence that the image or term in the mark is in fact culturally offensive, racist, or derogatory.[119]

To some, it is obvious that the sports mascots for the Cleveland and Washington professional sports teams are racist and derogatory. It also seemed obvious to many that the band No Doubt's "Looking Hot" video was racist, degrading, and appropriated indigenous cultural property in an unacceptable way – in fact, the band deleted the video within days of releasing it due to overwhelming criticism from fans, members of the public, and many in indigenous communities throughout the United States. However, many National Football League fans, players, owners, and corporate sponsors support the Washington football team's continuing use of its mascot, even while condemning the league's treatment of African American football players who began silently protesting violence against African American men by the police at the beginning of each game during the playing of the national anthem in 2018. In 2019, the President of the United States also continues to use the name Pocahontas in a derogatory fashion to degrade presidential aspirant Senator Elizabeth Warren, and the Supreme Court indicated its tacit acceptance of the use of racially derogatory terms and images in the *Matal* v. *Tam* opinion in 2017.

The racism still evident in these acts of cultural appropriation and cultural assault, combined with the broader societal antipathy and apathy toward racial inequities faced by indigenous peoples in the United States, are remarkable. This cultural assault has been aided by the silence, participation, or acquiescence of those at the highest levels of the federal government. In this environment, cultural appropriation will continue to be accepted, or even overlooked, until the reality of this social pandemic sinks into the collective conscience of nonindigenous society.

But, in the face of centuries of historical and continuing racism, cultural theft, intellectual property encroachment, and other forms of cultural assault, often under the color of law in which these latent hatreds are deeply imbedded, indigenous

[115] *Id.*
[116] *Id.*
[117] *Id.* at 126–27.
[118] *Id.*
[119] *Id.*

cultures persist while continuing to assert claims based on the ideals professed as supporting those very same laws. In addition to their continued advocacy, tribes and their allies have also been incredibly effective stewards of their cultural property and traditional knowledge. As a result, that combination of indigenous advocacy and cultural stewardship is likely to result in continued challenges to the limits of existing federal and state intellectual property laws, which, in time, are likely to trend toward a new, more effective, way of protecting cultural practices, traditions, knowledge, and other intangible cultural elements; a new way rooted in – instead of preying upon – indigenous cultural values.

9

A Third Way for the Future

So many tribes, so many stories. The state of Indian culture and sovereignty, the state of the future, can be understood only through many stories from many places.

— Charles Wilkinson[1]

Deep in the heart of the Fort Peck Indian Reservation in northeast Montana, hundreds of bison now roam the rolling hills, grazing on the tall prairie grasses, wallowing in worn out patches of plains dirt, and representing the return of a vital, foundational element of the Tribes' culture and very existence. Though the story of the Tribes' effort to bring bison back to their homelands is only one of the many stories of cultural revival across Indian Country and beyond, it is emblematic of the changes to come, as indigenous leaders and their allies use laws to protect and empower their cultures. That story, like many, many others, is not just about the bison, their meaning to the tribes of Fort Peck, or the power that those massive beasts carry with them over their millennia of genetic memory across the continent's Great Plains. Beyond all of that, the story of bison returning to Fort Peck and the future of indigenous culture and sovereignty are tales of promise, showing the pathway of new laws and legal structures that meaningfully incorporate, respect, and are shaped by those cultures. The fulfill-ment of that promise requires a reckoning with the core tenets and assumptions of the entire American legal system, an accounting that has long been denied by the rigid structures and inherent biases of that system. But just like the wild bison that now roam the fields of the Fort Peck Reservation despite the near extermination of their ancestors and the legal, practical, and other barriers to their restoration, the call for that reckoning will soon overcome the barriers that have historically prevented it.

The return of bison to Fort Peck is an example of the third way of cultural protection. It shows how a new era of federal, state, and tribal cultural protection laws and standards might force innovative ideas of governmental collaboration and success.

---

[1] CHARLES WILKINSON, BLOOD STRUGGLE: THE RISE OF MODERN INDIAN NATIONS, 376 (2005).

Though wild bison are the national mammal and revered as a tourist attraction at Yellowstone National Park, Montana law does not consider a wild bison "wildlife" once the animal goes beyond the Yellowstone area. Instead, state law classifies such bison as a "species in need of management" subject to control by the state Department of Livestock, which, out of concern over the potential for the transmission of brucellosis, a disease that could be fatal to the state's treasured cattle industry, severely restricts how and whether bison can be moved throughout the state.[2]

In addition to strict state standards, permitting requirements, and controls, wild bison in Yellowstone are also subject to federal oversight and management, at least so long as they remain in or near the Park. In recognition of the state's concerns over livestock, and particularly the potential threats posed by bison migrating beyond the Park's boundaries, the federal National Park Service (NPS) has tried to manage bison populations in the Park since the 1970s. The agency's management efforts have included killing bison that approached park boundaries, hazing animals to herd them back toward the Park, and after ending the practice of killing bison inside the Park in 1978, relying on state game wardens and hunters to carry out this work outside of the Park's boundaries.[3] Following extensive litigation between the state of Montana and the federal government over bison management, government agencies developed environmental impact statements studying options for the joint management of bison in Montana and Yellowstone, which commenced after each government issued records of decision in late 2000.[4]

But the initial federal–state Joint Management Plan that arose from these studies ignored the tribal interests at stake in managing the nation's last herds of wild bison. In fact, the federal record of decision adopting the initial plan begins with the following narrative: "[e]arly European travelers to the Yellowstone area observed bison before and after the creation of Yellowstone National Park," omitting entirely the deep and lengthy connection between the region's tribes, the landscape, and this emblematic animal.[5] It was not until 2009 that tribal interests were represented in bison management discussions. That year, two local tribes, the Nez Perce Tribe of Idaho and the Confederated Salish and Kootenai Tribes located in northwest Montana, along with the group of tribes making up the Inter-Tribal Bison Cooperative, pushed federal and state bison managers for a role in what had become known as the Interagency Bison Management Plan (IBMP).[6] Almost immediately upon the

---

[2]   Mont. Code Ann. § 87-1-216.

[3]   Wildlife Management: Many Issues Unresolved in Yellowstone Bison-Cattle Brucellosis Conflict, General Accountability Office Report No GAO/RCED-93-2, 4 (Oct. 1992).

[4]   See Record of Decision for Final Environmental Impact Statement and Bison Management Plan for the State of Montana and Yellowstone National Park, US Department of the Interior & US Department of Agriculture (Dec. 20, 2000), http://www.ibmp.info/Library/IBMP_FED_ROD/3%20-%20Federal%20ROD.pdf.

[5]   Id. at 3.

[6]   See Summary Report from Interagency Bison Management Plan Meeting (Aug. 11–12, 2009), http://www.ibmp.info/Library/20090811/20090811Summary.pdf.

tribes' involvement in the process, discussion about the potential transfer of bison to tribes across the country began.[7] From the tribes' perspective, if the federal and state managers were interested in limiting the presence of wild bison beyond the boundaries of Yellowstone, the tribes must have an active role in accepting the transfer of bison or exercising their treaty rights to hunt bison to assist in those management priorities. Unlike the state and federal management priorities, however, the tribes sought avenues to reconnect with their historic and cultural roots through participation and leadership in the IBMP.

While many tribes now exercise their treaty rights to hunt bison around the boundaries of Yellowstone National Park, the Fort Peck Tribes sought a different connection. Because the IBMP called for the annual removal of a certain number of bison from the overall Yellowstone population in order to minimize conflicts with and threats to Montana and its livestock industry, the Tribes sought to have bison transferred to their reservation, rather than the animals being killed by state or tribal hunters or federal or state game management officials. Because the state of Montana and local livestock producers were concerned about the threat posed by transferring bison all the way across the state (it is about 500 miles from Yellowstone to the Fort Peck Reservation), that effort ran into repeated legal and political roadblocks. First, the IBMP needed to study the possibility of quarantining bison before transfer as a way to determine whether they were disease free and would pose a reduced risk to livestock.[8] After capturing and quarantining bison throughout the mid-2000s, an initial herd of 87 animals was transferred to a private ranch in 2010, but still managed by Montana's Department of Fish, Wildlife, and Parks (DFWP).[9] Thereafter, DFWP planned to transfer additional bison that had been quarantined and developed an environmental assessment to study the potential options for the transfer.[10]

In addition, many within Montana opposed the transfer of wild bison anywhere within the state, making the potential political costs of approving such a decision significant. By late 2011, however, DFWP identified the Fort Peck pasture as a likely transfer site, but transfer would occur only after the state reached agreement with the Tribes on the details, including the need for suitable fencing and the transfer of some bison to the nearby Assiniboine and Gros Ventre Tribes of the Fort Belknap Reservation.[11]

The outcry and opposition from local ranchers and agricultural interests was immediate and intense, with a group of concerned citizens filing a request for an injunction to stop the transfer and seeking to prohibit any further movement of bison across Montana without the state first complying with the provisions of

---

[7] *Id.* at 8.
[8] *See, e.g.,* Bison Quarantine Feasibility Study, Interim Summary (Apr. 2012), http://www .ibmp.info/Library/20120501/BQFS_summary_2012.pdf.
[9] *Id.*
[10] *See* Citizens for Balanced Use v. Maurier, 303 P.3d 794, 413 (Mont. 2013).
[11] *Id.*

Montana law regarding the transfer of "wild buffalo or bison" to "public or private land in Montana."[12] Under that provision, DFWP would have to engage in an extensive planning and analysis process, including taking public comments and responding to them and studying the carrying capacity of any such lands, prior to transferring any animals.[13] But, before the trial court ruled on that issue, the DFWP and then-Governor Brian Schweitzer entered into an agreement with the Tribes and approved the first transfer of about 60 bison to Fort Peck, which took place on March 19, 2012, "in the middle of a snowstorm and with no prior public announcement."[14] The plaintiffs in the pending state court action immediately requested and were granted an injunction preventing further transfers, a decision that was ultimately appealed to the Montana Supreme Court.[15] After reviewing the terms of Montana law on which the trial court relied, the supreme court unanimously determined, with one justice concurring, that transfers of bison to tribal lands (as opposed to "public or private land" as stated in the statute) were not covered by provisions of law relied on by the plaintiffs and, therefore, the law's extensive procedural steps were also inapplicable.[16] The court also noted in passing that, because they had been quarantined, the bison at issue "arguably are not 'wild buffalo or bison.'"[17] Instead, DFWP was free to enter in the agreements with the Tribes to transfer bison without complying with the state's procedural requirements.

Despite that victory and the implicit approval of the initial transfer of nearly 60 bison to the Tribes, it would be another two years, until 2014, before the tribes would receive more bison from Yellowstone. During those years, hundreds more bison were slaughtered outside of the Park and opponents continued to press for bison to be considered livestock and managed for disease control rather than according to tribal priorities. In fact, the bison transferred in 2014 had been allowed to move across the state only because they were from the herd that was quarantined and monitored on a private ranch since 2010.[18] After 2014, repeated proposals and further efforts to transfer more bison to the Tribes fell through, largely because of disagreements over whether and how much of the quarantine process and responsibility the Tribes could assume.[19] It would be another five years, until April 2019, before the tribes would receive additional bison, in a transfer that brought five bulls, with the attached condition that the Tribes must conduct a final brucellosis quarantine and

---

[12] *Id.* at 415–16 ; *see also* Mont. Code Ann. § 87-1-216.

[13] *Id.* § 87-1-216.

[14] *See* Associated Press, *Yellowstone Bison Arrive at Fort Peck*, BILLINGS GAZETTE (Mar. 19, 2012).

[15] Citizens for Balanced Use, 303 P.3d, *supra* note 10, at 414.

[16] *Id.* at 418.

[17] *Id.*

[18] Associated Press, *Yellowstone Bison to Be Transferred to Fort Peck*, MISSOULIAN (Nov. 5, 2014).

[19] *See* Joseph Bullington, *Transfer of Park Bison to Ft. Peck Hits Another Roadblock*, THE LIVINGSTON ENTERPRISE (Nov. 29, 2018, 12:00 AM), https://www.livingstonenterprise.com/content/transfer-park-bison-ft-peck-hits-another-roadblock.

testing procedures.[20] The Tribes continue to seek to assume additional authority over earlier stages of brucellosis testing and plan to develop their resources to help support the broader pasturing and transfer of bison from Yellowstone to other tribes and tribally owned entities.[21]

The potential for the Fort Peck Tribes to become a resource for Yellowstone bison and to help that species make a significant recovery and be protected from culling by state and federal officials is a microcosm of the broader modern movement to protect and invigorate indigenous cultures. In addition to the barriers of federal and state legal and administrative bureaucracies, the Tribes' battle to bring bison back to their cultural and historical homes on Assiniboine and Sioux lands faced the nearly insurmountable competing legacies and visions of American identity that have driven the laws of cultural protection profiled throughout this book. At the federal level, the protection of Yellowstone as a national park without due regard for the natural migratory habits of bison or the human environmental and cultural values surrounding the area motivated the National Park Service's efforts to restrict the movement of bison from the park and to capture or kill them to prevent them from leaving the park's boundaries. The purpose was to protect a valuable federal "natural resource." But, that perspective, illustrated by the initial record of decision quoted earlier, recognizing the "[e]arly European travelers" to the Yellowstone area who witnessed bison, echoes the sentiment from the early 1900s that natural resources should be protected for the benefit of white America and erases the longstanding presence of indigenous people on the landscape. It also conveniently ignores their traditional and cultural connections to those resources.[22] The knowledge borne of those connections would have foretold of the challenges of keeping bison from following their natural tendencies and likely demonstrated a more realistic management scheme – one based on respect for the inherent value of bison and a deep long-standing relationship with the species – instead of focusing on potential methods of control.

Competing with that federal perspective are the concerns of state livestock producers and local non-Indians who view bison returning to Fort Peck as a threat to their livelihood and way of life. Although there's never been a documented transmission of brucellosis from a wild bison to a cow in the greater Yellowstone Area,[23] the conflict between the Tribes' interests and those of the livestock industry

---

[20] Michael Wright, *After 5 Yellowstone Bison Moved to Fort Peck Reservation, Managers Laud Quarantine Process*, BILLINGS GAZETTE (Apr. 26, 2019), https://billingsgazette.com/news/state-and-regional/after-yellowstone-bison-moved-to-fort-peck-reservation-managers-laud/article_415c 1936-7290-5273-b57f-8fae8d3a4828.html.

[21] *Id.*

[22] *See* Chapter 5.

[23] J. C. Rhyan, P. Nol, C. Quance, A. Gertonson, J. Belfrage, L. Harris, & S. Robbe-Austerman *Transmission of Brucellosis from Elk to Cattle and Bison, Greater Yellowstone Area, USA, 2002–2012*, 19(12) EMERGING INFECTIOUS DISEASES 1992–95 (2013), https://dx.doi.org/10.3201/eid1912.130167.

and local non-Indians is reminiscent of historical conflicts between homesteading non-Indian settlers moving west and the tribes who called those lands home for generations before their arrival.[24] Montana law restricting bison transfers in the state sought to respond to and protect the history and pride of homesteading western lands by cattle ranchers who were concerned about the presence of bison near their cows and operations. In short, these ranchers saw bison as a threat to their domestic cattle herds and, contrary to the nonindigenous conservation perspective motivating the federal management of bison, the state law restrictions on bison transfers stemmed instead from this legacy of rugged American cowboys taming the West (and its indigenous inhabitants). Opposition to the Tribes' acquisition and maintenance of bison still runs hot in many of these rural communities.

But, despite these deeply ingrained values and perspectives and the laws and challenges they presented, the Tribes insisted on bringing bison back to their homelands. Because of that persistence, not only has the reservation seen a resurgence of important cultural values and innovative pathways to achieving deeper connections with those values, the stage has been set for broader benefits to accrue to all Americans. For example, bison in their natural plains habitat improve the ecology of the area and begin, in some small measure, to restore historical ecosystems that were long ago decimated by fractionation, illogical jurisdictional and political boundaries, and development.[25] Beyond these ecological benefits, however, the tribes' effort, like that of many other Tribes raising and protecting bison, presents the promise of protection for America's national mammal, recognized in 2016 as an important symbol of shared national identity.[26]

Thus, like the Oceti Sakowin, who raised their voices in opposition to the Dakota Access Pipeline and were joined by thousands of supporters in North Dakota and around the world, or the Bears Ears Inter-Tribal Coalition, whose proposal to protect the sacred lands around the Bears Ears buttes was supported by millions of Americans from across the country, the efforts of the Fort Peck Tribes to bring bison back home may initially have been centered on indigenous cultural values, but connected with broader shared national values. Although the legal barriers that confronted these efforts may not have aligned with the cultural protections demanded by tribal voices, the Tribes' efforts and the support they received signal an important moment in the continuing development of the laws and legal structures that apply, and still often frustrate, the recognition and protection of indigenous cultures. This achievement demands a collective reassessment of the history and context in which those laws and structures were created, the implicit and explicit perspectives they

---

[24] See generally JOSHUA SPECHT, RED MEAT REPUBLIC: A HOOF-TO-TABLE HISTORY OF HOW BEEF CHANGED AMERICA (2019).

[25] See, e.g., Matthew D. Moran, Bison Are Back, and That Benefits Many Other Species on the Great Plains, THE CONVERSATION (updated Jan. 24, 2019, 10:48 AM), https://theconversation .com/bison-are-back-and-that-benefits-many-other-species-on-the-great-plains-107588.

[26] Pub. L. 114-152, 130 Stat. 373 (May 9, 2016).

represent, and the ways in which they have viewed (or ignored) indigenous cultures. Only by acknowledging the rightful claims of tribal nations, communities, bands, and other indigenous groups to protection under time-honored and universally applicable established legal doctrines like the Constitution's Supremacy Clause or the First Amendment, and by rectifying the subordination of indigenous cultures and cultural values, can the nation successfully engage in that reassessment. Tribes, their leaders, members, and allies are leading the way, through the exercise of their sovereign authority to develop their own laws and legal structures and by demanding that both federal and state laws rightfully accommodate and incorporate their cultural values. This trend opens the door to a new way for the future of indigenous cultural protection.

In his thoughtful, humorous, and prescient essay "You can't Rollerskate in a Buffalo Herd Even if You Have All the Medicine': American Indian Law and Policy," Rennard Strickland recounted the evolution of Indian law and policy from the dark days of termination during the 1950s to the dawn of the self-determination era of the 1970s. Recalling the story of a tribal elder describing a meeting between the Lummi Tribe and Bureau of Indian Affairs (BIA) officials at which the BIA told the tribal representatives that the tribe would be terminated, Strickland related the following:

> The man from the BIA told them it was going to happen one of two ways: either the 'easy way' with the tribe helping the Bureau make a smooth transition or the 'hard way' with the Bureau doing it alone. With tears in her eyes, a tremor in her voice, and pride on her face, she [the tribal elder telling the story] reported that her previously shy husband [who had recently returned from service in World War II] stood up, drawing upon his military demeanor and experience [and] said, 'No, there is a third way and that is with the tribe saying 'NO' and, if necessary, going to congress to stop you . . . Their way ultimately became the way. The Tribe survived termination and this led to many changes that culminated decades later in *U.S. v. Washington*, the Boldt decision that recognized the birth of West Coast Indian fishing rights.[27]

Like the tribal elder's husband, tribes are now finding a "third way" for the law to protect their cultures and cultural values – a way that provides legal protections for cultural values, while simultaneously incorporating those values into the law. This movement marks both the continuing presence of tribes as third sovereigns in the United States and the coalescing of two prior approaches to indigenous cultures. Since time immemorial and prior to the arrival of European colonists, indigenous peoples across the continent engaged in their various cultural practices. During this "first way," those cultures were free from the imposition or oppression of external legal doctrines conceived by foreigners and based on foreign mores. They were

---

[27] RENNARD STRICKLAND, TONTO'S REVENGE: REFLECTIONS ON AMERICAN INDIAN CULTURE AND POLICY, 49 (1997) (emphasis in original).

rooted only in indigenous values, often tied closely to the land, and connected with others through vast networks of trade, commerce, warfare, and other interactions.

But, following the arrival of Europeans, the decimation of indigenous people and their cultures brought about the second way. Eventually, this second way was marked by laws based on European legal traditions and inspired by American hubris, racial subjugation, religious doctrines like Manifest Destiny, and misconceptions of indigenous cultural inferiority. Tribes and indigenous communities have preserved their cultural practices in the face of these purely external and foreign laws, the military and political power of the federal government, and the laws and legal structures imposed on them, all of which were often aimed directly at destroying those cultures. Even laws that appeared facially neutral toward such cultures, like the National Historic Preservation Act or the Archaeological Resources Protection Act, still imported the historical conceptions of indigenous cultures as unworthy of protection or only of scientific or museum value to non-Indians. This was also true of generally applicable legal rights like the free exercise of one's religion, which the Supreme Court has interpreted broadly in the nonindigenous context but refuses to honor when it comes to indigenous practices.

Yet, with the self-determination era of the 1970s and the growth of a broader indigenous rights movement, both in the halls of legal and political power and across the country, there is now emerging a third way. One could see this new approach at work on the plains of North Dakota, as members of the Sioux Nation opened the eyes of the world to the cultural threats posed by the Dakota Access Pipeline, and now in the halls of Congress, with the first two indigenous women representatives in US history co-sponsoring a bill to restore the Bears Ears National Monument and advance other vital legislation proposed by tribes and tribal members. It can be seen in Alaska with the efforts to incorporate indigenous languages into the halls of state government, and in Maine with the nation's first Truth and Reconciliation Commission to study and document the harms resulting from the removal of Passamaquoddy, Penobscot, Maliseet, and Micmac children from their homes in the early twentieth century. Similarly, the Fort Peck Tribes continue to overcome the hurdles of federal and state laws to bring their bison back home, providing an example to other tribes in the process. That work is not strictly within the parameters of existing legal systems, but shows the potential for a new approach, driven by indigenous cultural values and stretching those external systems to account for them.

Throughout the United States, tribes and indigenous interests are overcoming the limits and strictures of the second way and, as demonstrated throughout the preceding chapters, succeeding in bending federal and state laws toward their own cultural lodestars: they are engaging the third way. More importantly, these efforts are resulting in innovative approaches that rely on the creation of new tribal laws and the blazing of new pathways, like using the Antiquities Act to protect Bears Ears and the use of existing federal and state laws, like the Native American Graves Protection and Repatriation Act (NAGPRA) and its state-level progeny. While the successes of this third way may still be difficult for many outside indigenous communities to see, the continuing efforts of tribes and their allies toward legal reform will surely bear fruit, just as their work to protect their ancestors resulted in NAGPRA.

To build the third way, reshaping the laws of cultural protection to reflect indigenous cultural values will require a reckoning with the history and values imbedded in those laws. Unless federal laws are understood with an eye toward the implicit assumptions that led to their enactment and recognizing the lingering American tendency toward assimilation and away from cultural independence, efforts at reform will remain incomplete.[28] Similarly, state laws cannot simply be changed to better respect tribal or indigenous interests without understanding the potential for collaborative and cooperative efforts at ensuring that respect is meaningful, and certainly not without an understanding of the proper situation of tribes as external sovereigns, not de facto subjects of state law.[29] Even where tribes are working to reform their own laws and exercise broader sovereignty within their territories to protect important cultural values, the legacy of allotment and the subjectivism of the US Supreme Court limit their authority over nonmembers and their lands.[30] Importantly, however, the third way and the new movement to decolonize the laws and practices of cultural protection may not require abandoning foundational legal tenets, but it will demand that the legal systems built on those foundations reject the generations of subsequent developments premised on the erasure of indigenous people and their cultures.

The result of this effort will not be that indigenous interests always prevail or that those are the only concerns that the law will recognize. Instead, the third way leads to a new approach for considering and balancing the difficult decisions required of federal, state, and tribal leaders; judges and agency officials; and law and policy makers. Ideally, like the co-management framework proposed for the Bears Ears National Monument by the Inter-Tribal Coalition or the role provided for indigenous oral histories and traditions in NAGPRA, the third way leads to a more robust legal system that goes beyond simply accommodating indigenous people and their beliefs in name only. Instead, the third way will lead to a new era in which laws and policies value the role of distinct indigenous cultures within the legal system and look to tribal laws and practices for guidance without marginalizing them or their wisdom. While some might view such reform as inconsistent with notions of equal treatment under the laws and other long-standing myths associated with the US Constitution, the third way provides a measure of justice, both restorative and actual – not just for tribes and indigenous cultures but for all Americans.

Felix S. Cohen, the progenitor of federal Indian law and driving force behind ending the federal government's allotment and assimilation policies, once famously

---

[28] *See* Chapter 4 and Chapter 5.
[29] *See* Chapter 7.
[30] *See* Chapter 2 and Chapter 6.

lamented the dominant perception of indigenous Americans during his time, saying "[i]t is a pity that so many Americans today think of the Indian as a romantic or comic figure in American history without contemporary significance."[31] Instead, Cohen saw the law's mistreatment of indigenous people – and, we would add, their cultures – as a telltale sign of governmental demise. "Like the miner's canary," Cohen famously wrote in 1953, "the Indian marks the shifts from fresh air to poison gas in our political atmosphere; and our treatment of Indians, even more than our treatment of other minorities, reflects the rise and fall in our democratic faith."[32] While Cohen's view reflected paternalistic notions about the nation's treatment of "the Indians," his underlying message rings true. Just as the return of bison to their ancestral home on the Great Plains of the Fort Peck Reservation is beginning to heal century-old wounds there, following indigenous voices toward the third way could finally align the laws of indigenous cultural protection with the truest ideals of America's shared democratic faith.

[31] Felix S. Cohen, *The Erosion of Indian Rights*, 62 Yale L. Rev. 349, 390 (1953).
[32] *Id.*

Index

Index

CPSIA information can be obtained
at www.ICGtesting.com
Printed in the USA
BVHW041808281120
594417BV00007B/36